STUDY COMPOSITION AND RHETORIC

UNIVERSITY OF MICHIGAN

SCHOOL OF EDUCATION

DEPARTMENT of ENGLISH

Joint PhD Program in English and Education

Bringing together the best of research, scholarship, and pedagogy from both English and Education, this interdisciplinary program draws on top-flight resources to provide a satisfying and rich doctoral experience. Among our strengths, we offer a supportive and engaging community of scholars that includes both students and faculty, and we provide the flexibility for students to craft a program centered on their individual interests. These interests have included rhetorical theory, literacy studies, new media composition, applied linguistics, English language studies, teacher education, and writing assessment; our faculty are happy to work with you to craft a program centered on your research and teaching interests.

This PHD program is designed for students who hold master's degrees in English or education and who have teaching experience. We have an excellent record of placing graduates in tenure-track positions in education and English departments in colleges and universities.

Phone: 734.763.6643 • Email: ed.jpee@umich.edu

soe.umich.edu/jpee

Education Faculty
Chandra L. Alston: teacher education, English education, adolescent literacy, urban education

Barry Fishman: technology, video games as models for learning, reform involving technology, teacher learning, design-based implementation research

Elizabeth Birr Moje: adolescent and disciplinary literacy, literacy and cultural theory, research methods

Mary J. Schleppegrell: functional linguistics, second language learning, discourse analysis, language development

Co-Chairs
Anne Curzan: history of English, language and gender, corpus linguistics, lexicography, pedagogy

Anne Ruggles Gere: composition theory, gender and literacy, writing assessment, and pedagogy

English Faculty
David Gold: history of rhetoric, women's rhetorics, composition pedagogy

Scott Richard Lyons: Native American and global indigenous studies, settler colonialism, posthumanism

Alisse Portnoy: rhetoric and composition, rhetorical activism and civil rights movements

Megan Sweeney: African American literature and culture, ethnography, pedagogy, critical prison studies

Melanie R. Yergeau: composition and rhetoric, digital media studies, disability studies, autistic culture

Reviewers

All essay submissions are reviewed blind by two external readers; those listed below are members of the active reader pool. We thank them for their critical contributions to scholarship in the field.

Tom Amorose
Valerie Balester
Cheryl Ball
Nicholas Behm
Patricia Belanoff
Patricia Bizzell
Bill Bolin
Darsie Bowden
Colin Brooke
Robert Brooke
Nancy Buffington
Beth Burmester
Paul Butler
Mary Ann Cain
Carol Lea Clark
Kirsti Cole
Lisa Coleman
James Comas
Juanita Rodgers Comfort
Thomas Deans
Jane Detweiler
Ronda Leathers Dively
Sidney Dobrin
Whitney Douglas
Donna Dunbar-Odom
Lynell Edwards
David Elder
Janet Carey Eldred
Michelle Eodice
Heidi Estrem
Sheryl Fontaine
Helen Fox
Tom Fox
Christy Friend
Richard Fulkerson
Catherine Gabor

Lynée Lewis Gaillet
Alice Gilliam
Maureen Daly Goggin
Angela González
Lorie Goodman
Heather Brodie Graves
Roger Graves
Paul Hanstedt
Dana Harrington
Jeanette Harris
Cynthia Haynes
Paul Heilker
Carl Herndl
Brooke Hessler
Charlotte Hogg
Bruce Horner
Sue Hum
Brian Huot
James Inman
Asao Inoue
Rebecca Jackson
T. R. Johnson
Judith Kearns
Martha Kruse
bonnie kyburz
Mary Lamb
Donna LeCourt
Neal Lerner
Carrie Leverenz
Min-Zhan Lu
Brad Lucas
William Macauley
Tim Mayers
Lisa McClure
Moriah McCracken
Dan Meltzer

Laura Rose Micciche
Ruth Mirtz
Clyde Moneyhun
Roxanne Mountford
Gerald P. Mulderig
Joan A. Mullin
Joddy Murray
Marshall Myers
Gerald Nelms
Jon Olson
Peggy O'Neill
Derek Owens
Irv Peckham
Donna Qualley
Ellen Quandahl
Kelly Ritter
Duane Roen
Randall Roorda
Blake Scott
Ellen Schendel
Carol Severino
Wendy Sharer
Steve Sherwood
Donna Strickland
William Thelin
Peter Vandenberg
Deirdre Vinyard
Zachary Waggoner
Kathleen Welch
Thomas West
Katherine Wills
Rosemary Winslow
Vershawn Ashanti Young
Janet Zepernick

Member of the Council of Editors of Learned Journals

composition STUDIES

Volume 41, Number 1
Spring 2013

Editor
Jennifer Clary-Lemon

Book Review Editor
Asao B. Inoue

Editorial Assistant
Carmela Fabros

Former Editors
Gary Tate
Robert Mayberry
Christina Murphy
Peter Vandenberg
Ann George
Carrie Leverenz
Brad E. Lucas

Advisory Board

Linda Adler-Kassner
*University of California,
Santa Barbara*

Tom Amorose
Seattle Pacific University

Chris Anson
North Carolina State University

Valerie Balester
Texas A&M University

Robert Brooke
University of Nebraska, Lincoln

Sidney Dobrin
University of Florida

Lisa Ede
Oregon State University

Paul Heilker
*Virginia Polytechnic Institute
and State University*

James Inman
*University of Maryland
University College*

Laura Micciche
University of Cincinnati

Peggy O'Neill
Loyola College

Victor Villanueva
Washington State University

SUBSCRIPTIONS

Composition Studies is published twice each year (May and November). Subscription rates: Individuals $25 (Domestic) and $30 (International); Institutions $75 (Domestic) and $75 (International); Students $15.

BACK ISSUES

Recent back issues are now available through Amazon.com for $12. To find issues, use the advanced search feature and search on "Composition Studies" (title) and "Parlor Press" (publisher). Photocopies of earlier issues are available for $3.

BOOK REVIEWS

Assignments are made from a file of potential book reviewers. To have your name added to the file, send a current vita to the Book Review Editor at asao@inoueweb.com.

SUBMISSIONS

All appropriate essay submissions will be blind reviewed by two external readers. Manuscripts should be 3,500-7,500 words and conform to current MLA guidelines for format and documentation; they should be free of author's names and other identifying references. *Electronic submissions are preferred*: consult our Web site for details. (For print submissions, submit three titled, letter-quality copies with a cover letter including the title and author contact information, loose postage sufficient to mail manuscripts to two reviewers, and a #10 SASE for the return of reviewer comments.) *Composition Studies* will not consider previously published manuscripts. We discourage the submission of conference papers that have not been revised or extended for a critical reading audience. Those wishing to submit Course Designs should first consult our Web site for specific instructions. Letters to the editor and responses to articles are strongly encouraged.

To ensure a blind review, *Composition Studies* requests
1. The authors of the document have deleted their names from the text, with "Author" and year used in the references and endnotes, instead of the authors' name, article title, etc.
2. With Microsoft Office documents, author identification should also be removed from the properties for the file (see under File in Word), by clicking on the following, beginning with File on the main menu of the Microsoft application: File > Save As > Tools (or Options with a Mac) > Security > Remove personal information from file properties on save > Save.
3. With PDFs, the authors' names should also be removed from Document Properties found under File on Adobe Acrobat's main menu.

Direct all correspondence to:

    Laura Micciche, Editor
    Department of English
    University of Cincinnati
    PO Box 210069
    Cincinnati, OH 45221-0069

Composition Studies *is grateful for the generous support of the Dean of Arts and the Department of Rhetoric, Writing, and Communications at the University of Winnipeg.*

© Copyright 2013 by Jennifer Clary-Lemon, Editor
Production and printing is managed by Parlor Press, www.parlorpress.com.
ISSN 1534-9322

www.compositionstudies.uwinnipeg.ca

composition STUDIES

Volume 41, Number 1
Spring 2013

Editor's Note   9

Articles

Institutionalizing Normal: Rethinking Composition's
Precedence in Normal Schools   10
   Ryan Skinnell

Transitioning Writers across the Composition Threshold:
What We Can Learn from Dual Enrollment Partnerships   27
   Christine Denecker

Truth, Memory, Selectivity: Understanding Historical Work
by Writing Personal Histories   51
   Duncan Koerber

Where Professional Writing Meets Social Change:
The Grant Proposal as a Site of Hospitality   70
   Kenna Barrett

The Historical Problem of Vertical Coherence: Writing,
Research, and Legitimacy in Early 20th Century Rhetoric and
Composition   84
   Annie Mendenhall

Course Design

ETC 408/508: Technical Editing   101
   Michael Charlton

Reviews

Agency in the Age of Peer Production, by Quentin D. Vieregge, Kyle D. Stedman, Taylor Joy Mitchell, and Joseph M. Moxley   117
   Reviewed by Peter Brooks

Redesigning Composition for Multilingual Realities, by Jay Jordan   121
   Reviewed by Pisarn Bee Chamcharatsri

Agents of Integration: Understanding Transfer as a Rhetorical Act, by
Rebecca S. Nowacek **124**
    Reviewed by José M. Cortez

*Beyond the Pulpit: Women's Rhetorical Roles in the Antebellum
Religious Press,* by Lisa J. Shaver **127**
    Reviewed by Paul Dahlgren

*Composing (Media) = Composing (Embodiment): Bodies, Technologies,
Writing and the Teaching of Writing,* edited by Kristin L. Arola
and Anne Frances Wysocki **131**
    Reviewed by Lauri Bohanan Goodling

Listening to our Elders: Working and Writing for Change, edited by
Samantha Blackmon, Cristina Kirklighter and Steve Parks **134**
    Reviewed by Cantice Greene

Literate Zeal: Gender and the Making of a New Yorker *Ethos,*
by Janet Carey Eldred **137**
    Reviewed by Kerri Hauman

Writing Home: A Literacy Autobiography, by Eli Goldblatt **141**
    Reviewed by Ted Kesler

*Collaborative Learning and Writing: Essays on Using Small Groups in
Teaching English and Composition,* edited by Kathleen M. Hunzer **145**
    Reviewed by Sean R. Maddox

*Autism Spectrum Disorders in the College Composition Classroom:
Making Writing Instruction More Accessible for All Students,*
edited by Val Gerstle and Lynda Walsh **149**
    Reviewed by Adam M. Pacton

Feminist Rhetorical Resilience, edited by Elizabeth A. Flynn,
Patricia Sotirin, and Anne Brady **153**
    Reviewed by Kristin Ravel

Exploring Composition Studies: Sites, Issues, and Perspectives,
edited by Kelly Ritter and Paul Kei Matsuda **157**
    Reviewed by Bryna Siegel Finer

Announcement   162

Contributors   163

Editor's Note

This spring's issue marks my last as Editor of *Composition Studies*. I am pleased to announce that *Composition Studies* will make its new home at the University of Cincinnati, under the leadership of Editor Laura Micciche. Following nomination and review by the journal's Advisory Board, Micciche was elected from a short-list of excellent candidates. It is a pleasure to close my tenure with CS by passing it on to an Editor with the passion, expertise, and dedication of Laura Micciche.

Laura Micciche

Laura Micciche is excited to serve as editor of *Composition Studies*, beginning with 41.2. She is the former Director of Composition at the University of Cincinnati, where she teaches rhetorical theory, writing pedagogy, and various composition courses, including digital composing. Her research has focused on rhetoric and affect, theories of writing, WPAing, and pedagogical issues. She currently serves as Editor of *Queen City Writers* (qc-writers.com), an open-access journal for undergraduate writing, and, not so recently, she was poetry co-editor for *The Cream City Review*. Laura looks forward to continuing the good work of Jennifer Clary-Lemon and past editors as well as to reaching new audiences, publishing new voices, and contributing in substantial ways to ongoing conversations in the field. Composition Studies has never been a single-minded field; our practices, tools, communities, research methods, and orientations to practice and theory continue to proliferate, stimulating our forward movement. She seeks submissions that illustrate this point. Laura is especially interested in article submissions that address any aspect of the journal's entitled term, composition, in association with its many complements, including but not limited to pedagogy, theory, administration, research, history, identity, community, assessment, creativity, rhetoric, digitality, and embodiment. Laura looks forward to serving our diverse group of teacher-scholars through the editorship, and invites your comments and feedback about the journal and its content along the way.

Institutionalizing Normal: Rethinking Composition's Precedence in Normal Schools[1]

Ryan Skinnell

Composition historians have recently worked to recover histories of composition in normal schools. This essay argues, however, that historians have inadvertently misconstrued the role of normal schools in American education by inaccurately comparing rhetorical education in normal schools to rhetorical education in colleges and universities. Consequently, claims that normal schools set useful historical precedents for rhetoric and composition are misguided. In order to understand normal schools' importance for contemporary teachers and scholars, composition historians need to account more precisely for larger institutional objectives—common objectives that constitute an institution type across individual cases—that shaped the conditions for rhetorical education.

A normal school is a school established for the academic and professional preparation of teachers. It is a technical school differing from academies and colleges in its objects and methods of work. The objects of the academy and college are general culture and the acquisition of knowledge; the object of the normal school is to impart culture, discipline, skill, and learning to its students for a specific and technical purpose, viz, that of fitting them to teach others.

—Eliphalet Oram Lyte, "The State Normal Schools
of the United States," 1903 (1104)

The normal school under this name or some equivalent title has been established in all lands where there exists a system of state-supported schools. It is a vital part of the public school system because well-trained teachers are a prime requisite for efficient schools.

—David Felmley, "The Collegiate Rank
of the Normal School," 1923 (41)

As David Felmley, president of the State Normal University in Normal, Illinois, indicates in the epigraph, normal schools[2] served an essential function in American education for many decades—training teachers to teach. Normal schools are now relics of education history, but they were once prominent, if not exactly preeminent, teacher-training institutions.[3] Hundreds of normals were founded in communities in nearly every state in the nation, and in some cases, cities and towns aggressively lobbied state governments for the right to open normal schools (Ogren 26, 57-59).

They educated tens of thousands of students each year during the height of their popularity, and although they ultimately produced only a fraction of the teachers needed, in the last decades of 1800s, normal schools enrolled more students than any other type of institution of higher education (Burke 216; Harris xiv-xix). Furthermore, because they were often founded in rural settings and open to students without regard to race, class, or gender, education historian Jurgen Herbst argues that "[n]ormal schools, rather than land-grant universities, were the pioneers of higher education for the people" ("Nineteenth-Century" 227). It is not an exaggeration to say that normal schools played an integral role in the spread of universal education in America; without them, large numbers of students—especially underprivileged students, non-white students, and female students—would not have been exposed to formal rhetorical education or composition instruction.[4] In recognition of normal schools' significance during the nineteenth and twentieth centuries, composition historians have recently begun researching their role in providing rhetoric and writing education (see Bordelon; Fitzgerald, "Platteville," "Platteville Revisited," and "Rediscovered"; Gold; Gray; Lindblom, Banks, and Quay; Ritter; Rothermel, "Our Life's Work" and "Sphere").

By and large, composition historians have found in the normal school "a site that turns out to harbor rich intellectual, methodological, and political implications for composition's tradition" because "several contemporary attitudes about composition theory, methods, teachers, and students have precedent in the normal schools" (Fitzgerald, "Rediscovered" 225). There is some question about the degree to which normals embraced theories and pedagogies that existed in colleges and universities, but there is widespread consensus that normals belong to what David Gold calls "a rich, alternative tradition of rhetorical education in America" (x). As such, composition historians have argued that studying normal schools is important for understanding how large numbers of students were taught to write, as well as for discovering historical precedents that have shaped the modern field of rhetoric and composition. Like Fitzgerald and Gold, I agree that normal schools merit closer attention from historians. However, in service of discovering the rich intellectual, methodological, and political implications of normal schools, composition historians have significantly misconstrued the role of normal schools in American education. By focusing their scope of inquiry on disciplinary norms and practices (c.f., Gannett, Brereton, and Tirabassi), historians have not accounted for important institutional issues that framed how students were taught to write. As a consequence, claims about normal school precedence for contemporary rhetoric and composition teachers and scholars are problematic.

One critical concern with normal school histories is that they rely on a flawed comparison of rhetorical education in normals to rhetorical education in colleges and universities. That is, historians have sought to understand normal schools by drawing comparisons from pedagogies, curricula, and theories at colleges and universities. But, as I discuss below, normals were not colleges or universities, nor were they meant to be. In fact, they were specifically designed in contrast to colleges and universities. So, while such comparisons may potentially yield some valuable insights, they are substantially limited. As well, discussions of historical precedence overlook crucial aspects of normal schools' objectives and histories, such as normal schools' objective of providing both secondary and post-secondary instruction. Consequently, the lessons composition historians have drawn from normal schools—about writing pedagogy, rhetorical curricula and extra-curricula, and historical precedence—are misguided inasmuch as they fail to appreciate the ways in which normal schools' unique institutional objectives shaped the conditions for rhetoric and writing.

If composition historians are to learn significant lessons from normal schools, it is imperative that we consider more carefully normals' unique role in American education—especially given the fallacies that constitute many widely held beliefs about them. In *Feminist Rhetorical Practices*, Jacqueline Jones Royster notes that when she began researching African-American women's rhetorics, she was met with "deep disbelief" about their contributions to nineteenth century rhetorical history (Royster and Kirsch 9). "[T]he growth of the historical documentation of lives and contributions of women of African descent," which countered entrenched understandings about African-American women, was necessary for Royster's claims to be understood. The same, I contend, is true of normal schools. That is, in order to draw useful conclusions about normal schools' significance, historians must first upset entrenched understandings of normals by developing broader historical documentation of normal schools' functions in American education.

In this paper, I begin the work of developing a more precise historical account of normal schools' functions in American education, first by analyzing normal schools' distinctive institutional objectives—the common objectives that constituted normals across individual cases. Then, I turn to the example of a single institution, Tempe Normal School (TNS). I use Tempe Normal as a case study because it exemplifies the qualities of normals that are supposed to qualify them as part of the "alternative rhetorical tradition"—it was rural, in the West, served primarily female students, and offered students a robust rhetorical curriculum and extra-curriculum. TNS is also notable because it eventually transformed into Arizona State University, one of the country's most prominent twenty-first century research universities. I use the example of TNS to argue that, despite parallels with other post-secondary institutions, rhetorical education differed significantly at the normal because of institutional objectives. Finally, I draw out some of the potential lessons that can be learned from normals when they are considered apart from the search for historical precedence.

"It Wasn't Much of a College"[5]

As I noted, composition historians have generally compared rhetorical education at normal schools to that at colleges and universities.[6] Even when historians have recognized important distinguishing characteristics of normals, these comparisons persist and they strongly inform claims to precedence. For example, even after noting complex differences between normal schools and colleges in her influential article, "A Rediscovered Tradition: European Pedagogy and Composition in Nineteenth-Century Midwestern Normal Schools," Kathryn Fitzgerald contrasts the Pestalozzian intellectual traditions at normal schools to current-traditionalism in college composition. She concludes that normal school values (e.g., student-centered pedagogy, intellectual freedom, etc.) strongly reflect contemporary values in rhetoric and composition, and therefore deserve historians' attention. Fitzgerald's comparison is understandable inasmuch as it echoes similar characterizations of normal schools in education histories more broadly (see Ogren 2-3). However, it significantly oversimplifies normal schools' purposes for existing by describing them as institutionally parallel to colleges and universities, which they were not.

Of course, normal schools did resemble colleges and universities in important ways. For instance, normal schools offered rhetoric and/or writing courses that resemble courses offered at other types of institutions (see Gray for a good example). However, as Fitzgerald notes, "Normal schools were established in a completely different social and educational environment from the elite schools on which historians have primarily focused so far" (225-226). I would extend Fitzgerald's analysis by noting that normal schools were established in completely different social and educational environments than virtually all colleges and universities, elite or otherwise. Most pointedly, normal schools differed from colleges and universities in that they were not exclusively post-secondary institutions. Rather, normal schools were designed to be simultaneously secondary and post-secondary. As superintendent of Denver schools, Aaron Gove, wrote in his contribution to the 1903 *Report of the Commissioner of Education*, "The education covered in the average normal school corresponds well to that of the secondary school, with the increased task of professional work" (357). Gove's description of normals is neither apologetic nor accidental—normal schools were expressly intended to overlap secondary and post-secondary levels in order to meet the institutional mission of training teachers for public schools. This characteristic overlap had serious effects on normal schools in general, and as I argue later, on rhetorical education in particular.

Before looking specifically at rhetorical education, it is worth considering the more general curricular objectives defined by normals' overlapping secondary and post-secondary education. A fundamental assumption of normal school proponents was that normal students (often called "normalites") would receive an education that differed significantly from that given at colleges and universities. Whereas colleges were expected to offer students a liberal education (see Cohen 145-147) and universities were designed to facilitate content-specific research (see Lucas, *American* 194-195), normal schools were conceived of and established to impart teaching methods and classroom administration, irrespective of content knowledge (Ogren 32-33). These objectives were geared toward preparing students for the demands of public school teaching, where teachers simultaneously taught and administered schools; students ranged in age from 6 to 15, and had radically diverse levels of academic preparation; and teaching conditions (i.e., materials, attendance, etc.) varied dramatically from one school to another.

Meeting the distinctive curricular objective of preparing future teachers, not surprisingly, required that normals adopt a distinctive curriculum. In "Nineteenth-Century Normal Schools in the United States," Jurgen Herbst explains that normal schools were "created for a two-fold purpose: to review the basic subjects taught in the elementary schools as proper objects of the teacher's pedagogical expertise and to instill in the future teacher a few basic precepts of professional knowledge" (220). In short, normal schools provided (1) an academic curriculum that focused on elementary (and secondary) school subjects, often called the "common branches,"[7] and (2) a professional curriculum that trained normalites in methods.[8] The academic curriculum refreshed students' acquaintance with subjects they would be expected to teach, and the professional curriculum provided teachers with skills necessary for efficient teaching and classroom management.

In addition to refreshing normalites' acquaintance with basic subjects, the academic curriculum also addressed practical realities. An important consequence of normal schools' broad admissions policies was that many students who attended normal schools had little or no formal education. In fact, normal schools were sometimes the first schools established in a given area. Therefore, it was not uncommon for normalites to need introduction to and review of basic subjects, including reading, writing, and arithmetic. As Ogren writes, "Basic liberal-arts subjects were a necessary part of the curriculum at all state normals from the beginning," because most students "arrived with limited exposure to anything beyond what was offered in the common schools" (45). Some students arrived without any prior formal education, and normals were often not in a position to deny admittance based on students' qualifications or lack thereof. Therefore, the academic curriculum enabled normals to address students' widely varying academic preparation under the guise of meeting the second, and central, purpose of the normal: providing general methodological, meta-discursive knowledge—"sound techniques for teaching"—deemed necessary for teaching (Lucas, *Teacher* 29).[9]

According to normal school proponents, the genuine and distinctive function of normal schools was imparting general teaching methods—what Edward Everett, an early advocate of normal schools, called "those principles of our nature on which education depends; the laws which control the faculties of the youthful mind in the pursuit and attainment of truth; and the moral sentiments on the part of the teacher and pupil which must be brought into harmonious action" (qtd. in Ogren 32).[10] Everett indicates that teacher training started from general methods, which could be used to teach any subject to any student in any classroom (e.g., recitation, study skills, organization, etc.). These methods fitted students for the essential demands of teaching and prepared them to be effective irrespective of the conditions in which they taught. Normal instruction then moved to subject-specific methods—the "peculiar methods, applicable to each branch of knowledge"—that made teaching biology or history more effective (Ogren 32).

The focus on methods was seen as normal schools' greatest strength, in part because it distinguished normals from colleges and universities and countered the accusation that normals duplicated other institutions' offerings. This was especially an issue in places where institutions had to justify the expenditure of state funds for establishing and maintaining institutions of public education. The importance of the distinction can be seen in education reports filed around the turn of the twentieth century. In 1895, for example, the National Education Association (NEA) formed a normal school committee. According to the committee's 1899 report:

> The work of the normal school is unique. It means more than teaching subjects; it means more than the developing of the character; it means the teaching of subjects that they in turn may be taught; it means the development of character that it in turn may be transfigured into character; it means such a preparation for life that it in turn may prepare others to enter fully, readily, and righteously into their environment. Thus to prepare an individual to lead and direct a little child is a grave responsibility. ("Report" 838)

As this passage indicates, the committee put strong emphasis on articulating normal schools' professional, methodological focus. Although the report makes occasional reference to the importance of liberal education, it attaches far greater importance to normal schools' unique professional work: "It is this kind of work that distinguishes normal school work in the branches from academic work proper as we find it in the high school. It is professional" (840). In other words, the professional curriculum represented normals' distinct value in contrast to high schools, colleges, or universities.

The NEA committee's comparison of normal schools to high schools—not colleges or universities—is telling. It reinforces the point that normals cannot be easily equated to colleges. But equally important is the committee's focus on differentiating "academic work" from "professional work." The committee's report reiterates the conception of academic work as elementary and/or secondary and professional work—that is, teaching methods—as normals' only properly post-secondary subject matter. To put it another way, as a general rule, normal schools' post-secondary curriculum was solely focused on teaching methods. This distinction has important ramifications for studying rhetorical education in normal schools because, as I discuss in more detail below, courses in rhetoric, writing, composition, and literature and language were usually considered "academic." They were, therefore, generally confined to the secondary level.

In detailing normal schools' institutional objectives to this point, I do not mean to suggest that all normals were identical. Nevertheless, normal schools' institutional objectives remained relatively stable across individual examples. In his description of the national condition of normal schools for the 1903 *Report of the Commissioner of Education*, Eliphalet Oram Lyte writes, "As a rule all the normal schools of a State have the same general course of study, and there is no great variation among the States of a division of the Union. There is more difference in the standards applied by the faculties of different institutions than in the courses of study" (1132). Individual normal schools had particular emphases, and rigor could vary greatly from one normal to another, but there was still significant uniformity with regard to normal school objectives, including what constituted appropriate elements of the post-secondary curriculum.[11]

Given the relative uniformity among normal schools, and given the general tendency to restrict post-secondary training in normal schools to teaching methods, composition historians' inclination to compare rhetorical education in normal schools to rhetorical education in other post-secondary institutions necessitates serious scrutiny. When, for example, Kathryn Fitzgerald notes that "normal teachers [in 1900] reported using texts by Scott and Denney, Buck and Woodbridge, and A.S. Hill" ("Rediscovered" 231), it bears examining whether those texts were used: (1) to teach rhetoric and writing at the post-secondary level, (2) to teach rhetoric and writing at the secondary level, or (3) to teach future teachers to teach rhetoric and writing at the elementary and secondary level. Fitzgerald strongly implies the first case, but in light of normals' post-secondary focus on methods as outlined above, it seems unlikely. If, in fact, the texts Fitzgerald identifies were used in the secondary-level "academic curriculum," then direct comparisons to first-year composition are problematic, to say the least, considering the different levels of instruction comprised by the comparison. Likewise, if the texts were being used to impart teaching methods—that is, if A.S. Hill's textbook was used to teach normalites how to teach writing in elementary and secondary schools, as opposed to teaching normalites how to write—the comparison seems equally problematic. There may be meaningful connections, in the latter case, between the normal curriculum and TA training, but even that comparison would be somewhat artificial because of the different populations students would eventually teach. Ultimately, Fitzgerald's comparison of normals to other post-secondary institutions is untenable, as are all normal school histories that rely on similar comparisons, because it strips away the effects of normals' institutional objectives on rhetorical education.

It should be sufficiently clear by now that normal schools were not merely second-class colleges, and normals' rhetorical education cannot be understood without broader reference to institutional objectives. In the next section, therefore, I describe normal schools' rhetorical education more specifically in light of the institutional objectives I've already laid out. In particular, I develop the claim that normals offered rhetoric and writing courses exclusively at the secondary level in order to demonstrate that more precision regarding institutional objectives can augment the lessons of disciplinary histories.

Rhetoric and Writing in the Normals

One benefit of the relative uniformity among normal schools is that focusing on circumstances at an individual institution can help composition historians locate broad themes that tell us about rhetorical education in normals more generally. Therefore, I turn now to a brief history of one normal school, Tempe Normal School (TNS).[12] TNS was founded in 1885 in Tempe, Arizona—a rural outpost approximately ten miles east of Phoenix—to address Arizona's teacher-shortage problem (Hopkins and Thomas 43-44). When it was founded, TNS was the only institution of higher education within 400 miles, and although TNS was not without idiosyncrasies, it represents well the conditions in which normal schools existed around the turn of the twentieth century—it was founded in a rural community, enrolled predominantly underserved populations of students, and evolved similarly to other normals. By looking more closely at TNS's example, it is possible to discuss more precisely the conditions in which rhetorical education existed in the normals, particularly given the distinction between "academic" and "professional" curricula.

Tempe Normal was established as part of a broad legislative agenda in Arizona in 1885, which included the allocation of a land-grant university, the University of Arizona, to Tucson. According to TNS's charter, the school was established for "instruction of persons . . . in the art of teaching and in all the various branches that pertain to good common school education" ("An Act"). In short, by legislative act, the focus of the normal education was primarily defined as "the art of teaching," which referred specifically to the professional curriculum focused on teaching methods, and "the various branches," which referred specifically to the academic curriculum focused on elementary and secondary level subjects. Students as young as sixteen could enroll at Tempe Normal, provided they had already completed the equivalent of a 7th grade education. Students could begin coursework at TNS in what were called "Sub-normal" courses, covering the 8th and 9th grades (McClintock 10), for one year prior to enrolling in the secondary curriculum.[13] Once students completed the equivalent of a 9th grade education, they could enroll in the "normal course," which began with two years of high school equivalent "academic" coursework. According to TNS's first archivist, Alfred Thomas, Jr., "For several years after its beginning, the work of the Normal was carried on largely at the high school level with a small portion of the program being devoted to teacher training work" (315). In fact, TNS was the only high school in the greater Phoenix area for a decade after it was founded, so even students who had no intention of becoming teachers enrolled at TNS to earn a high school diploma. Following the secondary coursework, students could enroll in the post-secondary "professional" curriculum, the completion of which qualified them to teach in Arizona's schools.

Rhetoric, writing, and language and literacy courses constituted a significant portion of TNS's curriculum. In 1888, for example, students took "Grammar—Analysis and Parsing," "Spelling, Oral and Written," "English Composition," "Reading," and "Word Analysis—especially in the Greek and Latin Elements of English" in their first year ("Prospectus"). In the second year, students took "Rhetorical Work—Orations, Essays and Declarations," "Rhetoric," "English Literature," and "Rhetorical Work—Orations and Discussions" ("Prospectus"). Rhetoric and writing courses were distributed throughout the curriculum to reinforce the lessons normal students would be expected to teach in the state's elementary and secondary classrooms. However, rhetoric and writing were remanded to the first two years of TNS's curriculum (three for "Sub-normal" students), which were wholly "academic" in the sense delineated by the NEA committee.[14] They were equivalent to high school courses and were meant to refresh students' acquaintance with subjects they would be expected to teach in Arizona's public schools. Alongside the rhetoric and writing courses listed above, students also took other "basic subjects," including math, geography, history, science, and civics. When read in the broader normal school context, all the evidence of rhetoric and writing education at TNS must be understood as secondary in nature.

In contrast, the post-secondary curriculum at TNS required no coursework in rhetoric or writing. After completing the secondary coursework (or after demonstrating "advanced standing" by passing an examination), TNS students enrolled in the post-secondary courses, which included: "Primary Methods," "Arithmetic Methods," "Pedagogy," "School Management," etc. (Farmer 3). With the exception of Latin and Geometry, the professional curriculum was entirely focused on methods, and rhetoric and writing courses were no longer offered, much less required. The only courses even related to rhetoric and/or writing were Latin and potentially "Professional Work," in which students were required to teach "at least one class in Arithmetic, Geography, Grammar, Reading, Spelling, and Penmanship for half a term under the supervision and criticism of the principal" ("Prospectus"). But any relation to rhetoric or writing was incidental. As soon as students embarked on the post-secondary course of study, they were involved in rhetoric and writing education only inasmuch as they were expected to (1) learn methods that would enable them to teach rhetoric and writing, and (2) practice teaching them.

It is easy to see why researching rhetorical education at normals is inviting to composition historians. Without needing to look much further than course catalogs, there are many apparent parallels that can be drawn between rhetorical education at Tempe Normal, as one example, and rhetorical education at colleges and universities. There is ample evidence to suggest that rhetoric and composition at TNS were simplified, instrumentalized, and inflected with current-traditional sensibilities between 1885 and the early 1900s. According to the 1896-97 "Circular and Catalogue," for instance, writing was taught using the infamous modes of discourse, "advancing by easy steps from simple description to exposition and to the construction of argument" (18). Theories, pedagogies, and texts[15] reflect what has long been known by composition historians about rhetoric and composition at colleges and universities at and around the turn of the twentieth century. Add the founding of literary societies at TNS in 1896, the establishment of a school newspaper and literary journals around the turn of the century, and the introduction of intercollegiate debates with the University of Arizona starting in the early 1900s, and Tempe Normal School's history naturally aligns with histories describing the state of rhetorical curricula and extra-curricula at colleges and universities across the country during that period. But read in the context of normal schools' institutional objectives, all of these comparisons become dubious because the parallels that are so apparent meet different objectives at different levels of education for different populations of students.

This history of TNS is necessarily abridged, but even this condensed version challenges the belief that normal schools set useful precedents for contemporary rhetoric and composition teachers and scholars. Certainly the notion that "contemporary attitudes" have precedence in the normal school is troubling when we consider the different objectives for rhetorical education in nineteenth century normals and contemporary colleges and universities. If the attitudes praised by Fitzgerald and others were considered better suited to secondary education a century ago, and if we feel that such attitudes effectively define us as a field in the twenty-first century, there are serious implications for rhetorical education to be contemplated, including whether we should teach rhetoric and writing in colleges and universities at all. Add the fact that normal schools were systematically eradicated from American education before World War II because they became obsolete, and normal schools offer historical precedents we should be loathe to repeat.

Normal Lessons

The conclusion that rhetorical education at normal schools cannot be compared to rhetorical education in colleges and universities might be understood to suggest that composition historians should abandon normal school research altogether; I think that would be a mistake. Even if normal schools do not exemplify the kind of "rich, alternative tradition of rhetorical education in America" (Gold x) that historians have imagined, there are still important lessons to be learned from studying normal schools. In the remainder of this essay, then, I sketch out some tentative lessons that can be drawn from normal schools for contemporary scholars and teachers.

One of the important lessons of normal schools is that institutional objectives have played a crucial role in shaping the conditions for rhetorical education. To some degree, composition historians have known this for some time—it is commonplace, for example, that the institutional requirement of first-year composition in colleges and universities has had lasting consequences for rhetorical education (e.g., Crowley, especially Chapter 10). But it is a point that needs to be made more forcefully because institutional objectives are often considered contextual, rather than formative. Most historians ultimately resort to cultural, local, or disciplinary exigencies to explain various developments in rhetoric and writing education. For example, in "Mid-Nineteenth-Century Writing Instruction at Illinois State Normal University," Kenneth Lindblom, William Banks, and Risë Quay explain writing pedagogy at Illinois State Normal University by reference to the increasing cultural value placed on academic credentials in the last half of the nineteenth century (96); David Gold contends that local exigencies at East Texas Normal College, specifically President William Mayo's pedagogical ideals, shaped the rhetorical education students received (114); and Kathryn Fitzgerald argues for the importance of normal school pedagogies by contrasting them with classical rhetoric (230). These cultural, local, and disciplinary lenses are unquestionably illuminating, but they generally relegate institutional objectives to background information.

As the example of normal schools demonstrates, however, institutional objectives played a primary role in how hundreds of thousands of students were exposed to rhetorical education. Normal schools' common objectives of (1) reinforcing basic subjects, (2) training teachers, and (3) remaining distinct from high schools, colleges, and universities determined that rhetoric and writing were secondary, not post-secondary. Even granting variations in academic standards and possible exceptions, normal schools' institutional objectives were common enough that most normalites would have taken similar classes at similar times for similar reasons. Although institutional objectives were certainly not independent from cultural, local, or disciplinary concerns, neither were they less consequential. Furthermore, institutional objectives often shaped the conditions of rhetoric and writing more directly than cultural, local, or disciplinary exigencies. Therefore, for historians interested in how rhetoric and writing were taught in bygone eras, attention to institutional objectives is essential.

The importance of studying institutional objectives is even more striking when one realizes that around the turn of the twentieth century, students could earn some form of post-secondary education at colleges, universities, normal schools, women's colleges, black colleges and universities, junior colleges, law and medical schools, seminaries, institutes, technical colleges, and more (see Cremin). Each type of institution competed for students, to a greater or lesser degree, with other institutions, and each had distinct objectives that differentiated them from other types of institutions. If historians want to understand how vast populations of students were taught rhetoric and writing, and how different systems of rhetorical education related to one another, considering how rhetoric and writing education were inflected by various institutions' objectives is vital.

A second lesson normal schools can teach composition historians is that the resemblance of theories, pedagogies, and curricula across institutions cannot be the sole basis for historical research. To put it another way, composition historians cannot look for normal schools, or any other institution for that matter, to mirror contemporary perspectives about rhetoric and writing. Rhetoric and writing in normal schools strongly resembled rhetoric and writing in colleges and universities during the late-nineteenth and early-twentieth centuries, but as I have argued, the resemblance is misleading. In drawing comparisons historians have neglected—or worse, assimilated—the characteristics that make normals distinct, and therefore worth studying in more depth. Obviously, this is not intentional misrepresentation, but it is a function of historians' search for research subjects, based on resemblances, linked to the search for precedence.

Detached from the search for precedence, however, the fact of resemblance can be indispensible. Kathryn Fitzgerald asserts in "The Platteville Papers Revisited" that "the most significant contribution historical research makes to the contemporary field" is "to enable us to critique still current practices from an outsider's point of view" (116). In other words, the proper objective of historical research is to understand the present by reference to the past, and it is an important point for historians to recognize. The fact of historical resemblance, coupled with the realization of fundamental differences between historical and contemporary subjects, helps to reveal the limits of contemporary thinking in order to aid the critique of current practices from an outsider's point of view. Less abstractly, the fact that normals provided rhetorical education at the secondary level which strongly resembles rhetoric and writing education in contemporary post-secondary institutions should raise a red flag for historians. The resulting dissonance can help historians evaluate current practices and their attendant values and beliefs by provoking questions about why we believe what we believe. The goal of historians, ultimately, is to critique current practices so as to improve them, rather than finding historical precedence that appeals to contemporary convictions and reinforces current practices.

I should note that this lesson—that resemblance can be useful, but is not sufficient, for identifying research subjects—has implications far beyond normal school histories. To extend Fitzgerald's point, critique of current practices is as necessary for digital humanists as it is for composition historians, as important for cutting edge theorists as for classroom practitioners, and so on. Critique enables teachers and researchers to evaluate our own beliefs and values with an eye toward improving the work we do to the benefit of our institutions, our fields, and our students rather than simply affirming beliefs we already hold. So while this essay is specifically calling for composition historians to be more critical in their search for normal school precedents, it is a reminder for all researchers and teachers that a critical attitude is a necessary component of all scholarly work.

A third lesson proceeds from the first two: composition historians need to expand their scope of inquiry to consider more specifically institutional conditions that shaped the possibilities for composition's existence in higher education. Doing so compels composition historians to become much better acquainted with education history. The history of rhetorical education for much of the past 200 years is largely a history of American education. Certainly rhetoric and writing were taught outside of educational institutions, as historians including Royster have powerfully demonstrated. At the same time, the majority of formal education in America was predicated on basic subjects which included rhetoric and writing instruction; and as education developed, so too did rhetoric and writing. Historians would do well to investigate that relationship more closely. Education history—as opposed to the history of rhetoric and composition, cultural history, or local history—can provide us with an important frame for understanding how educational institutions developed, how different institutions reacted to similar cultural exigencies, how institutional objectives shaped the conditions for rhetorical education, and ultimately how students and teachers encountered rhetorical education. Moreover, education history can help us to better recognize the resemblances and differences among institutions that enable us to critique, and thereby improve, current practices.

Composition historians' focus on disciplinary norms and practices is invaluable, and education history cannot replace disciplinary, cultural, or local historical research. But it must become a more central part of historians' repertoires if we are to understand the lessons of nineteenth- and twentieth-century rhetorical education. An added benefit is that the history of American education is well documented. There are vast collections of primary sources available for study, many of them available in digital collections, which can help us find resemblances that invite deeper study, if not easy comparisons. The combination of important avenues of research and relatively ready access is fortuitous and should be embraced by composition historians.

Normal schools continue to represent one such avenue of research. In the first three decades of the twentieth century, as a result of many complex educational, political, and cultural factors, normal schools came under sustained attack as inferior institutions that provided inadequate training for the nation's teachers (Ogren 2-3; Rettger). By the time David Felmley gave his talk in 1923, normal schools were under siege from colleges and universities, which increasingly offered four-year, liberal arts-based teaching degrees. In the subsequent decade and a half, normal schools virtually disappeared, either shuttering their doors or transforming into teachers' colleges in the 1920s, 30s, and 40s. In 1925, Tempe Normal followed the national trend and transformed into Tempe State Teachers' College, replete with four-year liberal arts curriculum and a required, two-course, first-year composition sequence. In fact, the rhetoric and writing curriculum at Tempe State Teachers' College strongly resembled the curriculum that exists to this day in thousands of colleges and universities across the country, despite radical differences in institutional objectives at teachers' colleges and other post-secondary institutions. Questions about how and why are potentially enlightening for contemporary teachers and scholars, but they have not yet been asked. In short, composition historians have much work still to do.

Notes

1. I want to thank Kyle Jensen and Matthew Heard for their invaluable contributions to this essay.
2. In this essay, "normal" refers to the normal school tradition and is not a qualitative judgment (e.g., "Normal department" is a teacher education department).
3. According to Felmley, "We use the term teacher training [as opposed to 'teacher education'] because we recognize that teaching is an art in which skill is to be acquired rather than a science of which knowledge is to be gained" (47).
4. Teachers in American schools were traditionally male, but many education reformers believed that women were ideally suited to teaching. During his time as Massachusetts Secretary of Education, Horace Mann defended training female teachers, writing: "Is not woman destined to conduct the rising generation, of both sexes, at least through all the primary stages of education? Has not the Author of nature preadapted her, by constitution, and faculty, and temperament, for this noble work?" (qtd. in Herbst, *And Sadly Teach* 28). Herbst and Ogren discuss the relationship between women and teaching at length. Ogren also discusses the normals' tradition of courting other types of nontraditional students (see esp. Chapter 2).
5. I borrow this title from Ogren. "[A]lthough it 'wasn't much of a college,'" she writes, "the state normal school was a revolutionary institution in the field of higher education" (4).
6. Colleges and universities differed significantly during this period as well, both in missions and methods. Nevertheless, the conflation of colleges and universities has predominated in composition histories, and I maintain it here on the grounds that rhetorical education seems to have existed in similar measure at both institution types. I recognize the probability, inherent in my own argument, that closer examination would prove the conflation unsustainable.
7. The "common branches" (i.e., "basic subjects") constituted the curriculum in the vast majority of American public schools. Although there was considerable disagreement about what constituted the common branches, basic literacy was a ubiquitous component.
8. Mariolina Salvatori claims that the professional focus of normal schools became a political problem in the 1880s when some people "began to argue for the inadequacy of normal schools 'to educate' teachers [. . .] because of their exclusive and limiting reliance on 'methods'" (xiv). Despite the political opposition, normal school proponents continued to champion normal schools' methodological focus for at least another forty years.

9. Normal schools were not in a position to turn students away for a number of reasons, including the desperate need for teachers to teach in public schools. But there were also pressing economic and political considerations that militated against rigorous admissions policies (Ogren 61-62). If normals failed to attract sufficient enrollment, for example, legislators threatened to withdraw state funding. In Tempe Normal's case, according to Hopkins and Thomas, TNS faced a series of challenges—particularly legislative challenges—that threatened to shutter the school permanently in its first two decades in existence (97-114; see also Hronek 81, 98).
10. John Ogden, a prominent figure in teacher education during the nineteenth-century, lists the general methods as: school-room duties, study, recitation, school business, recreation, and school government (iii-iv). The title of Ogden's book, *The Art of Teaching*, was a commonly used phrase to describe the aim of teacher training. There is a fairly extensive literature on "the art of teaching" that is informative for understanding what goals normal schools were attempting to meet (e.g., Barnard).
11. Normal schools evolved over time and their objectives gradually shifted, but there remained significant uniformity across institutions well into the twentieth century. It is not within the purview of this essay to detail normal schools' evolution of over time, but such a project would no doubt reveal that rhetorical education changed significantly as normals' institutional objectives shifted to meet various exigencies.
12. TNS had four different names during its forty years as a normal school. For the sake of brevity and consistency, I refer to the institution as Tempe Normal School or TNS.
13. The "Sub-normal" curriculum was disestablished in 1905 ("Tempe Normal").
14. TNS's rhetoric and writing curriculum changed significantly over the years, but two important things remained constant: (1) the courses were always widely distributed throughout the curriculum, but (2) they were confined to the secondary level.
15. TNS's textbooks should be familiar to composition historians. Between 1890 and 1906, students used textbooks by Adams Sherman Hill, John Genung, Fred Newton Scott and Joseph Villiers Denny, Gertrude Buck, Virginia Waddy, and George Quackenbos, among others (see Carr, Carr, and Schultz for discussion of these authors' books with regards to composition history).

Works Cited

"An Act to Locate, Establish, and Endow, and Provide for the Maintenance of a Territorial Normal School, 1885." [legislative act]. (UM USM-343). ASU Libraries, University Archives. Arizona State University.

Barnard, Henry. *Normal Schools, and Other Institutions, Agencies, and Means Designed for the Professional Education of Teachers*. Hartford: Case, 1851. Print.

Bordelon, Suzanne. "Participating on an 'Equal Footing': The Rhetorical Significance of California State Normal School in the Late Nineteenth Century." *Rhetoric Society Quarterly* 41.2 (2011): 168-90. Print.

Burke, Colin B. *American Collegiate Populations: A Test of the Traditional View*. New York: New York UP, 1982. Print.

Carr, Jean Ferguson, Stephen L. Carr, and Lucille Schultz. *Archives of Instruction: Nineteenth-Century Rhetorics, Readers, and Composition Books in the United States*. Carbondale: Southern Illinois UP, 2005. Print.

"Circular and Catalogue of the Arizona Territorial Normal School, Tempe, AZ, 1896-1897." [general catalog]. (UE ASU 0.3). ASU Libraries, University Archives. Arizona State University.

Cohen, Arthur M. *The Shaping of American Higher Education: Emergence and Growth of the Contemporary System*. San Francisco: Jossey-Bass, 1998. Print.

Cremin, Lawrence A., ed. *Reports of the Mosely Educational Commission to the United States*. New York: Arno, 1969. Print.

Crowley, Sharon. *Composition in the University: Historical and Polemical Essays*. Pittsburgh: U Pittsburgh P, 1998. Print.

Donahue, Patricia, and Gretchen Flesher Moon, eds. *Local Histories: Reading the Archives of Composition*. Pittsburgh: U of Pittsburgh P, 2007. Print.

Farmer, Hiram Bradford. "Course of Study, 1886-1887." [general catalog]. ASU Libraries, University Archives. Arizona State University. Web. 18 Jun. 2012.

Felmley, David. "The Collegiate Rank of the Normal School." Rettger 41-52.

Fitzgerald, Kathryn. "The Platteville Papers: Inscribing Frontier Ideology and Culture in a Nineteenth-Century Writing Assignment." *College English* 64.3 (2002): 273-301. Print.

—. "The Platteville Papers Revisited: Gender and Genre in a Normal School Writing Assignment." Donahue and Moon 115-33.

—. "A Rediscovered Tradition: European Pedagogy and Composition in Nineteenth-Century Midwestern Normal Schools." *CCC* 53.2 (2001): 224-50. Print.

Gannett, Cinthia, John C. Brereton, and Katherine E. Tirabassi. "'We All Got History': Process and Product in the History of Composition." *Pedagogy* 10.2 (2010): 425-50. Print.

Gold, David. *Rhetoric at the Margins: Revisiting the History of Writing Instruction in American Colleges, 1873-1947*. Carbondale: SIUP, 2008. Print.

Gove, Aaron. "Chapter VII: The Public Schools Systems of the United States." *Report* 351-8. Print.

Gray, Patrice K. "Life in the Margins: Student Writing and Curricular Change at Fitchburg Normal, 1895-1910." Donahue and Moon 159-80.

Harris, William T. "The Commissioner's Introduction." *Report* ix-lxxvi. Print.

Herbst, Jurgen. *And Sadly Teach: Teacher Education and Professionalization in American Culture*. Madison: U Wisconsin P, 1989. Print.

—. "Nineteenth-Century Normal Schools in the United States: A Fresh Look." *History of Education* 9.3 (1980): 219-27. Print.

Hopkins, Ernest J. and Alfred Thomas, Jr. *The Arizona State University Story*. Phoenix: Southwest, 1960. Print.

Hronek, Pamela Claire. *Women and Normal Schools: Tempe Normal, A Case Study, 1885-1925*. Diss. Arizona State University, 1985. Ann Arbor: UMI, 1985. Print.

Lindblom, Kenneth, William Banks, and Risë Quay. "Mid-Nineteenth-Century Writing Instruction at Illinois State Normal University: Credentials, Correctness, and the Rise of a Teaching Class." Donahue and Moon 94-114.

Lucas, Christopher J. *American Higher Education, A History*. 2nd ed. New York: Palgrave, 2006. Print.

—. *Teacher Education in America: Reform Agendas for the Twenty-First Century*. New York: Palgrave, 1999. Print.

Lyte, Eliphalet Oram. "The State Normal Schools of the United States." *Report* 1103-36. Print.

McClintock, Jas. H. "Biennial Report of the Normal Schools of Arizona, 1900." [report]. (2.2 B4771 1900). ASU Libraries, University Archives. Arizona State University.

Ogden, John. *The Art of Teaching*. New York: American, 1879. Print.

Ogren, Christine A. *The American State Normal School: "An Instrument of Great Good."* New York: Palgrave, 2005. Print.

"Prospectus and Circular of the Arizona Territorial Normal School, Tempe, Arizona, 1888-1889." [general catalog]. (UE ASU 0.3). ASU Libraries, University Archives. Arizona State University.

Report of the Commissioner of Education, 1903, Volume 1. Department of the Interior. Washington DC: Government Printing Office, 1904. Print.

"Report of the Committee on Normal Schools." *Addresses and Proceedings, National Education Association of the United States, Volume 38*. Chicago: U Chicago P (1899): 836-54. Print.

Rettger, L.J., ed. *Proceedings of the Centennial Conference on Teacher Training, Terre Haute, 1923*. Spec. issue of *Indiana State Normal School Bulletin* 17.1 (1923). Print.

Ritter, Kelly. *To Know Her Own History: Writing at the Woman's College, 1943–1963*. Pittsburgh: U of Pittsburgh P, 2012. Print.

Rothermel, Beth Ann. "'Our Life's Work': Rhetorical Preparation and Teacher Training at a Massachusetts State Normal School, 1839-1929." Donahue and Moon 134-58.

—. "A Sphere of Noble Action: Gender, Rhetoric, and Influence at a Nineteenth-Century Massachusetts State Normal School." *Rhetoric Society Quarterly* 33.1 (2003): 35-64. Print.

Royster, Jacqueline Jones, and Gesa E. Kirsch. *Feminist Rhetorical Practices: New Horizons for Rhetoric, Composition, and Literacy Studies*. Carbondale: SIUP, 2012. Print.

Salvatori, Mariolina Rizzi, Ed. *Pedagogy: Disturbing History, 1819-1929*. Pittsburgh: U Pittsburgh P, 1996. Print.

"The Tempe Normal School of Arizona at Tempe, Annual Catalogue, 1905-1906." [general catalog]. (UE ASU 0.3). ASU Libraries, University Archives. Arizona State University.

Thomas, Alfred, Jr. *Arizona State University: A Documentary History of the First Seventy-Five Years, 1885-1960: Volume 2*. (LD 179.28 T6 A3X v.2). ASU Libraries, University Archives. Arizona State University.

Transitioning Writers across the Composition Threshold: What We Can Learn from Dual Enrollment Partnerships

Christine Denecker

> Crossing the threshold from high school to college-level writing expectations constitutes a challenge for many students since secondary and post-secondary composition instructors often work under different constraints and are guided by different curricular philosophies. Dual enrollment classrooms provide a space where these differences can be delineated, discussed, respected, and perhaps even reconciled by instructors on both sides of the divide.

Dual Enrollment and the Composition Threshold

A century ago, the National Council for the Teachers of English was formed, in part, to empower high school educators against the top-down demands of university English programs ("Forum"; "NCTE's History"). Today, the relationship between secondary and post-secondary English programs remains a complex one, most particularly, in the area of composition studies. Questions such as "What is College-Level Writing?" posed by Patrick Sullivan, Howard Tinberg, and Sheridan Blau as well as Kristine Hansen and Christine Farris's query into the "business" of granting college credit to high school writers suggest the on-going conversation. Meanwhile, Mary Jo Reiff and Anis Bawarshi's research into the discursive resources high school students transfer into first-year college composition courses implies a lack of uniformity in writing instruction across secondary/post-secondary boundaries. However, as David Foster and David R. Russell point out, an inherent reciprocity exists between secondary and post-secondary writing instruction since, "students' writing development plays an important—though often unacknowledged—role in the crucial transition from secondary school to university" (1). To borrow from Larry Weinstein, this transitional movement might be seen as an intellectual "threshold" which secondary students are challenged to cross as they enter into the demands of post-secondary education (xi).

Unfortunately, this threshold is not easily traversed, due, in part, to the uneven juncture where the paths of secondary and post-secondary writing expectations meet. In fact, to borrow the words of Foster and Russell, a "profound mismatch in expectations" exists among "teachers in secondary and in higher education" regarding "student writing and writing development" (42). To this point, according to Herb Budden, et al., "many college composition faculty berate secondary school teachers, blaming them for college students' inability to punctuate, to cite, to synthesize" (75). And, it is not uncommon to hear college composition instructors "complain that the students in their various first-year English classes [are] not ready for the course" (Blau 368) or "wonder whether high school English teachers are aware of their students' incompetence in writing" (Mosley 59–60). In frustration, some college writing instructors find themselves "un-teaching" many elements of students' high school writing instruction in order to "ready" students for the college writing experience.

At the same time, secondary English teachers such as Gregory Shafer resist the notion that he and his colleagues merely "reject the double negative, the first person narrative, [or] the contraction" (67) in their writing instruction. His comment delineates the "catch 22" of many high school teachers who face top-down pressure to rely on prescriptive pedagogies for instruction. According to Merrill Davies, "The often-berated five-paragraph essay is an attempt to teach students how to [organize material]" ("Whistling," 33), and Ellen Andrews Knodt explains that many secondary teachers utilize the five-paragraph format because of its usefulness "for beginning writers who have little sense of organization" (148). Still, Jeanette Jordan and her colleagues in "Am I a Liar? The Angst of a High School English Teacher," argue that secondary educators also "value nonformulaic writing and struggle to push [their] students beyond the very limiting five-paragraph structure that they find so comforting and familiar" (38). However, she wonders, "Am I doing a disservice to my low-level writers . . . if I throw out the scaffold that they are still trying to master?" (38). Secondary instructor Lesley Roessing also feels this squeeze and struggles with teaching "high school" concepts such as the five-paragraph essay while, at the same time, fostering her students' ability to have voice, choice, and style in their writing (41)—in other words, traditional college-level writing requirements.

To further complicate matters, as Katherine Nolan of Project Alignment notes, "Colleges have rarely defined what students need to know and be able to do in order to be successful writers" (qtd. in Nagin 64). Consequently, countless former and current secondary English teachers such as Roger Shanley have faced the challenge of trying to make "their writing instruction serve as the natural segue from high school to . . . university writing programs" (14) in a climate where "college theory and high school practice differ greatly" (Mosley 60). Likewise, the students, themselves, are left to "negotiate between the resources of their previous writing expectations and the expectations of new academic contexts" (Reiff and Bawarshi 313).

Dual enrollment composition courses add yet another layer of complexity to the relationship between high school and college writing instruction. In the mid-1980s, a nationwide trend of dual enrollment[1]—high school students attending college for both high school and college credit—came into existence with claims of providing, among other features, a mode of transition for students from the familiarity of secondary education to the demands and challenges of the post-secondary environment (see McCarthy). Dual Enrollment, also known as Postsecondary Education Options (PSEO), dual credit, or concurrent enrollment[2] grew exponentially in the 1990s, and according to researcher Hans Andrews, all fifty states currently have some form of dual enrollment opportunities for eligible high school students.

The most recent report (2005) on dual enrollment from the U.S. Department of Education puts participation at upwards of 800,000 or the equivalent of five percent of all high school students (National Center for Education Statistics). No complete data exists on the nationwide number of students dual enrolled in composition courses. However, for the purposes of this study, as of 2006, composition ranked as number one among Ohio's "Top 15 Courses" for dual enrolled students with 2,571 participants—nearly 700 more than in psychology, which ranked number two (ODE, *The Promise* 22). It should be noted that these statistics only account for those students enrolled in public institutions; the number of students dual enrolled in composition courses at private institutions has not been captured. Finally, a cursory web glance at institutions nationwide suggests that many routinely offer first and even second-level composition courses to dual enrolled students—students poised to navigate the threshold from secondary to post-secondary writing expectations.

A Space for Examining the Disconnect between High School and College Writing Expectations

The dual enrollment composition classroom provides a unique space where students simultaneously experience both high school and college expectations. As a result, it is in this space that the tensions and inconsistencies between secondary and post-secondary writing instruction have the potential for becoming more clearly defined. Such has been my experience as I have segued professionally from high school English teacher to college writing instructor and director of a dual enrollment writing program. Thus, the findings that follow are the result of observations of, interviews with, and surveys completed by high school teachers, college instructors, and students participating in three distinct dual enrollment/dual credit options at The University of Findlay (in Ohio): 1) on the college campus in a traditional composition classroom setting; 2) on the high school campus (with a trained high school instructor); and 3) on the college campus in a classroom populated exclusively by high school students.

Methodology

From 2006–2007, I conducted an initial pilot study of the three University of Findlay (UF) dual enrollment settings.[3] During that time, I observed three College Writing I classrooms (one at each setting), surveyed/interviewed seven teachers, surveyed seventeen students, and then personally interviewed fifteen of the seventeen students. From 2007-present,[4] I have maintained a follow-up study of the dual enrollment composition classroom.[5] During this follow-up phase, I have surveyed and held formal bi-annual discussions/grading sessions with twenty-two UF concurrent enrollment composition instructors.[6] These instructors have also shared a minimum of three representative student papers[7] with me per year for individual calibration and discussion purposes.

In each setting of writing instruction, students follow the same general syllabus for UF's College Writing I course and are given the same writing assignments (narrative, analysis, and argument). Likewise, all students must submit a final portfolio for communal review upon completion of the course.[8] All of the instructors, regardless of setting, have had experience teaching secondary and post-secondary writing. Unique to each situation are the obvious physical surroundings as well as *who* does the teaching and *how*. In the on-campus, self-contained classrooms, the instructor was (most often) a former high school teacher turned college instructor, while in the on-campus mixed population, the instructor has traditionally been either a faculty member or an adjunct. On the high school campus, the instructor is a high school English teacher, who has successfully completed UF's dual enrollment training course and continues to participate in UF's summer professional development opportunities for dual enrollment instructors. Similar to the diversification found among instructors in the program, the dual enrollment student population is diversified as well. While all students enrolled are high school junior or seniors (presumably in the 16–19 year-old age range), the majority of students taking dual enrollment composition classes on The University of Findlay's campus are rural or suburban students who live in close proximity to the university; those students participating in the high school setting are from urban areas or remote rural areas across the state of Ohio.

In terms of methodology, I employed Robert Bogdan and Sari Knopp Biklen's "constant comparative method" in order to collect and assess data from both the on-campus and off-campus sites (73). In addition, as noted earlier, I gathered the voices of students and their instructors through survey questionnaires and face-to-face interviews. Rosanna Hertz stresses the importance of authentic voice in research and also legitimizes the inclusion of my own voice in the research process. A similar approach can be seen in the work of Cindy Johanek, who cautions (auto)ethnographic researchers to "balance" abundant qualitative information with a quantitative approach, which includes the coding of data (124). Thus, the survey and interview data for this study were coded for analysis. Specifically, participants (both students and instructors) discussed and ranked elements of "good" writing in both the survey and interview portions of the study. For purposes of this study "good" writing was defined as that which moves beyond a formulaic structure (five-paragraph essay) and includes attention to style, audience, organization, development, thesis, and grammar. While this study was put into place before the publication of "High School Teaching and College

Expectations in Writing and Reading," the elements of "good" writing used here mirror those found by Joseph Patterson and David Duer in their research: "Selecting a topic, formulating a thesis"; "Editing and proofreading"; "Developing logical arguments" and "Analyzing an issue or problem" (82).

With that said, it should be noted that this study was *not* carried out with the assumption that a single, clear-cut definition exists for "good" writing at either the high school-level or the college-level. *What is "College-Level" Writing? Volumes 1* and *2,* in particular, point to the complexity of that discussion. Still, as Howard Tinberg and Jean-Paul Nadeau argue, "To be effective, dual-enrollment programs require a clear understanding among all interested parties as to the core principles, practices, and outcomes for first-year college composition" (710). Even before that caveat was issued, this research went forward with, to borrow from Kristine Hansen, some "fairly safe generalization[s]" (10) that college-level writing should challenge and meet, in the words of Budden, et. al, "students' diverse needs" through discussion "about ideas" that "generate theses about topics of interest that they then defend and support with specific details and concrete examples—skills that will be essential no matter where they attend college" (76). In addition, recent literature indicates that current college-level writing instruction privileges, among other elements, analysis, argument, voice, audience, and process (see Sullivan and Tinberg; Lujan; Davies; Harris; Lunsford; Schorn; Kearns; Alsup and Bernard-Donals; Yancey and Morrison; Reiff and Bawarshi). Finally, this study borrows the notion of Larry Weinstein that the threshold between high school and college writing expectations consists "of that which, at any age, leads from doing slavish or derivative thinking to doing real, engaged thinking of one's own" (xi).

And while the intent of my research was to uncover inconsistencies between high school and college-level writing instruction in order to discern best practices for transitioning high school students across the composition threshold, I came to recognize that the most powerful element for moving students from point A to B as writers may lie not with the students themselves but with those who plan, oversee, and carry out dual enrollment composition instruction. In other words, transitioning writers across the composition threshold is not so much about what the *students* do as it is about what the *instructors* know or understand about composition practices on both sides of the divide. As Foster and Russell write, "if teachers, examiners, and policymakers on either side of the secondary/higher education divide do not talk to each other, directly and/or indirectly, about student writing and writing development, then the mismatch [in writing instruction] will continue" (42). Thus, while the initial pilot study (2006–2007) for this research focused primarily on students, the follow-up phase (2007-present) has sought to discern what dual enrollment instructors—especially high school instructors teaching college writing on the high school campus—have to offer in unearthing inconsistencies that exist between high school and college-level writing expectations.[9]

Differing Expectations

Specifically, three basic factors surfaced in this study as contributing to the inconsistencies between high school and college writing instruction. First is the sheer scope of material public school English teachers are challenged to cover in their classes—from vocabulary to grammar to literature to writing. In other words, composition is rarely taught in a stand-alone fashion in high schools as it is on college campuses. In fact, at a May 2012 meeting of the High School and Higher Education Northwest Ohio Regional Consortia for High School and Higher Education Curricular alignment, secondary English teachers noted that the majority of high school writing instruction is traditionally embedded in *literature* instruction. A second difference between secondary and post-secondary writing instruction is the state and national standards to which high school English teachers must adhere. As Merrill Davies notes, "the teaching of writing in high school, as compared to college, is permeated by the need to get ready for the standardized writing test" ("Making the Leap" 119). These standards, to be discussed in detail later, impact the nature and quality of high school writing instruction. The third basic factor separating high school and college level writing instruction is the paper-load/grading dilemma. Teaching upwards of one-hundred (or even one-hundred-fifty plus) students per day,[10] every day, makes assigning and grading writing assignments a prohibitive venture for many high school teachers. These three factors suggest that, from the start, a dual enrolled student entering a college composition classroom is crossing the threshold into somewhat foreign territory—a place where writing alone is king, a place where the expectations for writing are *not* dictated by state or national mandates, and a place where the instructor's time and energy are (presumably) focused on the needs of fewer students.

Although factors of content coverage, testing mandates, and the grading load have consistently dominated the conversations I have had with instructors in this study over the past six years, three additional factors (with complexities all their own) have also surfaced as we have worked collaboratively to better understand how "good" writing is defined at each level of instruction. The factors have elements that intertwine. However, for purposes of this discussion, I have organized them into the following overarching groups: "Reporting" and the Argumentative Thesis, Surface Writing and Deep Writing, and The Writing Process.

"Reporting" and the Argumentative Thesis

Dual enrollment students in this study expressed that college-level writing's[11] intense focus on "thesis" is one element that differentiates it from typical high school writing instruction.[12] According to Jean,[13] a student in this study, "I only had it [thesis] one time in high school," and still another student, Kasey, shared that although she had learned about thesis statements in high school, "college was stronger on thesis and development."

Kristie added that, in her experience, "High school focuses more on grammar and presentation [than thesis]." One dual enrollment instructor, Kim, also cites attention to thesis as one of the noticeable differences between secondary and post-secondary instruction. Furthermore, specific to this study, and that of others (see Yancey and Morrison) is the acknowledgement that high school writing instruction generally focuses on analyzing literature or reporting information rather than creating thesis-driven works meant to "join a conversation." As a result, it was no surprise that many instructor participants pointed to "thesis" as the main disconnect between how they have approached the teaching of writing at high school versus college.

To put the issue of thesis into context, it is important to know that in Ohio, the tenth grade Ohio Graduation Test (OGT) writing requirements include composing narratives, responding to literature, writing letters, and crafting "a persuasive piece that states a clear position, includes relevant information and offers compelling evidence in the form of facts and details" (ODE *Academic Content Standards* 45–47). In addition, the final Ohio 12th grade Writing Process indicator requires that, prior to graduation, students exhibit the ability to compose persuasive pieces that "articulate a clear position" and display the development of "arguments" (124).

At first glance, the OGT benchmark and the 12th grade Writing Process indicator, which are both aligned with persuasive writing, seem to suggest the need for a "thesis-driven" stance in student writing, since each, respectively, calls for work that "states a clear position." However, the benchmark does not delineate *whose* position that might be—that of the student? the teacher? the writer of the source(s) the student happens to be using? Furthermore, the lone high school grade-level indicator for thesis writing (tied to the OGT) requires students to demonstrate the ability to "Establish and develop a clear thesis statement for *informational*[14] writing or a clear plan or outline for narrative writing" (107). In other words, these particular benchmarks/indicators may indeed suggest or even directly speak to the development of thesis. However, the type of thesis being described here is one that "reports" information rather than one that argues a position or strives to add something new to an on-going conversation. To apply the words of Kathleen McCormick, "[high school students] have been asked to write research reports, which are basically summaries, rather than researched essays—that is, carefully integrated arguments in which student writers enter into genuine conversation with a group of experts" (211). Thus, since secondary writers are often required to *report* information in their writing assignments[15] or on state tests, such as the OGT, rather than *research* information or *argue a position*, the definition of "thesis" differs between high school and college writing instruction.

The structure expected of these types of writings—think five paragraph essay—also presents a conundrum for high school writing students and their instructors, since movement beyond writing formulas stands, among many university educators, as a benchmark of college-level writing conventions. "Success" via writing formulas has been dubbed a "mythrule," and in the words of Kenneth Lindblom:

> lead[s] to one thing: boring swatches of writing intended to do nothing other than result in a high score on a test of writing that tests nothing real about writing. But if people who assess the writing expect to see school-writing mythrules followed, not following them can have serious consequences for students. (105)

The statement of Sharon, another dual enrollment instructor in this study, corroborates Lindblom's remarks. She notes that an emphasis on format is a distinctive element of high school writing instruction and explains that since a five-paragraph essay has typically allowed students to pass the 10th grade Ohio Graduation Test, it can be difficult, in her words, "to get [students] beyond that point. They have a hard time with that."

In regard to formulaic structures, another instructor, Janet, explains, "At high school, they're *learning* the essay form. At college, they're *using* the essay form. They're expected to think outside the box and do more with it"—an explanation not unlike the advice of The Writing Center at North Carolina at Chapel Hill, which challenges writers "to move beyond the five-paragraph themes" they "learned to write in high school and start writing essays that are more analytical and more flexible." The instructors in this study note that they often see their dual enrollment students moving out of the five-paragraph-mindset, in the words of one participant, about "a month or so" into the College Writing I course when students "find they do have something to say." Janet describes this move as a "natural progression" and admits that while some students never get past the five-paragraph essay format, others, in her words, "bleed out of it." Reiff and Bawarshi might describe these students as "boundary crossers" who have broken down their prior knowledge "into useful strategies" and "repurpose[d]" it for a new context (314). Or perhaps it is at this point that students have experienced a shift in audience from writing for their teacher or faceless standardized test assessor to writing for a more specific group (Foster and Russell 15). Still another possibility is that students have begun to initially internalize the importance of finding and contributing their own voices to an on-going conversation (Budden et al. 91). Despite these conjectures, some students' movement from the five-paragraph essay to more sophisticated writing forms remains difficult because, to them, the five paragraph essay marks the pinnacle of "good" writing; after all, it stands as the benchmark for standardized testing.[16]

Perhaps, at least for Ohio high school students, the new College and Career Ready (Common Core) State Standards,[17] poised to replace the OGT, will provide stronger avenues for alignment of writing instruction, K-16. The Common Core will assess students on three writing types: Argument, Informational/Explanatory Writing, and Narrative Writing (Common Core

23), and its accompanying curriculum will challenge high school writers to grapple with a proportionately higher number of non-fiction texts than past curriculums which predominately focused on literature study (10). In the meantime, the current "report" versus "research" binary leads to the argument that, although high school and college-level writing instruction may each strive to equip students with the abilities to write strong essays—essays with thesis and structure—the goals behind these essays may be inherently different. As a result, student (and instructor) attempts to transition across the writing threshold may be tricky if not confounding and frustrating.

Surface Writing and Deep Writing

An application of Ellen Lavelle and Anthony J. Guarino's theories on "surface" and "deep" writing also helps unpack the notion that differing goals impede students' transition from high school to college-level writing expectations. Lavelle and Guarino state: "The emphasis on minimal involvement and sticking to the rules is suggestive of a surface approach [to writing]" (298). With that said, high school's aforementioned report-like stance in thesis writing would, indeed, involve "minimal involvement" on the part of the student writer, since he or she would not have to risk the vulnerability of posing a new perspective to the on-going conversation regarding the topic being written about. Likewise, secondary writing instruction's incorporation of writing "formulas" such as the five-paragraph theme—although necessary to meet state testing requirements—still smacks distinctively of "sticking to the rules." Here's the conundrum then: report writing needs to be informational and broad, and, in turn, informational, broad writing lends itself to reporting about a topic instead of grappling with the complexities or intricacies of an issue. In other words, surface writing lends itself to a re-inscription of its own elements. Now to be fair, report writing definitely has its place and its own usefulness, but this difference in alignment or expectations can result in quite a jolt for dual enrollment students who feel that the rules of writing have been changed when they enter the college composition classroom and are expected to analyze information rather than report on it.

For example, many times the students in this study individually recalled instances where they composed their high school essays "the night before" a due date and still would "get an 'A.'" Given the linear nature of "report" writing, such an approach makes sense: gather the information, put it into essay form, proof-read, add a works cited page, and the assignment is complete. However, when student writers at the college level were asked to take an analytical and informed position on a topic many found their previous approach to writing inadequate. To apply the terminology of Reiff and Bawarshi, these students may have engaged in "low road transfer" practices (315) by "resort[ing] to well-worn paths—routinized inclinations and default uptakes" (331) that had served them well in the past despite the fact that their writing contexts had changed. One student noted, "Before [prior to

College Writing I], I'd write the whole paper in one night. Now I pre-write, plan, and think about what needs to go where . . . [I] slowly write more over a longer period." Other student respondents in this study also noted that they could not expect similar success with the "night before" approach in their college composition classes.

Arguably, the students' "night before" writing approach failed because the students were encountering expectations of a different outcome; simply "reporting" information would no longer suffice. Said another way, to borrow again from Reiff and Bawarshi, perhaps students' "*incomes,* or the 'discursive resources' that students bring with them" (313) to college writing were mismatched to the expectations of the assignment, even though some students did not perceive the dissimilarity. Joseph M. Williams and Lawrence McEnerney argue that one of the reasons high school students often struggle with the transition from secondary to post-secondary writing instruction is that university instructors are often asking students not just to write "something *better,* but something *different.*" This may explain why, one student, Andrea, describes college writing as "a lot more involved" and states that she "needed more preparation" in order to achieve "a decent grade." She adds, "With high school writing, I could get away with a lot more." Another student, Shelley, calls college writing "time consuming" and claims she had "second thoughts at first" about the course. She states, "I wasn't sure I could get to that level of writing . . . [In the past], I was lackadaisical, never proof-read—just threw them [essays] together and hoped for the best. I got away with a lot then." Tonya also notes time and effort as factors as new elements in her college writing experience: "It [College Writing I] takes a lot of time and hard work . . . you can't do half the work, you have to go all the way. It's a lot harder but a lot more beneficial." Shelley adds that she and the other students "found out how mediocre our writing really was [before taking the course]!"

The instructors in this study also witnessed the students' struggle to transition from "surface" writing to "deep" writing in the College Writing I course. As Kay explains, students "had to step back and evaluate how much of themselves they were going to put into this [class]." Kay also notes that the transition from surface to deep writing can be especially difficult for some students who have been labeled "great writers" by their former teachers. She states, "They [the former 'great writers'] want to write a big paper, but they don't want to read the articles or follow the examples from the book. They just want to write." According to Kay (and others in the study), these "great writers" have often earned their labels largely in part to writing formulaic essays that are grammatically clean rather than essays that display a clear focus and well developed, complex arguments. She describes the result as a kind of "smoke and mirrors with no substance that other teachers have bought into." The words of Amanda Winalski, in her essay, "Bam," further explicate this point: "During high school, I operated under the assumption that what I wrote was much less important than how I wrote . . . I realized that teachers concentrated so intensely on revising dangling modifiers and comma splices that they tended to ignore the actual ideas embodied in the essay" (303). The struggle of this study's "great writers" echoes findings from a longitudinal study at Harvard, which suggests "that those student writers who identify themselves as experts early on tend to develop less as writers in the long term than those who are willing to accept a temporary novice status" (Reiff and Bawarshi 313).

Thus, while students in this study were awarded for and accustomed to a routine of formulaic reporting and editing for surface errors, these strategies stand in sharp contrast to the "reflective-revision" skills necessary for the "deep writing" they were being asked to do at the college level. Lavelle and Guarino argue that reflective-revision "is viewed as a tool for creating meaning and exploring ideas rather than for just telling what is known" (298). And Reiff and Bawarshi might describe reflective revision as a "high-road transfer" skill, which "requires metacognition—an ability to reflect on one's cognitive processes—as well as the related ability to see connections between contexts and to abstract and draw from prior skills and knowledge" (315). Said another way, deep writing asks students to analyze, interpret, question, and offer individual insights rather than to "report" given information to a generalized audience. Alfredo Celedon Lujan's contention that "Good writing is a student thinking on paper, using words unique to her or him—voice, a rhetorical stamp, citing the text, attributing quotes, answering the question thoughtfully, creating intelligent prose, poetry, or poetic prose" (55–56) is also reminiscent of the definition of deep writing. Similarly, Edward White in "My Five-Paragraph-Theme Theme," explains that "most of what [he] value[s] about writing is . . . reflection, understanding of the issues, awareness of other perspectives on the topic, and an understanding of the relation of writing to thinking" (139).

These are the same issues, though, with which writers in this study as well as those in Kara Taczak and William Thelin's dual enrollment study grappled. For example, in Taczak and Thelin's study, Shannon "had trouble seeing herself as a knowledge-maker and did not feel that she learned more about herself through writing" (13), while Juliet "did not revise to clear up . . . contradictions" and "showed no signs of understanding the needs of an audience" (14). Specifically, two of the students interviewed for this study indicated at semester's end that their approach to writing would return to surface-level concerns when they exited the College Writing I course.

The Writing Process

Deep writing, then, requires a reflective and recursive writing process that goes beyond writing formulas and surface-level issues—a territory many students have not encountered due to the constraints of high school writing instruction. To this point, the majority of instructors in the pilot study and all those in the follow-up study have either made specific comment to or alluded to the prohibitive nature of teaching a recursive writing process given the average English teacher's workload. In her article "The Truth about High School English," Milka Mustenikova Mosely writes of the dilemma of incorporating writing instruction when so many other elements vie for attention in the English classroom. She states: "it is important for college educators to understand that our English classes are not composition classes, but are *surveys of literature classes* . . . We also cover study skills, grammar, and vocabulary" (61). Kim concurs: "You have to understand that high school teachers have literature, vocabulary, and a lot more students to teach; in other words, there's not enough time [to teach writing thoroughly]. We did four-five major writings per year. I fault the education system . . . I fault the state mandates."

The sheer number of students for which a solitary high school teacher might be responsible also creates a dilemma. One year alone, I taught 170+ high school students per day. Sharon, who has also shouldered large class loads, explains: "When dealing with 65–85 students per day in regular high school classes, assigning lots of writing becomes basically impossible (at least not too often). Grading becomes overwhelming and conferencing individually is nearly impossible." According to instructors in this study, high student-to-teacher ratios results in a decrease in writing assignments. Their responses shed additional light on the findings of Vanderbilt's Steve Graham whose national survey of high school teachers revealed that "There's very little writing going on" in secondary classrooms and "very little teaching of writing" ("Interview"). Kim explains that prior to teaching College Writing I she typically gave her high school students a writing assignment and a due date; in between she incorporated virtually no pre-planning pedagogy and required very little revision upon the part of her students. Thus, although "process" is hardly a new approach to writing, it might be regarded as novel for the transitioning high school writers, since their writing experiences have heretofore been integrated among other curricula and impacted by class size—factors that constrain most secondary English teachers from devoting much instructional time to recursive writing practices.[18]

It should also be noted that, in an effort to thwart plagiarism, some high school teachers (whether the in English classroom or in other courses) often mandate that students craft writing assignments during school hours or under the watchful guidance of the teacher. As Jean notes, her high school English instructor "had us compose on the spot." Mark experienced similar scenarios, as did Jack, who states, "At high school, in some classes, all the writing has to be done at school, so time is an issue for doing rough drafts and final drafts." Jean described a similar "hand-held" approach to writing instruction that occur predominantly within the confines of the school day. This approach, unlike the aforementioned "hands-off" method used by Kim, "walks" the students through a writing assignment. Jean explains: "in high school, the teacher does each step with you." Sharon adds an instructor's perspective, stating, "In high school we spoon feed them [the students] step-by-step." Another student, Tonya, adds, "At the college level, there is no hand-holding; you have to keep up. They're not going to walk you through every step."

These findings suggest that implementing a writing "process" in the high school classroom might range on a continuum from a hands-off, find-your-own-process approach to a step-by-step process formula. As a result, many high school students in this study were not accustomed to independently drafting various versions of a writing assignment. Kasey claims she "didn't get much direction in revision in high school," and Mark cites process work and reflective revision, in particular, among the new concepts he learned in College Writing I. Likewise, Kristie admits that she "never thought about rewriting things, [but] I found out [from the dual enrollment writing course] it's better if you rewrite." And Gabe claims he had to "steadily revise" while crafting his College Writing I assignments, a step he did not incorporate in writing assignments prior to the course. Participants in Taczak and Thelin's study expressed a similar dissonance in regard to revision in the dual enrolled composition classroom; specifically, Juliet wanted to see sample essays without "mistakes" in them when her instructor modeled writing of his own in the drafting stage (15). Students' perception of revision was even more clearly revealed when those in the study described the multiple drafts, revisions, and re-writes of their work in their college composition course as a "difference in instruction"—reminiscent of Williams and McEnerney's comment that "something *different*" is being asked of students when they enter college writing classrooms.

All this is not to say, though, that some form of "process" does not occur in high school writing instruction. In fact, at least in the state of Ohio, K-12 English Language Arts teachers are required to instruct students as early as kindergarten in "writing processes," which according to Ohio Department of Education's *Academic Content Standards* "includes the phases of prewriting, drafting, revising and editing and publishing" as well as "revision strategies to improve the content, organization and language of their writing" (96). In fact, Jean states that she had "already been doing process work" on the high school level prior to entering the dual-enrolled college writing class; however, she described the process as "more chunked up" than what she was doing in college, since, at the high school level, she was required to do "a little bit each night, because the work was due the next morning" (read this as the aforementioned "step-by-step" process). As such, the "process work" described by Jean suggests an act more linear than recursive and may indicate "steps" in the writing process rather than process as part of reflective revision. To gloss this point a bit—if, as Lavelle and Guarino claim, "Active, comprehensive revision is the defining element of deep writing," and deep writing functions as a "tool of thinking" (302), then "reflective-revision" is unlikely to happen among writers at the secondary-level given teacher's heavy instructional loads and differing definitions of (as well as approaches to) process. Instead, in the words of Taczak and Thelin's subject, Shannon, revision remains for many high school students a process of "fixing and deleting" (13). Furthermore, state mandated tests such as the writing portion of the OGT are timed; as a result, these types of tests lend themselves mainly to proof-reading and editing processes—*not* reflective-revision processes.

Unfortunately, the dual enrollment students in this study gave very little indication they would continue to replicate the recursive processes they had learned when composing papers for courses or writing assignments outside their college composition course. For example, at the end of the semester, only 33% of the students included revising as one of the necessary steps to writing a good essay. And although each student surveyed demonstrated a cognizance of the need for process (at least when it came to writing "English" papers), their responses for writing in general indicated that process would not be part of their writing routine. Greg states that there is a "different approach to writing an English paper than a science paper," and Luke admitted that only "sometimes" did he "get a peer review or go to the writing center" for papers outside of English class. Still, Kim has witnessed some "buy in" and comments that she routinely sees change in her students' approach to process by the end of the semester, as they engage in "more pre-planning and are more willing to change the entire focus if the paper is not going in the direction they want; they start over; change topic; I see a lot more interest and effort."

Since composition theory has demonstrated that engaging in process can help students think more deeply about *what* they are communicating in their writing and *how* they are communicating, then it is reasonable to assert that clear definitions of and instruction in the process of writing may improve student transition from high school to college-level writing expectations. As Lavelle and Guarnio state, "Reflective-revision strategies involve taking charge in order to create meaning when writing. Writing is viewed as a tool for creating meaning and exploring ideas rather than for just telling what is known" (298). Lavelle and Guarnio's words on process and revision seem especially pertinent in that the students in this study described their writing experience prior to taking the college writing course as mainly in the area of "research" and "reports" ("just telling what is known") (298) rather than in a more argumentative, thesis-driven vein ("creating meaning") (298). Again, what may be further extrapolated is that writing instruction that utilizes a reflective and recursive process has the likelihood of increasing student awareness of and ability to compose works that create rather than report information. To that point, Lavelle and Guarnio's suggestion that "Teaching and modeling revision, as opposed to editing, is key both in college *and earlier*"[19] seems worthy of note (302).

The gap between editing for "surface" issues versus the "deep" revision measures expected of college-level writing should be approached with caution here in order to avoid the impulse to simply read surface writing as "bad" and deep writing as "good." Instead, Lavelle and Guarino emphasize the necessity of both skills when they state: "We are not suggesting that surface skills are not important: only that alone they do not constitute deep writing and that mastery alone is not enough" (302–303). In other words, good writing can be achieved when the two work in tandem; the trick is intertwining the surface and the deep within the context of the college writing classroom. According to Winalski:

> The transition from high school to university writing is not as simple as the memorization of a few grammar handouts; rather, it consists of a student's willingness to learn, understand, and modify the rules that govern language in order to communicate ideas. (307)

Winalski's words suggest that students must gain a rhetorical awareness ("rules that govern language in order to communicate ideas") in order to don the "writerly identity" of a college student, a point which calls to mind Foster and Russell's contention that, ultimately, at the college level "students must develop a chameleon rhetorical capacity" to tailor their word choice and writing style to suit the needs of different contexts and/or disciplines (43). This capacity allows students "to draw from their full range of discursive knowledge . . . in order to negotiate what they perceive as new and future rhetorical situations" (Reiff and Bawarshi 331). Again, though, all these comments imply that the onus of transitioning the composition threshold lies solely on the students—students who have spent their high school years *reporting and editing* instead of *creating meaning through revision* in their own writing.

The Call for Collaboration, Conversation, and Professional Development

To put it simply, while students certainly own some responsibility in transitioning themselves from high school to college-level writing expectations, the real key to ameliorating gaps between secondary and post-secondary writing instruction is open, respectful, and productive dialogue among instructors on both sides of the composition threshold. Furthermore, as revealed in this study, it is likely that instructors exist on either side of the divide who *do* possess an understanding of each level's differing foci. To be certain, some secondary English teachers obviously see (if not name) the "surface" and "deep" writing dichotomy, and as a result, push their students (sometimes successfully, sometimes not) from the surface to the deep—even if this is not their particular charge. It is also likely that some university writing professors may "adjust their instruction to capitalise on well-honed" surface skills as well as "offer appropriate remediation" (Lavelle and Guarino 303) to students who have not been exposed to deep writing assignments.

Still, if an awareness of each level's writing expectations were uniformly true on the part of secondary and post-secondary writing instructors, there would be less need for this discussion or for remedial writing classes[20] at the post-secondary level. Until then, there will continue to be high school writing instruction which overvalues and over-rewards surface elements just as there will continue to be university professors who perceive their students' struggles with deep writing as an indication of inadequacies in previous instruction. In the meantime, writing students may find themselves stranded somewhere between what they know and what they are supposed to know.

Moreover, this study reveals that a possible re-inscription of the writing divide may be occurring. In explanation, at the end of the semester, the dual enrollment participants, overall, described themselves as "better" writers. As mentioned earlier, Tonya described College Writing I as "more beneficial" than her high school writing instruction, and Shelley commented on "how mediocre" her writing was prior to taking the course. And Kasey remarked that she "learned more from this college class than writing other papers in high school." Whether Kasey and the others actually learned *more* or learned *different* elements in her college writing instruction is open for debate. However, if students interpret the foci of college-level writing as superior to that of high school writing instruction—read "I am a *better* writer, because my college composition course stressed *different* elements of writing that my secondary writing instruction never did and now I am privy to those elements"—then *better* fails to acknowledge the existence of *different*. In the words of Kim, "It worries me, because I don't want them [the dual enrollment students] to . . . say 'we're doing things all wrong at the high school level.'" I harbor similar concerns. Since high school teachers bear heavier instructional, curricular, and assessment loads than many of their post-secondary counterparts, they often view instructional advice from those "in the tower" with suspicion: the day-to-day practicalities of secondary writing instruction do not meet neatly with the ideals espoused by college composition instructors.

Fortunately, dual enrollment writing classrooms, such as the ones in this study, can serve as conduits for collaboration, conversation, and professional development since these are spaces where high school and college students and instructors come together. A host of educators and scholars either acknowledge the need for or explicitly call for increased communication across the high school/college writing divide (see, for example, Davies, Mosely, Kittle, Bauman, Alsup and Bernard-Donals, Kapanke and Westemeirer, Jennings and Hunn, Thompson and Gallagher, Taczak and Thelin, and Sehulster). And the potential for success through collaboration and conversation is evidenced in efforts described in the works of Katherine Hughes, Michael Vivion, Wendy Strachan, Peter Kittle, Herb Budden et al. and Sheridan Blau, respectively. However, the caution here is in regard to what constitutes those conversations and how those conversations evolve. Specifically, *these must be two-way dialogues* among affected parties at both levels—a point not consistently noted by those lobbying for such conversations. Taczak and Thelin describe this "outreach" as "a historically difficult bridge to cross" (21) And as Kittle argues, unless participants from both sides of the discussion bring the proper attitudes, introspections, and respect to the table, such conversations may serve to intensify tensions between the two camps. He warns:

> I fear that, without being able to establish the kinds of professional relationships that are predicated on mutual respect for teaching abilities, subject matter knowledge, and academic values, any ideas being propounded by college writing teachers will be seen as just another mandate from above. (143)

Since Kittle has (as have I) resided on both sides of the writing threshold, we are sensitive to the assumptions and suspicions that may cloud these needed dialogues.

With that said, when broached with a spirit of openness, dual enrollment collaborations have the potential to inform and energize those who genuinely yearn to understand the unique charges and constraints inherent to each level of instruction. Kathleen Blake Yancey and Brian M. Morrison describe a summer program at The University of North Carolina at Greensboro where dual enrollment teachers from high school campus sites "gather on the college campus to think about how they teach composition, to share assignments and response strategies, and to compare what they do with practices in the college writing program" (274). Likewise, Patricia Sehulster outlines sample activities, agendas, and readings with which high school and college participants have engaged during "Writing Forums" at her community college (349–352). Even less formal ventures such as university instructor Tom Thompson's guest lectures in Andrea Gallagher's high school classroom (see Hansen and Farris's collection) can lead to rich exchanges of ideas and practices and can help pave the way for "shaping better messages about writing instruction" (Taczak and Thelin 21).

Both formal and informal opportunities to discuss writing instruction are embedded in The University of Findlay's dual enrollment mentorship program where high school English teachers and UF English instructors collaborate to build, sustain, and provide high-quality dual enrollment instruction. Those training to become dual enrollment composition instructors participate in a week-long intensive course in composition theory that challenges them to reflect upon their own philosophies as writing instructors. During the week, seasoned dual enrollment instructors and faculty from The University of Findlay's English Department spend time sharing their experiences of teaching college writing. The dual enrollment instructor candidates then spend the next several weeks building their syllabi and assignments. In this process, they maintain freedom to choose materials and pedagogical approaches while working within the framework of the English department's expectations. Most importantly, though, is the exchange of information: university faculty members become more aware of the trends and demands in secondary writing instruction, and the dual enrollment instructors (new and seasoned) become increasingly cognizant of college-level writing expectations.

As a continued form of professional development and support at The University of Findlay, dual enrollment composition instructors come to campus twice per year to calibrate grading, share pedagogical techniques, contribute to the development of course assignments as well as the portfolio grading rubric, and discuss the challenges of teaching writers from high school to college-level writing expectations. Technology has added another layer of collaboration in that college writing faculty can now easily "enter" high school dual enrollment writing classrooms via Skype for collaborative exchanges.

Overall, anonymous survey results as well as face-to-face conversation, and email exchanges from instructors in the program describe initial training and on-going professional development opportunities as "transformational" in regard to their approaches to writing instruction. One instructor reflects, "I spend more time evaluating, set higher expectations, and try to influence my fellow teachers in the English department to do a better, more thorough job of teaching writing—beyond the formulaic OGT required writing!" Another instructor states, "I feel that the training I've had as a DE [dual enrollment] instructor has made me more confident and more prepared for the CC [Common Core]." Still another instructor adds, "Because of teaching College Writing I, I have revamped and up-graded the Jr./Sr. composition classes I teach. In fact, students of mine who have gone on to college thank me for how well prepared they were [for college writing]." Similarly, one veteran in the program states, "I didn't realize how much I had integrated the philosophy [of writing instruction] into the lower [high school] levels [I teach]." "Now that I am totally aware of what is expected in a college writing class, I push my high school students to aspire to the same level," says another.

When asked to describe the impact teaching College Writing I has had on her instruction in her other courses, Janet remarked, "I don't know where to begin . . . there were gray areas, weaknesses in my teaching that have been strengthened . . . I'm learning so much." She reiterated this point on her written survey by describing the impact teaching in dual enrollment classroom has had on the pedagogies she employs when teaching writing in other situations; she writes, "I go back into the high school with new strategies from the college-level . . . I took what I had from [College Writing I] and then expected more from my high school juniors—[I decided to] bring it up a notch." Not only have Janet's high school student felt the impact of her College Writing I teaching experience; her colleagues have as well, since she openly shares with them the new ideas, information, and techniques she has garnered from collaborating with her dual enrollment instructor-peers.

College faculty members, too, have benefited from the collaboration. One, in particular, shared that "it [the dual enrollment partnership] challenges me to think beyond my own classroom space and consider how what I do in my classroom intersects with what other teachers have done in theirs." Furthermore, I have benefitted professionally in numerous ways from the exchange of pedagogical strategies that occurs during our collaborative sessions. From supplementary text suggestions to providing a clearer picture of how students might "come to recognize a task" (Reiff and Bawarshi 332), my writing instructor peers at the high school level have enriched my ability to "cue," "prime," and "guide" (331) my students through College Writing I. Simply put, collaborating across dual enrollment spaces makes good sense: formerly frustrated college composition and high school English teachers can finally quit un-doing one another's work and move toward the common goal of transitioning student writers from one level of instruction to the next.

Conclusion

In *High School-College Partnerships: Conceptual Models, Programs and Issues,* Arthur Greenburg writes that "the future" of high school and college writing instruction "is dependent on the performance of the other" (xv). Likewise, Taczak and Thelin argue that "if we are to shape a consistent, strong, effective message [of writing instruction], we cannot ignore this collaboration" (21). Historically, a lack of open communication across the writing threshold has served to hinder rather than to pave a smooth pathway for students transitioning from high school to college-level writing expectations, and, as a result, each side often has differing goals and ways of defining elements of writing even while "depending" on the other. In the meantime, organizations such as the Alliance for Excellent Education claim that high schools need to "revamp instruction" in order to "be aligned to the expectations of colleges." Such moves evoke the top-down theory of education that groups such as NCTE have long fought against. A better answer, to borrow from Sehulster, is to "consciously work to inform one another's teaching and ultimately our students' learning and readiness for college-level writing" (343) via candid, reciprocal conversation between high school teachers and college instructors. The voices of students should also be included in these dialogues and research as, ultimately, the writing they produce—and the struggle or ease with which they produce it—are indicators of how well we, as composition instructors, speak the same language.

And perhaps, as this study suggests, the dual enrolled composition classroom may be a place "to make changes, to train a new generation, and *to talk to one another*" (Brantley and Brantley 220), since it is in this space that high school teachers, college instructors, and students all have a stake in the learning outcomes. What remains to be seen is whether the limited findings indicative of this small-scale study of UF's dual enrolled writing programs hold true at similar universities among like populations. For example, how prevalent is the dilemma of "reporting" versus "creating meaning" through writing? What are best practices for addressing issues of practicality and efficacy in high school writing instruction? How might instructors better aid students in their transfer of high school writing strategies such as formulas and surface writing skills to new contexts and for new purposes while simultaneously maintaining the goals and integrity of each level of instruction? And, finally, how might clearer, shared definitions of revision and process improve students' abilities to balance and integrate elements of surface and deep writing as they move from secondary to post-secondary writing expectations? Transitioning writers across the composition threshold is challenging, labor-intensive, rewarding, and collaborative work. Paying attention to what the dual enrollment classroom can teach us may make that work a bit easier.

Notes

1. According to the U.S. Department of Education, "The term 'dual enrollment' refers to an arrangement where students are enrolled in courses that count for both high school and college credit. These programs are also called 'dual credit' or 'concurrent enrollment'" (1).
2. Recent definitions differentiate "concurrent enrollment" from "dual enrollment." NACEP defines a concurrent enrollment program as one "in which the high school student travels to the college campus or college faculty travel to the high school"; it is also defined as "programs where the student takes a course from a college instructor via distance education" ("What is concurrent enrollment?") "Dual credit" refers to students earning both high school and college credit for the successful completion of a college-level course (Allen 2).
3. This study was approved by The University of Findlay's IRB. The author utilized consent forms and has changed students' as well as teachers' names to protect their anonymity.
4. The follow-up phase of the study is on-going; findings shared in this article represent the initial pilot study (2007) and four years of subsequent data.
5. In 2009, The University of Findlay discontinued its dual-enrolled-only on-campus sections of College Writing I.
6. The number of concurrent enrollment instructors for The University of Findlay fluctuates per year. The number twenty-two is the number of individual UF concurrent enrollment instructors that have taught in the program from 2007–2012.
7. "Representative" is defined as one "high" or A paper, one "medium" or B/C range paper, and one "low" or C-/below paper.
8. When this study began in 2007, students in College Writing I took a final exam (worth 10% of their overall grade) at the end of the course. In Fall 2009, The University of Findlay implemented a portfolio review system for College Writing I students; this serves as the exit assessment for the course, and student work is scored as "satisfactory" or "unsatisfactory" via a common rubric.
9. Similar to dual enrolled students, the dual enrollment instructors in this study are in the unique position of teaching college writing while being simultaneously immersed or well studied in the elements of high school writing.
10. These numbers are based on experience as well as on survey and discussion responses from participating instructors.
11. Given the arbitrary nature of the definition of "college-level writing," the "college-level" writing elements discussed here refer to those stressed by The University of Findlay in its College Writing I syllabus template.

12. Elsewhere in this study it has been noted how difficult it is to define both "high school-level writing" and "college-level writing" since some core elements and certainly subtleties of each vary greatly from instructional institution to instructional institution. However, for the sake of this study and due to the credentials of the instructor-participants, who (with the exception of one) have taught or currently teach in secondary and post-secondary writing classrooms, some assumptions are made here regarding the characteristics of writing taught at each level.
13. The students' and instructors' names in this study have been changed to protect their anonymity.
14. Italics added.
15. According to student respondents in this survey and per my own experience as a high school teacher, this statement generally holds true for disciplines on the secondary level outside of English as well. For example, the student respondents noted history and science as other courses in which they had been required to write "reports."
16. As noted elsewhere, the testing described here is based on that in the state of Ohio.
17. In 2010, the Ohio Department of Education (along with 44 other states) adopted a Common Core Curriculum (CCC) of standards to replace the current English Language Arts Content Standards. The CCC is scheduled to be phased into public school systems over a four year period with full implementation by 2014.
18. It is also worth noting that, while most college writing instruction includes one-on-one instructor-student conferencing sessions, such sessions are rare at the secondary level given the typical high school English teacher's workload.
19. Italics added.
20. According to Susan Aud, et al.s' U.S. Department of Education's report, *The Condition of Education 2011*, one-third of undergraduate students and 42% of students at two-year institutions reported taking remedial courses.

Works Cited

Allen, Drew. "Dual Enrollment: A Comprehensive Literature Review and Bibliography." *CUNY Collaborative Programs*, Office of Academic Affairs. August 2010. Print.

Alliance for Excellent Education. "High School Teaching for the Twenty-First Century: Preparing Student for College." *IssueBrief*. Washington, D.C. Sept. 2007. Web. 28 July 2012.

Alsup, Janet, and Michael Bernard-Donals. "The Fantasy of the Seamless Transition." Thompson 115-35.

Andrews, Hans A. "Dual-Credit Research Outcomes for Students." *Community College Journal of Research and Practice* 28.5 (June 2004): 415-422. Print.

Aud, Susan, et al. *The Condition of Education 2011*. U.S. Department of Education, National Center for Education Statistics. Washington, DC: U.S. Government Printing Office. 2011. 28 July 2012. Web.

Bauman, Amy. "What is College-Level Writing?" *The Council Chronicle* 16.3 (March 2007). 1+. Print.

Blau, Sheridan. "College Writing, Academic Literacy, and the Intellectual Community." Sullivan and Tinberg 358-77.

Bogdan, Robert and Sari Knopp Biklen. *Qualitiative Research for Education: An Introduction to Theory and Methods*. Boston: Allyn and Bacon, 2007. Print.

Brantley, Richard E., and Diana R. Brantley. "Sleeping with the Enemy: Communiques From a Pedagogical Marriage." Thompson 214-20.

Budden, Herb, et. al. "What We Talk About When We Talk About College Writing." Thompson 73-93.

Common Core Standards Initiative: Preparing America's Students for College and Career. *Common Core State Standards for English Language Arts and Literacy in History/Social Studies, Science, and Technical Subjects*. Appendix A: Research Supporting Key Elements of the Standards. Glossary of Key Terms. Common Core Standards Initiative. 2012. 28 July 2012. Web.

Davies, Merrill J. "Making the Leap from High School to College Writing." Sullivan, Tinberg, and Blau 119-33.

—. "Whistling in the Dark." Sullivan and Tinberg 31-35.

"Forum." *English Journal* 82.6 (Oct. 1993): 13. Print.

Foster, David, and David R. Russell, eds. *Writing and Learning In Cross-National Perspective: Transitions from Secondary to Higher Education*. Urbana, Illinois: NCTE, 2002. Print.

Greenberg, Arthur. *High School-College Partnerships: Conceptual Models Programs and Issues*. Washington, D.C.: School of Education and Human Development. George Washington University, 1991. Print.

Hansen, Kristine, and Christine R. Farris, eds. *College Credit for Writing in High School*. Urbana, Illinois: NCTE, 2010. Print.

Hansen, Kristine. "The Composition Marketplace: Shopping for Credit versus Learning to Write." *College Credit for Writing in High School: The "Taking Care of" Business*. Ed. Kristine Hansen and Christine R. Farris. Urbana, IL: NCTE, 2010. 1-39. Print.

Harris, Muriel. "What Does the Instructor Want?" Sullivan and Tinberg 121-33.

Hertz, Rosanna, ed. *Reflexivity and Voice*. Thousand Oaks, CA: Sage Publications, 1997. Print.

High School and Higher Education Curriculum Alignment Grant: EHOVE-Penta Consortium. Northwest Regional Center Ohio College Tech Prep, 2012. Print.

Hughes, Katherine L. "Dual Enrollment: Postsecondary/Secondary Partnerships to Prepare Students." *Journal of College Science Teaching* (July/August 2010): 12-13. Print.

"Interview with Steve Graham on Improving Primary Grade Writing Instruction." *Vanderbilt University* 17 April 2009. YouTube. 19 Oct. 2012.

Jennings, Chris, and Jane Hunn. "'Why Do I Have to Take Remedial English?': A Collaborative Model to Solve a National Problem." Thompson 182-200.

Johanek, Cindy. *Composing Research: A Contextualist Paradigm for Rhetoric and Composition*. Logan, Utah: Utah State University Press, 2000. Print.

Jordan, Jeanette, with Karena K. Nelson, Howard Clauser, Susan E. Albert, Karen M. Cunningham, and Amanda Scholz. "Am I a Liar? the Angst of a High School English Teacher." Sullivan and Tinberg 36-40.

Kapanke, Susan, and Melissa Westemeier. "The University of Wisconsin Oshkosh and Area High Schools Strike a Partnership." Thompson 153-68.

Kearns, Chris. "The Recursive Character of College Writing." Sullivan and Tinberg 341-57.

Kittle, Peter. "It's Not the High School Teachers' Fault: An Alternative to the Blame Game." Sullivan and Tinberg 134-45.

Knodt, Ellen Andrews. "What is College Writing For?" Sullivan and Tinberg 146-57.

Lavelle, Ellen and Anthony J. Guarino. "A Multidimensional Approach to Understanding College Writing Processes." *Educational Psychology* 23.3 (2003): 295-305. Print.

Lindblom, Kenneth. "Teaching English in the World." *English Journal* 94.1 (Sept. 2004): 104-108. Print.

Lujan, Alfredo Celedon. "The Salem Witch Trials: Voice(s)." Sullivan and Tinberg 41-57.

Lunsford, Ronald R. "From Attitude to Aptitude: Assuming the Stance of a College Writer." Sullivan and Tinberg 178-98.

McCarthy, Sarah Rohrer. "Dual-Enrollment Programs: Legislation helps High School Students Enroll in College Courses." *Journal of Secondary Gifted Education* 11.1 (Fall 1999): Academic Search Premier. Web. 5 Nov. 2005.

McCormick, Kathleen. "Do You Believe in Magic? Collaboration and the Demystification of Research." Sullivan and Tinberg 199-230.

Mosley, Milka Mustenikova. "The Truth about High School English." Sullivan and Tinberg 58-68.

Nagin, Carl. *Because Writing Matters: Improving Student Writing in Our Schools.* San Francisco: Josey-Bass. 2006. Print.

National Center for Education Statistics. *Dual Enrollment of High School Students at Postsecondary Institutions: 2002-2003.* U.S. Department of Education. Washington, D.C. 2005. Print.

"NCTE's History." *National Council of Teachers of English.* NCTE. 2011. Web. 3 Aug. 2011.

Ohio Department of Education. *Academic Content Standards: K-12 English Language Arts.* Center for Curriculum and Assessment. Columbus, OH. Feb. 2002. Print.

—. *The Promise of Dual Enrollment: Assessing Ohio's Early College Access Policy.* KnowledgeWorks Foundation and the Western Interstate Commission for Higher Education. 2007. Print.

Patterson, Joseph P., and David Duer. "High School Teaching and College Expectations in Writing and Reading." *English Journal* 95.3 (2006): 81-27. Print.

Reiff, Mary Jo, and Anis Bawarshi. "Tracing Discursive Resources: How Students Use Prior Genre Knowledge to Negotiate New Writing Contexts in First-Year Composition." *Written Communication* 28.3 (2011): 312-337. Print.

Roessing, Lesley. "Toppling the Idol." *English Journal* 94.1 (Sept. 2004): 41-46. Print.

Schorn, Susan E. "A Lot Like Us But More So: Listening to the Writing Faculty Across The Curriculum." Sullivan and Tinberg 330-40.

Sehulster, Patricia. "Forums: Bridging the Gap between High School and College Writing." *TETYC* (May 2012): 343-354. Print.

Shafer, Gregory. "Reforming Writing and Rethinking Correctness." *English Journal* 84.1 (Sept. 2004): 66-71. Print.

Shanely, Roger. "ReformIng Wri Ing Instruction." *English Journal* 94.1 (Sept. 2004): 13-15. Print.

Strachan, Wendy. "Talking about the Transition: Dialogues between High School And University Teachers." Thompson 136-50.

Sullivan, Patrick, and Howard Tinberg, eds. *What is "College-Level" Writing?* Urbana, IL: NCTE, 2006. Print.

Sullivan, Patrick, Howard Tinberg, and Sheridan Blau, eds. *What is "College-Level" Writing?: Volume 2: Assignments, Readings, and Student Writing Samples*. Urbana, IL: NCTE, 2010. Print.

Taczak, Kara, and William H. Thelin. "(Re)Envisioning the Divide: The Impact of College Courses on High School Students." *TETYC* (September 2009): 7-23. Print.

Thompson, Thomas C., ed. *Teaching Writing in High School and College: Conversations and Collaborations*. Urbana, IL: NCTE, 2002. Print.

Thompson, Tom, and Andrea Gallagher. "When A College Professor and High School Teacher Read the Same Papers." Sullivan, Tinberg, and Blau. 3-28

Tinberg, Howard and Jean-Paul Nadeau. "Contesting the Space between High School and College in the Era of Dual-Enrollment." *CCC* 62.4 (June 2011): 704-725. Print.

The University of North Carolina at Chapel Hill. *The Writing Center*. The Writing Center at UNC Chapel Hill. 2012. Web. 30 July 2012.

United States Department of Education. *Dual Enrollment: Accelerating the Transition to College*. The High School Leadership Summit. Denver, CO. Dec. 2004. Print.

Vivion, Michael J. "High School/College Dual Enrollment and the Composition Program." *Writing Program Administration* 15.1-2 (Fall/Winter 1991): 55-60. Print.

Weinstein, Larry. *Writing at the Threshold: Featuring 56 Ways to Prepare High School and College Students to Think and Write at the College Level*. Urbana, Illinois: NCTE, 2001. Print.

"What is Concurrent Enrollment?" *National Alliance of Concurrent Enrollment Partnerships*. NACEP. 2012. Web. 30 July 2012.

White, Edward M. "My Five-Paragraph-Theme Theme." Sullivan, Tinberg, and Blau 137-41.

Williams, Joseph M., and Lawrence McEnerney. "Writing in College, Part 1." *Writing Program*. University of Chicago. 2007. Web. 11 April 2007.

Winalksi, Amanda. "Bam." Sullivan and Tinberg 302-08.

Yancey, Kathleen Blake, and Brian Morrison. "Coming to Terms: Vocabulary as a Means of Defining First-Year Composition." Sullivan and Tinberg 267-80.

Truth, Memory, Selectivity: Understanding Historical Work by Writing Personal Histories

Duncan Koerber

> This paper considers the use of a simple assignment, the personal narrative, in teaching students the discursive issues involved in doing academic history. Focusing on autobiography, I present the results of a survey of Canadian university students into their experiences with writing personal histories. Specifically, the survey asked students to think about three major epistemological issues in doing history: truth and subjectivity, problems of memory, and selectivity. Exemplary excerpts from three students' portfolios show the kind of work they produced. From the results, the paper argues that university history classes—not just writing courses—should employ personal history as a first assignment to allow students to work as historians and encounter the issues historians regularly face when constructing accounts of the past.

Personal writing comes in many forms, and it may at first glance seem to hold little value for teaching the work of the historian in the university setting. The expectations and characteristics of university writing differ depending on the academic field in question, raising further difficulties. This article shows, however, that personal writing and academic writing might be congruent in one way. Personal narrative can be used as a starting point to help students understand the discursive pressures of work in one particular field: history.

The value of using personal writing—a typical expressivist writing assignment—to teach students about historical work may not be readily apparent. The emphasis of expressivist pedagogy on voice and personal experience has been criticized by social constructivists on the grounds that it does not help writers "master the accepted practices of a discourse community" (Fishman and McCarthy 647). David Bartholomae, a proponent of this view, argued that students need to be taught the discourses of academic writing (63). He says student writers must be "aware of the forces at play in the production of knowledge" (66)—personal writing may avoid such questions, he argues. Without this attention to discourse, he says, students do not learn how to combat the power inherent in those discourses (64). Stephen Fishman and Lucille McCarthy describe social constructivist writing pedagogy as a concern for an apparent neglect for "academically valued ways of thinking" and "ignoring the social settings of specified skills and bodies of knowledge" (648). At first glance, the expressivist focus on the personal seems at odds with the social constructionist goal of "introducing students systematically to the rules of a disciplinary language that would otherwise be inaccessible to them" (Fishman and McCarthy 654). Candace Spigelman describes this as contrary to "expressive rhetoric's insistence on students' private voices, visions, and ultimate authority over their texts . . . Such an approach, they say, overemphasizes the power of personal insight and ignores the ways that knowledge is constructed socially" (70). Taken together, these arguments suggest that personal writing blinds the student writer to the discursive production of meaning and convinces the student writer that all meaning comes from within.

However, another strain of thinking has shown that the discursive production of meaning is best taught, particularly in history, through the emphasis on 'doing history,' not simply reading about history (VanSledright 1092). Personal writing, also called autobiography, life writing, or memoir, is a form of this 'doing history.' Personal writing is defined by Spigelman as "the ways in which writers make sense of their lives by organizing their experience into first-person stories" (65–66).

In the 'doing history' pedagogy, students are encouraged to bring the personal to their work to encourage engagement. As Deborah Vess argues, "Techniques which encourage active learning will better convey a sense of history as a vivid, exciting subject in which the past continues to speak through those who encounter it in the present" (46). A number of scholars have reported successful active learning classroom projects such as classroom histories (see Wallace and Beidler), family histories (see Culbert; Jeffrey), local histories (see Underwood; Candeloro), creative historical fiction (see Vess) and oral histories (see Long; Whitman). These studies found that through doing history students learned epistemological foundations of historical work. They understood historical generalizations, grappled with missing evidence and conflicting perspectives, and came to appreciate the preservation of history.

All of these active classroom projects required students not to receive historical wisdom from academic historians, but to understand the problems that those historians deal with every day in the construction of historical accounts. These approaches position history "not just there, awaiting the researcher's discovery . . . history has no existence before it is written" (Howell and Prevenier 1). Rather than seeing history as a collection of facts or a work of "voiceless men and women in textbooks" (Whitman 470), students who do historical work learn that history is a "confrontation between the investigator and the evidence" (McClymer and Moynihan 361). These projects do what Bruce VanSledright argues many history teachers typically *do not* do, which is illuminating the "interpretive paradox inherent in the practice of history itself" (1091). In theory, these kinds of 'doing history' approaches help students become immediately aware of the inherent constructedness—not just the factual excavation involved in historical work.

In the study of teaching history, however, there has been no research into using autobiography, life writing, and memoir as a way for university students to work as historians and, at the same time, encounter and reconcile history's epistemological realities. In his examination of personal writing's value, Stuart Green argues that it can help develop students' understanding of the "epistemological assumptions that inform its discursive practices" (138). In this light, perhaps writing teachers proper have simply not considered these kinds of personal writing as history at all, reflecting an earlier perspective of life writing, autobiography, and memoir as on or beyond the boundary of the historical field. Certainly academic historians have been skeptical of personal narrative as a historical source for reasons described later in this paper. Yet student responses in this paper suggest that personal narrative of this sort may help achieve the pedagogical goals set out by John Wallace and Paul Beidler to help history students

> realize the nature of historical inquiry[,] . . . appreciate the difficulties inherent in the reconstruction and interpretation of past events[,] . . . approach historical material with the healthy skepticism, sensitivity to uncertainty and discrepancy[,] . . . and [question the] objectivity of the properly trained historian. (24)

Personal writing also represents a relevant assignment for university history students because it is narrative, a form that has always been central to historical writing. Academic history writing today, despite shifts towards the theoretical and abstract, still includes a great deal of story-telling. While autobiography or memoir has always been seen as "not very respectable" in the field (Popkin 50), personal histories are growing in status (Caine 69). In writing personal histories, students produce a form that has become a useful source for academic historians. The personal narrative is also a reflection of 'history from below' and 'social history' approaches that gained popularity over the past five decades (Caine 70; Howell and Prevenier 14–16, 110). Carl Becker praises this kind of "living history" as the "history that does work in the world, the history that influences the course of history . . . that pattern of remembered events, whether true or false, that enlarges and enriches the collective present, the specious present of Mr. Everyman" (21). Personal narrative is distinctly within the academic history field today.

Personal writing can thus be respectably situated within academic history courses as an assignment. Assignments that require students to engage in this writing represent a way for "students to enter the academic conversation by bringing their own 'extratextual knowledge'" (Spigelman 71). Spigelman goes so far as to say that personal writing "can accomplish serious scholarly work" (64). Furthermore, Wallace and Biedler contend that "personal experience of students may provide a useful basis for teaching the more elusive attributes of the art of historical inquiry" (30).

Personal history writing draws on students' creative abilities in telling detailed stories with precision and bringing the past to life. In an assessment of creative writing more broadly as a writing tool in the history discipline,

Deborah Vess says it is "one way for students to realize that history is a discipline which is filtered through the lens of the present, and that each of them, as Carl Becker once said, must be their 'own historian'" (52). Furthermore, "Creative writing, which demands personal interaction with material and an inherently interpretive and critical approach, is often more successful in developing autonomous thought and the ability critically to evaluate sources" (Vess 46). Vess's ideas follow from Becker's notion that history is always a "story that employs all the devices of literary art" (Winks 17), a point often forgotten in the academic writing world of arguments and assertions. But as Ellen Somekawa and Elizabeth Smith have noted, this creative aspect of history writing is not typically taught to students; instead, teachers emphasize how to make inferences from evidence and how to cite evidence (152). The personal and its creativity are often left by the wayside. To introduce this missing element to history courses, the personal history assignment can help students understand this form both as historical evidence and as a project that can introduce them to the constructed discourse[1] of academic history.

The Survey

To connect the personal narrative assignment to broader discussions of academic history discourse, I engaged students through a short survey. The survey results present a look into the actual experience of students encountering the discourse of the academic history field. The voluntary, anonymous survey asked three questions corresponding to three key epistemological concerns in historical scholarship: truth and subjectivity, problems of memory, and selectivity. Recently, scholars of historiography have discussed a number of these at times contested and controversial concerns. Students who have an uncontested view of history—seeing history as a series of facts to be learned from others as is still often the case today (Díaz et al. 1218)—are students who have not had an opportunity to encounter or struggle with them.

Below, I describe the three concerns and present representative student writers' comments about each. Responses show that, in answering these questions after writing personal histories, students can encounter these major pressures of doing historical work. In some ways, students had already dealt with key academic historical research and writing problems before being prompted by the questions. This suggests that personal history assignments can serve as a useful beginning assignment in the history classroom to raise students' awareness of epistemological challenges of doing history.

The students who responded to the survey for this study took a course that was modeled upon a course for beginning writers taught by Guy Allen at the University of Toronto Mississauga (see Allen, "'Good-Enough'"; "Language"). The course encourages students to write non-fiction first-person narratives based on their experiences and observations, positions the instructor as an editor or supporting other, not as a judge, and has a clearly defined and rigorously maintained course frame (Allen, "Good-Enough" 148). Students wrote seven personal narratives (two to four pages in length) over twelve weeks on a number of themes (childhood, relationship, job, family) with regular revision based upon grammar and style lessons (eliminating wordiness, passive voice, clichés, and vague pronouns; employing strong verbs and nouns, active voice, parallelism, sentence length variation, rhythm, and pacing). Students shared their work with classmates in both one-on-one and group peer-editing sessions to encourage the understanding of audience reception in the editing process (additionally, each student met with me for two one-on-one editing sessions during the term). Students did not, however, receive grades on their work during the term. Instead, students had the opportunity to edit work until final submission day, when students e-mailed in their completed portfolios (worth 70% of the final grade). I examined how well students incorporated the grammar and style lessons from lectures into their writing and how well their work matched the peer model readings. Students did not read any writing by academic historians, only the best personal narratives written by previous students in the Professional Writing & Communication program at the University of Toronto Mississauga. Allen and students in the program have collected the best stories and published them in course textbooks (see Allen, *Make It New;* also see earlier collection: Allen, *No More Masterpieces*). As Allen has observed in his courses, students working in this method develop honest, subjective, first-person narrative voices, using direct experience for content, and employing an appropriate style for the subject ("'Good-Enough'" 144). While students were instructed to tell stories about their own lives, the course did not include any discussion of history, historiography, or academic writing.

In his classes, Allen reported "students making connections. They make these connections—between inner world and outer world, between self and other, between past and present" (150). Rather than seeing students as inward-looking, Allen found that students "use narratives to make links between their inner and outer worlds . . . and links between the academic and the personal" (159). The students' survey responses show the specific nature of those links.

At the end of three separate sections of the course (2009–2010), I asked students to complete the voluntary emailed exit survey after grades were submitted. Thirty-eight of 89 students answered the survey questions. The responses reveal how they dealt with the problems historians typically encounter. These answers provide further evidence for the assertion that rather than being close-minded or inward-looking, personal writing can connect students with discursive issues in an academic field.

The following sections include a short gloss on each of the three historical problems under consideration,[2] the questions asked, and a representative selection of students' answers. As students who were surveyed were promised anonymity, I have labelled answers only by an "S" for student and a unique number that represents each.

Student Commentaries Theme #1: Truth and Subjectivity

While truth has always been a central issue in all academic work, particularly in its relationship with fact-finding, historiography of the past half century or so has raised questions about the subjectivity of the historian and the constructed nature of historical accounts. In his famous book *What is History,* E.H. Carr spurred great debate when he questioned the notion of objective truth about the past, arguing that history is one's subjective interpretation (8). Barbara Tuchman, although contrary to Carr in many ways, agreed, saying there "is no such thing as a neutral or purely objective historian" (29). Philosopher of history Mark Day notes that "all history is constructed in some sense—we can never really 'test' the facts we use against the 'reality' of the past by some direct access to the past" (205).

At Indiana University, researchers of the History Learning Project found that students thought that facts "speak by themselves, and thus 'The Story' of the past has an objective quality in which 'truth' is found. They believe that their job in history courses is to regurgitate the dates and events they have memorized" (Díaz et al. 1213). On the contrary, the researchers argued, students

> must accept that sources are created by human beings and are as complicated as life itself . . . They may be asked . . . about the subjective perspectives that particular individuals brought to their experience. For students expecting a different kind of discussion this may seem like a walk into a confusing twilight zone. (1214)

In their research about students doing history, Somekawa and Smith argue further that this inherent subjectivity must be foregrounded so that "personal and limited perspectives, the institutional and social contexts in which we labor to produce history, and our political agendas for writing what we write would all become appropriate subjects for examination in our work" (158). Furthermore, they note that people must understand that "history does not portray a universal, objective truth about the past" (159). Autobiography has been a key genre in this truth debate, with some historians cautioning against giving too much weight to subjective accounts of the past (Howell and Prevenier 21). Caine and Carr counter that all historical writing, even if not explicitly personal, contains the subjectivity of the author (Caine 67; Carr 8).

Stemming from this short gloss on truth and objectivity in historical writing, the survey asked students to reflect on this question: *Do you think your stories represent the truth of what actually happened?* As the course was explicitly positioned as a non-fiction writing class, I expected many students would provide an uncritical affirmation. Indeed, a few students were certain their stories represented the truth:

S1: All the stories I wrote were true and actually happened.

S2: I think most of my stories told a fair representation of what happened.

S32: I feel that my stories conveyed the highest amount of truth. When I shared the stories with my family, they were surprised at how "real" I was being.

However, the majority of students responded with a more critical eye, clearly confronting the dilemma of their own subjectivity and truth of their personal histories. A number of students admitted—perhaps surprisingly given the non-fiction nature of the writing assignments—that their work *may not be true,* even if they felt they captured the story accurately. In particular, they recognized the bias of witness evidence:

S3: I do not think they represent the truth. I'm sure that the other "characters" in my stories would see it differently.

S4: In terms of dialogue, there could be many variations from what the portrayed character actually said. I believe that my characters would agree with the way events panned out, but they might argue that I made them appear a bit more extreme than they actually acted (or are willing to admit).

S8: Yes, I feel that my stories represent the truth of what happened, from my perspective. I mean, in a way, I feel like there is no such thing as "truth" because everyone sees things in a different way.

S9: I believe other characters in my stories must remember the events differently. There is no objective truth to the stories, only a subjective account.

S16: They are all told from my perspective, so subtleties of my diction reveal my interpretation of events. Had they been told from another person's perspective, maybe this person would remember different details or have perceived certain comments/actions differently.

These students were not questioning that their narratives did not attempt to correspond to the truth. However, they were willing to accept that witness testimony—their own testimony of history—may not be completely representative. They acknowledge that other witnesses to those events may have seen the situations somewhat differently and that incorporating those perspectives into the writing could fill in gaps or provide a broader view of what happened. Alternative viewpoints required to corroborate history were not problematic for these students despite their focus on expressing their own experiences of key moments in their lives.

This understanding is fundamental to the historian's work. Students who experienced this kind of dilemma in answering the question were forced to directly confront truth and subjectivity. In an academic history course, this realization could provide an opportunity or way in to discuss this major issue from the perspective of academic historians. This awareness is helpful whether one tells one's own history or researches and writes the histories of others.

The second set of responses in this theme shows that these writers do not see themselves as individuals disconnected from communities and audiences; neither are they attempting to find some essentialist meaning about their lives as they look within. Instead the students suggest an awareness of the nature of truth in historical retelling and their own position in relationships with others—audiences—as producers of meaning.

Student Commentaries Theme #2: Problems of Memory

Another major epistemological concern of academic historians is the issue of memory, specifically the reliability and distortions of individual memory found in personal narrative. Historians of the distant past thought they could "re[-]enter that mental universe and so recover the presence of those times" while today's historians are "suspicious of the distortions of memory, and they are watchful of the transference of their own memories onto the histories that they would write" (Hutton 535).

This concern for memory has caused historians to caution readers about the authenticity of testimony that comes from popular autobiographies. Testimony can be flawed, and "the 'truth' of these accounts lies as much in how the author chooses to tell them as it does in the historically verifiable 'past'" (Crane 21–22). Historian Rene Remond said that historians know "from experience the precariousness of recollection, the unreliability of first-person testimony" (qtd. in Popkin, *History* 62). Furthermore, as individual recollection, autobiography often includes evidence that just cannot be verified at all (Popkin, "Holocaust " 50). As such, academic historians have tended not to accept the "primacy of individual voices" (Caine 79). With this in mind, academic historians typically choose evidence that is available to the public and thus verifiable to supplement and confirm individual memory (Popkin, *History* 50).

Nonetheless, historians have come to appreciate *personal* narrative accounts even if they cannot be verified. Barbara Caine notes that individual voices can be valuable to "illustrate the experiences of a whole group" (80). In a specific example, Jeremy Popkin shows the importance of individual testimony in constructing greater accounts of the Holocaust ("Holocaust" 51). Crane similarly argues that "personal memory acquired from studying, thinking and learning is ultimately as much a 'source' of historical writing as the official sources, the artifacts and documents which historians use in research" (21).

To prompt students to think about the historian's concern for memory, the survey asked for responses to this question: *Did you have any problems remembering the details of your stories?* As with the first question, I expected some students would say no, particularly considering many of their narratives were about events that had happened recently. Surprisingly, only one respondent was relatively assured, saying "I had almost no difficulties remembering details." The rest of the students expressed varying degrees of concern. In the following responses, note in particular the recognition of individual memory and perspective:

S4: Yes, it was challenging to remember certain details because a lot of the stories took place when I was a lot younger.

S8: I found for some of my stories, I had a hard time remembering details, especially the one about childhood because it was so long ago.

S10: I think the memories we make are very individual though, so everybody would have a different interpretation of an event that took place. After thinking about it for so long, you form things in your brain, and it's hard to tell yourself whether that really happened, or if it's something you just thought up.

S21: People have selective memory, and some only remember certain aspects of a story, while others remember different aspects. However, I accurately described each story from my own perspective with my own selective memory.

Furthermore, in working like a historian—without having been told how historians work—many students said they got around memory problems by seeking out other sources, essentially trying to match their recollections with other people's memories and even documentary evidence from the events:

S6: For one story, I asked my sister what exactly John said because I knew she would read it and I wanted to get the dialogue right to satisfy her.

S11: I asked Mom about some details of the physical appearances and searched for pictures that were taken at that time.

S20: To help me remember I went through some family albums and talked to my family about how certain people looked at certain times. I also asked my parents if the character that I wrote about sounded like that person.

S26: Thankfully, I've kept journals since elementary school and I always keep my journals once they're filled. I was able to flip through them to remember certain events and better understand my emotional state at the time.

S32: For some of the events in my stories, I looked back at photo albums taken the day they occurred, just to refresh my memory.

Far from being certain that their personal experience was narrated accurately from memory, these students expressed a subtle doubt about what they had recollected. Like academic historians working with witnesses, they felt somewhat worried that perhaps those memories were not up to par. They understood that memories fade, and they showed the same skepticism as the historian for the ability of witness testimony to tell the complete story, even though it was their own. And just like the academic historian, they turned to other evidence in an attempt to ensure the stories corresponded to the truth. With this second question being asked *after* the writing of these personal histories, students were in a good position to reflect on memory concerns—this was not some abstract problem discussed by historians distanced from the students' world. On the contrary, students had directly experienced the problems of memory.

Student Commentaries Theme #3: Selectivity

A third major issue in doing history is the question of selection. What should historians include and exclude? How might the audience react to those inclusions and exclusions? Carr also discussed selectivity, arguing that history is "a process of selection in terms of historical significance" (105). This was not passing judgement on historians; Carr wrote that the "historian is necessarily selective. The belief in a hard core of historical facts existing objectively and independently of the interpretation of the historian is a preposterous fallacy" (12). The survival of certain documents and the preservation of some material over others emphasizes certain events in the historical record—the stories of history reflect the evidence that survives and was chosen to survive (Day 9; Carr 18).

Stuart Greene argues that personal writing illuminates this selectivity problem. Personal writing provides students with "opportunities to understand the extent to which the processes of selecting, arranging, and sequencing ideas are intimately related to the theoretical assumptions that guide one's thinking" (95). Naturally, "to narrate" and "to choose" are synonyms. To write a narrative—even a personal narrative—is to determine what details matter and what do not, what needs emphasis and what does not, and what deserves direct observation and what requires secondary sources. In his work on student family history projects, David Culbert notes that students who wrote family histories sometimes did not want to tell readers the bad things, a practical example of selectivity (16).

The next survey question dealt with the problems of selection, both as historian and as historical witness: *Were there any events or incidents that you avoided writing about?* Responses show that some things were off-limits in personal histories:

> S6: I altered one story to remove the part where someone in the story hurt me and let me down because I knew that person was going to read the story.

S8: There were some incidences that I tried to avoid writing about simply because they were too personal to be shared with anyone.

S26: I had a lot of difficulty with the last story, because it was about a relationship between a man and a woman. My home environment has always been abusive and I have not witnessed many loving relationships between men and women. I was unable to really write about the incidences I've witnessed because they're still too emotionally fresh. I know they say writing can be healing, but personal writing can also open up wounds that some would rather stay closed.

S30: There were some very personal things I did want to write about. But when I discussed it with my father (a second opinion) I decided against it. Some things are meant to be private I guess.

S33: I mainly avoided them because they were just too personal or traumatizing.

This set of responses shows students' encountering problems about publicizing the private, revealing the personal to the public. The students showed concern in the selection of what to choose to write about or include, reflecting on the possible judgements of audiences. Students recognized that telling one's history involves an act of selection at the very heart of the project and that such selection can hurt those involved. In this assignment, students were not simply expressing themselves freely and wholly, despite the assumed freedom found in personal writing. These experiences should help students develop sensitivity that historians have for documenting the witness testimony of others, such as Holocaust survivors or other survivors of trauma. This line of questioning also raised the students' consciousness of the self-censoring of historical witnesses.

Excerpts from Personal Histories

The students encountered these abstract concerns in doing history, but in the end, what kind and quality of history writing did this assignment, in the type of class described above, produce? Examples from the personal narratives[3] of three students show two main characteristics: clear, concise, detailed writing at the sentence level and the illumination of interesting eyewitness experiences of significant events—the characteristics of all good academic history. The stories are cultural and social histories that present groups, arts, and events from the perspective of ordinary people.

In one poignant story, Ariana Wardak writes about growing up in Kabul, Afghanistan. Depicting the factional strife of the Mujahideen, Wardak describes a moment in 1994 when a soldier enters an underground storage room where her family had taken refuge during bombings:

> Uncle Amaan holds the doorknob, twists it, pushes the door in and beckons us in. We hurry inside. Darkness fills the room except for the sunlight shimmering inside from a window. Mother walks towards the switchboard, flicks a switch, and light fills the room. Everyone looks around, up, and down. Spider-webs cover the four corners and a fireplace lies untouched in the other end of the room. Granny unfolds her shawl, dusts the ground with it, folds the shawl, places it on the ground, and we sit on it. Mother wraps her arms around me. Uncle Amaan's chest flares, his eyes turn red as he sits on the far corner of the shawl besides Granny.
>
> A tall *Mujahid* with a long beard and bulgy eyes walks in and raises his rifle in the air. His eyes dart from one face to another.
>
> "We are here for the Mujahideen. So just let us do our thing and we'll spare you all!" he says.
>
> Uncle Amaan stands up and shouts, "You just killed an innocent woman, you little piece of shit! Who are you to spare our lives? Allah gave us life and He will be the one to take it."
>
> "So you are not afraid to die?" the Mujahid says and stomps towards Uncle Amaan. He fixes Uncle Amaan a hard glare and places the end of his rifle on Uncle Amaan's chest. Granny mutters panicked prayers, and she rolls her turquoise prayer beads and tears moisten her wrinkled face. My stomach revolts, my lips purse, I let out a whimper, and cup my mouth with my hands. Mother gets up, races towards the Mujahid, kneels down and holds his thigh.
>
> "For Allah's sake, don't kill him. He is crazy. He doesn't know what he is talking about," she cries. The Mujahid looks down at Mother, then at Uncle Amaan, holds his rifle with both hands, puts it down, and glares at everyone in the room. The man raises his rifle again.
>
> "Does anybody else have a problem with what we are doing? 'Cause if you do, I'd be happy to blow your brains out!" the Mujahid says and walks out.

Wardak's personal narrative brings us directly into the action, documenting from the ground the human side of war. Academic historians aspire to this level of detail and immediacy. Understanding this testimony as historical source may broaden the student's scope in retelling past events. Accessing the experience of regular people, as Wardak's story does, may encourage student historians to go beyond official documents and artifacts. The focus on only one scene in personal narrative also demands attention to necessary selection on the historian's part: when to begin and end, what details of place, gesture, and clothing to include, and how to portray those participants accurately. If the personal narrative assignment is positioned as 'history' by the instructor, the student should quickly understand the truth questions raised in doing history.

With a long, colourful history, the cultural practices of Trinidadian society serve as fruitful material for Matthew Stollmeyer's tale of his experience at Carnival, an outdoor festival of dancing and music on the island:

> Perfectly synchronized metallic percussion resonated from the shiny silver drums and pans. The player's shoulders, arms and wrists moved in perfect

time, resulting in crisp ringing throughout the parade. Chaos followed. Couples everywhere outdanced each other with excessive gyrations and sexual expressions.

One couple in particular amused me. The man supported his body with his hands on the floor, resembling a failed limbo dancer. Four green straps sprouted from his chest piece; two of them wrapped around his shoulders while the other two wrapped around his lower back. The woman blocking the view of his pants practically sat on him. She wore a bikini costume adorned with stringed beads looping down her legs. His pelvis followed her waist regardless of how quickly she moved it.

I looked towards a Snow Cone vendor as he packed crushed ice into cups in time with the steelpan. With one pang he scooped ice, after another two he smacked it into the Styrofoam cup.

"Ahh ha, check de man fall!" Nicholas said, pointing at the couple.

The man lay face up on the ground, completely starfished. The girl stooped above him clutching her belly in laughter. An exhausted smile came over his face as another partier pulled him up.

The band advanced, people danced while walking, chippin' down the road. Others jumped forward, hands bobbing in the air while shouting along to the ever-present calypso.

In this excerpt, Stollmeyer presents his culture through a detailed scene. He includes the language of his friend as his friend actually sounds. The details of body movements and expressions, of dancing couples, and of a Snow Cone vender bring this scene to life for readers. Readers become immersed in the sounds and sights of the moment. The focused, detailed writing resembles the best of historical work that attempts to describe a cultural tradition. In this way, the personal narrative assignment allows the student to work within the realm of cultural history. While his story is obviously personal, the event itself represents group experience; the assignment connects the personal with the communal. Indeed, it may show the history student how to 'access' cultural history through witness testimony. Finally, Nishkruti Munshi describes the confusion of waiting with thousands of people in the Calgary, Alberta airport after her plane was diverted and grounded on the day of the September 11 terrorist attacks:

> People occupy different corners and personalize little patches of the blue carpet with their belongings that ooze out of their stuffed carry-on luggage.
>
> Airport officials appear from nowhere. They run about frantically in their ironed suits and polished shoes while they talk into hand held radios. At precise intervals, a recorder recites a message through the PA system, "Attention passengers, you are advised to be with your luggage at all times. Unattended luggage will be confiscated and destroyed."
>
> Armed men close in on the terminal. Stress swallows the stagnant air. I feel scared. A tall, stiff man with a megaphone tears through the crowd. A black wire creeps down his ear and disappears into his nape. The megaphone screeches into the air. The crowd goes quiet. The man bellows though the loudspeaker:

> "The reason everyone is gathered here today . . . *pause* . . . is that a terrorist attack . . . *pause* . . . has taken place in the United States of America."
> Murmurs ruffle through the crowd.
> "The World Trade Centre collapsed. Two United Airlines flights crashed into the twin towers. All flights going into the US are diverted. Airports in the US are closed. Outgoing flights from Canada are suspended . . . until further notice."
> A crescendo of confused gasps escapes from the swarm and tears instantly dribble down terrified eyes and people shrink to the floor and muffled wails reverberate in the dense air. Time pauses. I grab my Mummy's hand, close my eyes and think about my lost luggage, the people lost here at Calgary, and the lives lost in New York.

Munshi's tale shows the wide effect of the attack, connecting her personal history with the events in New York. It resembles oral history accounts of the attacks collected by the official 9/11 memorial. Just as greater understanding of the Holocaust was formed through the collection of individual stories, Munshi contributes her own individual testimony to a much larger cultural transnational experience. In choosing to tell this kind of personal narrative, the student may better recognize the role and appropriateness of participant histories in the retellings of larger events. As a result, the student broadens his or her perspective on the value of such specific, detailed testimony to a greater historical project.

All three stories show the best of historical storytelling, of important events and interesting cultures, produced in a beginner's writing course—not a history course—in a university environment.

Conclusion

The teaching approach outlined in this article represents a simple starting point for linking personal history writing to the epistemological issues of doing academic historical work. The survey answers show students wrestling with the power and responsibility inherent in the process of social construction of the past. This reflects Spigelman's observation that in personal writing students discover "the ways in which experiential evidence necessarily destabilizes certainty, the ways in which stories encourage contradiction and inconsistency and offer narrative layerings, all open to interpretation" (75). Most students showed a concern or care for truth even if they could not ultimately meet that high standard.

The survey results suggest that personal narrative and an ensuing discussion of students' work as historians can be useful not just as an assignment in the writing classroom but also as a beginning assignment in university history classes to engage students in understanding academic history's challenges. In constructing non-fiction narratives about their own lives—a respectable form in academic history today—they get to do what historians do: pull together historical details into coherent accounts. Students become producers, not just consumers, of history. Perhaps their singular drive to produce interesting, readable stories that they *care* about leads to the compelling, detailed historical narratives reprinted above.

As the survey comments suggest, personal experience writing need not produce an insular student writer unaware of the greater issues historians face. It can be employed to understand the discursive challenges of writing academic history, moving students away from seeing history as simply a collection of uncontested facts. Students reflected on possible audience reactions and the concepts of truth without reading secondary sources or receiving training in historiography. Personal narrative can thus accomplish goals of both expressivist and social constructivist pedagogies for the beginning history student: engaging students in writing—and writing history—while exposing them to the discursive production of knowledge. Personal narrative may also find a useful place, introducing students to other concepts, in other disciplines such as sociology, the hard sciences, and political science, among others.

The results of research into this specific form of the 'doing history' approach to history teaching reflect the importance of personalization to students' understanding of historical work and its challenges. Roger Long felt the need to add the personal dimension to his history courses—in his case oral history (308). However, these kinds of projects can be time-consuming, as Kirk Jeffrey recalls about his students' family history projects (367). Family history or local history projects can be more difficult to complete in one term for beginning history students than writing a traditional term paper based on secondary sources easily found on library shelves. The use of personal narrative of the sort described in this article, however, does not place unreasonable work demands on students in a single term. Students do not have to spend a great deal of time researching—the content is all in their heads—but they may choose to consult with others, as students in these classes did. The personal history assignment can provide students with "occasions to develop the thinking skills historians value through writing" (Greene 95). Of course, this assignment would not be the only part of a history course—it would only be the beginning. After writing the personal narrative, students may be assigned to visit local archives and research and write local history or tackle oral history projects. The University of Toronto Mississauga Professional Writing and Communication program asks students in a course called Writing History to produce local and personal histories, which have been published in two collections used as course textbooks (see Procter; Cunanan et al.). Later on, students may then be ready to deal with the secondary literature of the masterpiece academic historians and connect that material to their personal work, more fully able to relate from personal experience.

Yet traditional methods still reign in history courses. Many teachers assign argumentative and expository term papers based upon secondary sources in their attempt to help students understand the academic history discourse. They discuss truth and subjectivity, memory, and selectivity in terms of the work of academic 'others.' As a result, students may disengage. They do not get to experience the discourse from inside it as a practitioner—they work at a distance from secondary sources. Thousands of undergraduates are enrolled in history courses but rarely do they get to write accounts of history as the students in my study did. Rarely do they get to experience being a historian (they may not even realize this personal history is indeed legitimate historical work). Wallace and Beidler call for attention to that "experiential base" that allows history students to develop "sensitivity to discrepancy, awareness of uncertainty and disagreement and their potential sources, and the development of a healthy skepticism are intellectual attributes necessary in any field of scholarly inquiry" (29). The personal history assignment is clearly not antithesis to that goal.

On the other side of the equation, instructors in university history classes can introduce this assignment to their classes to introduce students to some of the major concerns of the field before they encounter them in textbooks. They can connect those abstract ideas to their personal experiences. Instructors may find students more willing to take on primary research projects with this experience behind them. As well, the assignment does not add a significant grading burden on the history teacher. It efficiently works on a number of levels—the practical and the abstract—and provides a chance for students to write.

These results reflects the idea that, as Richard Marius and Mel Page argue, "Historians must always put something of themselves into the stories they tell; never are they empty vessels through which the records of the past spew forth as if they were an untouched truth about the past" (6). When given a chance to put themselves into this work, they come to understand the historian's experience of subjectivity, the issues of truth, the problems of memory, and the power of selection.

Both personal writing pedagogy and the 'doing history' strain of historical pedagogy position students as active creators of meaning, and students' own experiences, whether as individual writer or historian, are valued. Adding this 'doing history' assignment and questions to the history classroom can, in Bruce Horner's terms, educate students about "material, social, and historical operating not only within and outside the classroom, but also, and more significantly, within as well as outside student consciousness" (513). As the survey answers show, most students can come to understand these issues even in writing their own personal histories. Academic historians understand these epistemological issues because they get to express their own ideas and experiences through this process of constructing works of history; beginning students of history should be encouraged to do the same.

Notes

1. I see discourse as the often unseen communicative pressures or structures that condition ways of thinking and acting in a given social domain (see

Fairclough, *Media Discourse;* Fairclough, *Language and Power;* Fairclough, *Discourse and Social Change;* van Dijk; Gee; Mills).
2. The descriptions of each section are naturally summary in nature. These summaries exist to suggest generally each epistemological before the presentation of student comments.
3. Students gave permission for their work to be reprinted here. The stories were written in other sections of the course that were not part of the anonymous survey. The full stories were significantly longer than these excerpts.

Acknowledgments

I would like to thank Robert Price for his helpful comments on an earlier version of this article.

Works Cited

Allen, Guy. "Language, Power, and Consciousness: A Writing Experiment at the University of Toronto." *Teaching Composition: Background Readings.* Ed. T.R. Johnson. New York: Bedford/St. Martin's, 2008. 65–98. Print.

—. ed. *Make It New: Creative Nonfiction by New Writers for New Writers.* Toronto: Life Rattle P, 2008. Print.

—. *No More Masterpieces: Short Prose by New Writers.* Canadian Scholars' Press, 1989. Print.

—. "The 'Good-Enough' Teacher and the Authentic Student." *A Pedagogy of Becoming.* Ed. Jon Mills. Amsterdam and New York: Rodopi, 2002. 141–176. Print.

Bartholomae, David. "Writing with Teachers: A Conversation with Peter Elbow." *CCC* 46.1 (1995): 62–71. Print.

Becker, Carl. "What is Evidence? The Relativist View." Winks 3–23.

Caine, Barbara. *Biography and History.* 1st ed. New York: Palgrave Macmillan, 2010. Print.

Candeloro, Dominic. "Undergraduates as Historians: Recovering the History of a Black Community." *The History Teacher* 7.1 (1973): 24–29. Web. 23 June 2011.

Carr, E.H. *What Is History?* New York: Penguin Books Ltd., 1986. Print.

Crane, Susan A. "(Not) Writing History: Rethinking the Intersections of Personal History and Collective Memory with Hans Von Aufsess." *History and Memory* 8.1 (1996): 5–29. Print.

Culbert, David H. "Undergraduates as Historians: Family History Projects Add Meaning to an Introductory Survey." *The History Teacher* 7.1 (1973): 7–17. Print.

Cunanan, Isa, Margaret Procter, Kornelia Telesz, and Julie Tyios. eds. *Writing History: A Collection by New Writers.* 2nd edition. Toronto: Life Rattle P, 2007. Print.

Day, Mark. *Philosophy of History: An Introduction.* London: Continuum, 2008. Print.

Díaz, Arlene et al. "The History Learning Project: A Department 'Decodes' Its Students." *The Journal of American History* 94.4 (2008): 1211–1224. Web. 5 Oct. 2012.

van Dijk, Teun Adrianus. *News as Discourse.* Hillsdale, NJ: L. Erlbaum Associates, 1988. Print.

Fairclough, Norman. *Discourse and Social Change*. Cambridge, Mass.: Polity Press, 1992. Print.

—. *Language and Power*. London: Longman, 1989. Print.

—. *Media Discourse*. London: E. Arnold, 1995. Print.

Fishman, Stephen M., and Lucille Parkinson McCarthy. "Is Expressivism Dead? Reconsidering Its Romantic Roots and Its Relation to Social Constructionism." *College English* 54.6 (1992): 647–661. Print.

Gee, James Paul. *An Introduction to Discourse Analysis: Theory and Method*. 2nd ed. New York: Routledge, 2005. Print.

Greene, Stuart. "The Problems of Learning to Think Like a Historian: Writing History in the Culture of the Classroom." *Educational Psychologist* 29.2 (1994): 89. Print.

Horner, Bruce. "Students, Authorship, and the Work of Composition." *College English* 59.5 (1997): 505–529. Web. 18 June 2011.

Howell, Martha C., and Walter Prevenier. *From Reliable Sources: An Introduction to Historical Methods*. Ithaca, N.Y: Cornell University Press, 2001. Print.

Hutton, Patrick. "Recent Scholarship on Memory and History." *The History Teacher* 33.4 (2000): 533–548. Print.

Jeffrey, Kirk. "Write a History of Your Own Family: Further Observations and Suggestions for Instructors." *The History Teacher* 7.3 (1974): 365–373. Print.

Long, Roger D. "The Personal Dimension in Doing Oral History." *The History Teacher* 24.3 (1991): 307–312. Print.

Marius, Richard A., and Mel Page. *A Short Guide to Writing About History*. 7th ed. London: Longman, 2009. Print.

McClymer, John F., and Kenneth J. Moynihan. "The Essay Assignment: A Teaching Device." *The History Teacher* 10.3 (1977): 359–371. Web. 23 June 2011.

Mills, Sara. *Discourse*. 2nd ed. London: Routledge, 2004. Print.

Popkin, Jeremy D. *History, Historians, and Autobiography*. University of Chicago Press, 2005. Print.

—. "Holocaust Memories, Historians' Memoirs: First-Person Narrative and the Memory of the Holocaust." *History and Memory* 15.1 (2003): 49–84. Print.

Procter, Margaret, ed. *Writing History: A Collection by New Writers*. 1st ed. Life Rattle Press, Toronto, 2004. Print.

Somekawa, Ellen, and Elizabeth A. Smith. "Theorizing the Writing of History or, 'I Can't Think Why It Should Be So Dull, for a Great Deal of It Must Be Invention.'" *Journal of Social History* 22.1 (1988): 149–161. Print.

Spigelman, Candace. "Argument and Evidence in the Case of the Personal." *College English* 64.1 (2001): 63–87. Print.

Tuchman, Barbara Wertheim. *Practicing History: Selected Essays*. 1st ed. New York: Ballantine Books, 1982. Print.

Underwood, Ted L. "Undergraduates as Historians: Writing Local History in a Seminar on Historical Research." *The History Teacher* 7.1 (1973): 18–23. Print.

VanSledright, Bruce. "Confronting History's Interpretive Paradox While Teaching Fifth Graders to Investigate the Past." *American Educational Research Journal* 39.4 (2002): 1089–1115. Print.

Vess, Deborah. "Creative Writing and the Historian: An Active Learning Model for Teaching the Craft of History." *The History Teacher* 30.1 (1996): 45–53. Print.

Wallace, John, and Paul Beidler. "Teaching History Through Personal Experience: An Experimental Inquiry." *The History Teacher* 1.3 (1968): 24–30. Print.

Whitman, Glenn. "Teaching Students How to Be Historians: An Oral History Project for the Secondary School Classroom." *The History Teacher* 33.4 (2000): 469–481. Print.

Winks, Robin W. *The Historian as Detective: Essays on Evidence.* 1st ed. New York: Harper & Row, 1969. Print.

Where Professional Writing Meets Social Change: The Grant Proposal as a Site of Hospitality

Kenna Barrett

> This essay builds upon prior attempts to foster linkages between the disciplines of Composition Studies and professional writing. I take up Jennifer Bay's suggestion that service learning is a site for connection and *hospitality* (in a Derridean sense) between these disciplines, advocating for and at the same time complicating Bay's proposal. Rather than offering straightforward hospitality, I posit, service learning sites present opportunities to critique, welcome, and revise the multiple demands of composing today.

In her 2010 *Composition Studies* article "Writing Beyond Borders: Rethinking the Relationship Between Composition Studies and Professional Writing," Jennifer Bay offers a path for rapprochement between composition studies and professional writing, fields that are often thought of as bounded by disciplinary ideology, compartmentalized by separate faculties, staff, students, and research pursuits. Bay proposes that the three sites of emerging technologies, work, and service learning comprise "threshold spaces" for the two disciplines to come together (29). In calling for rapprochement, Bay adopts the frame of the Derridean notion of hospitality as a way to invite scholars in both disciplines to "say yes to what shows up, say yes to all possibilities before we become engulfed in the moment of (self) identification as other" (30–31).

Derridean hospitality, I propose here, is not as straightforwardly welcoming as Bay's account might suggest, and it is this more complicated notion of hospitality that better fits the way in which our two disciplines could build accord in the offshore sites Bay proposes. Through a rhetorical analysis of a funding proposal framed by authethnographic reflections on my professional grant writing experience, I describe how service learning opportunities, focusing here on the case of nonprofit proposal writing, do serve as threshold spaces where hospitality is enacted. But these nonprofit sites are not neutral spaces any more than any other discourse community, and rather than offering the opportunity for uncomplicated syntheses or reconciliations, they offer a range of opportunities for students and researchers to acknowledge and critique the multiple demands of composing in today's world.

A note on methodology: ethnography as a research method in rhetoric and composition involves, as Matthew Ortoleva notes, techniques such as participant observation, interviews, and textual analysis, and is an approach to understanding social behavior as situated in time and place rather than as objectively renderable from a situation or text (60). I have chosen to include my textual analysis within an autoethnographic framework principally because I see this framework as best able to permit my drawing upon my 12 years of experience as a nonprofit grantwriter as part of my analysis. I use the term "autoethnographic reflections" to make clear that I intend my remarks as looking back from the present day, rather than drawing on field notes taken at the time.

The Call for Hospitality in Composing

Nonprofit writing *hosts* different rhetorical ideologies, and as I will propose, these ideologies hosted within nonprofit writing come into contact with one another in ways that echo Derrida's insistence that hospitality involves a measure of imposition. To motivate this project, let us look at the roots of the call for hospitality in rhetoric and composition.

Drawing from the essay "Writing Offshore" by Cynthia Haynes, Jennifer Bay shares Haynes' concern that Composition Studies has taught and prized the argument as a rhetorical mode, even though the logic behind professional decision-making in the workplace is not based on traditional argumentative forms such as rhetoric or dialectic. Corporate action is not based in anything that represents a process of reasoning, but on the profit motive, on "the logic of advanced multinational capitalism, which is *groundless*" (30). Bay uses Haynes' critique of argument as the dominant pedagogy in a groundless, capitalist world in order to draw attention to another disconnect in the landscape, the separation between Composition Studies and professional writing, by which she means business and technical writing and communication (43). Even as traditional argumentation cannot help structure our understanding of the tectonic shifts in the world today, neither can the boundaries of disciplinarity: "We need a new way of making sense of this constantly shifting ground, but as Haynes demonstrates, it can't be the ground of argument, and I would go farther to say that it also can't be the ground of disciplinarity" (33).

Bay calls for "a culture of hospitality" between professional writing and Composition Studies, a move that implies not only that the disciplines are disunified, but that the two disciplines *should* move closer together (29). Why are they not unified, and why should they move closer together? To answer the first question, Bay maintains that Composition Studies and professional writing have had a tension with one another due in part to the former's association with cultural theory and critiques of capitalist ideology. "Professional writing's connection to business and industry creates tensions with composition studies, which often aligns itself with cultural and post-Marxist critique" she writes, noting that Composition's "attachment to academic writing distances it from professional writing's focus on workplace writing situations" (36).

Certainly, the work of compositionists such as Lester Faigley and James Berlin, while not *prima facie* appearing to espouse disciplinary disunion, sought an ideological distinction between Composition Studies and what happens in the workplace. Faigley argued that Richard Lanham's *Revising Business Prose* was not only amoral but internally inconsistent with its own writerly tenets: it proposes that there are two main reasons for revising business prose, namely efficiency and ego (i.e., sincerity), but how is it possible, Faigley asks, for most of us to write sincere prose in a memo laying off mass numbers of workers? "Bottom line efficiency as practiced in business," writes Faigley, "continually conflicts with the human feelings that Lanham advocates" (136–7). In turn, Linda Flower and John Hayes' invitation to the writing student, that "whatever your goals are, you are interested in discovering better ways to achieve them" (672), concerned James Berlin, because it reinscribed the rational self-interest of the capitalist. "Nowhere," he writes of Flower and Hayes, "do [they] question the worth of the goals pursued by the manager, scientist, or writer" (672). Value-neutrality toward the commitments of writing is a recipe for training people to climb the corporate ladder, preserving the unfair class system.

Bay next argues that these disciplines that have "tried to forge separate disciplinary identities" (30) could benefit from greater solidarity, thus her call for hospitality. Bay points out that the disciplines are already connected and while they may hold distinct ideologies and goals, the idea that Composition Studies can critique the workplace from outside is mistaken:

> Look around and we see more change than stability: students change majors multiple times based on job possibilities; faculty spend years searching for full-time employment and often must pursue other careers due to the lack of positions; workers make career changes or return to school for job training and ensured future income; and elderly retirees must work to supplement their subsidized incomes. These are just a few images of the constantly shifting landscape on which Composition Studies attempts to build its constituency. (32)

In other words, professors already exist in a corporate hierarchy (and indeed, I would add, actively comply with it by sitting on appointment committees, developing labor policies for staff, admitting students through need-aware—not need-bind—admissions policies, and so forth). Even academic writing itself is not insulated from "corporate logic," as Bay points out, and I would support that observation by noting that funding often drives the direction that research programmes take; journal articles are written toward certain audiences, and so forth. Composition courses are often drafted to fulfill university objectives, such as retention initiatives, and first-year composition courses, as Ira Shor and others have noted, earn more money than they cost to run, thanks in part to their low-wage workforce (Parascondola).[1]

Bay realizes that the two disciplines can help one another: professional writing can help with integrating technologies into the curriculum, for instance, and "the critique of industry and culture" that one finds in composition courses "can be brought to bear on professional writing courses" in order to help students critique, and possibly creatively respond to, corporate culture and injustice (38).

Supporting this call for hospitality are the hybrid majors that some departments have created. Consider an analysis of 68 writing majors in American universities by Balzhiser and McLeod in 2010. As these researchers note, and as I have also found in an unpublished study of the University of Rhode Island's proposal for an undergraduate writing major in 2011, preprofessional education is a primary goal of a number of burgeoning undergraduate writing majors, tempting us to believe that the fields can and do go hand-in-hand. The Balzhiser and McLeod data indicates that within the 68 writing majors they reviewed (41 of these considered "professional/rhetoric" majors and 27 "liberal arts" writing majors), there were a total of 68 individual courses offered in the area of "technical/business/workplace/organizational communication/writing" (421).

Furthermore, the URI writing major is a locus where professional writing and Composition Studies are overseen by a single rhetoric and composition faculty, and the gateway course itself provides instruction in the canons of rhetoric even as it requires research on professional writers (Balzhiser and McLeod 419). In my analysis of URI's founding documents, I identified language pertaining to the proposed Writing and Rhetoric major that evokes the dual goals we have been speaking of, goals marking both professional and critique-driven demands. The URI writing major, for example, proposes to be a site where students can "recognize, value, and understand different cultural values" (URI 3–4) as well as a place that would emphasize "students' ethical development" and their "capabilities as critical and independent thinkers" (3). At the same time, however, this writing major designed as a liberal arts degree also "emphasizes the applied arts and technical skills that employers value" (1). In other words, rather than an "either-or" sensibility, the URI major proposes a "both-and" ethic.

Hybrid majors such as URI's suggest that the disciplinary distinctions between Composition Studies and professional writing are not essential, rigid boundaries: the properties of one discipline bleed into the other, making some form of disciplinary nominalism therefore in order. (For a discussion of nominalism, see Appiah's chapter in Appiah and Gutmann. Writing about the nature of the boundaries distinguishing biological species from one another and distinguishing the supposed races, Appiah describes nominalism as the position that such boundaries are "classificatory convenience[s]" rather than boundaries found "in nature" [67].) Indeed, one upshot of the following analysis of grant writing is that the difference in what we do when we ask students to think ethically and communally versus when we ask them to think profitably does not invoke disciplinarity, in the same sense that thinking mathematically may differ from thinking anthropologically. In other words, the Faigley and Berlin objections to business writing imply that the competition among different rhetorical goals in a given writing task can create ideological conflict. So sometimes thinking ethically and thinking profitably imply some level of incompatibility, for instance in their examples. But as we will see, thinking ethically and thinking profitably can work together toward the same goal, especially in domains such as grant writing.

In the discussion that follows, I borrow Steven Katz' labels of ethics and expediency to tease out the two core values that seem to be driving concerns that, in my view, have more to do with rhetorical goals than disciplinary boundaries. In 1992, Katz critiqued writing instruction, positing that technical communication (considered a form of deliberative rhetoric, or rhetoric concerning decisions about future action) places expediency over other values. Using the example of a Nazi-era memo discussing the specifications of vehicles that killed people with carbon monoxide, he charges that technical writing would evaluate positively all business correspondence that displayed formally desirable characteristics of deliberative writing (e.g., a purpose statement, use of *topoi*) regardless of moral content. "By any formal criteria in technical communication," he writes, "[the Nazi memo] is an almost perfect document" (256). Katz suggests that those who teach professional writing and even deliberative rhetoric (by extension implicating Composition Studies here too) are complicit in promoting an ideology that privileges efficiency. "[D]o we, as teachers and writers and scholars, contribute to this ethos by our writing theory, pedagogy, and practice, when we consider techniques of document design, audience adaptation, argumentation, and style without considering ethics?" Katz asks (271). These terms "ethics" and "expediency" I will use to denote the two different values that can be seen to drive rhetorical goals in writing, the first focused on doing what is good and the second on doing what brings about a desired end.

Bay's key insight, for my purposes, is her recognition that service learning can be a "threshold space" where a "culture of hospitality" can be fostered between professional writing and Composition Studies (31). As far as motivating service learning's role in this rapprochement, Bay suggests that community engagement is a practice "predicated on hospitality; it is the development of a relationship of trust and openness among teacher, student, institution, and community agency" and that in this space, professional writing and Composition scholars can "enact and learn hospitality" (41–2). In this utopian world, service learning sites would be zones of communal goodness where ethical reasoning prevails.

The reality of community agencies, however, is that they compete with other agencies for scarce funding streams, meaning that their goals are multivariate, encompassing rhetorical aims and acts of both ethics and efficiency. That is why, I suggest, we must explore what exactly the hospitality that Bay calls for would look like—how service learning sites can be sites of hospitality, and what shape that hospitality takes.

Writing the Nonprofit Grant Proposal: Ethics and Expediency

Writing in *Acts of Religion,* Derrida teases out a certain paradoxical nature of hospitality: "[I]f I welcome only what I welcome, what I am ready to welcome, and that I recognize in advance because I expect the coming of the hôte as invited, *there is no hospitality*" (362, italics mine). Derrida wants to say that the primary act of hosting, the act of extending a welcome to another, involves welcoming some measure of imposition. Hospitality connotes welcoming, then, even as it means being prepared to be overtaken (361). Hospitality is an aporia: not the unproblematic welcoming of another with open arms, hospitality involves countenancing the "other" and giving up or sacrificing something desired (e.g., time, space, dogma) in order to become the host. After all, we do not host what is already an integral part of us—our own beliefs or identities, for example. Bearing in mind this fuller conception of hospitality can help us make sense of how the rapprochement that Bay proposes could take form in the context of service learning.

To begin to explicate a Derridean conception of hospitality, consider that nonprofit organizations are hybrid entities—they are legally-recognized private corporations but they cannot distribute profits to any individuals and must instead use them toward public purposes (this is called the non-private inurement clause). As domains, they play host to professional aims and identities as well as social criticism and critique. These competing ideologies meet in many corners of the nonprofit organization, especially in the search for funding. In what follows, I analyze excerpts from a funding proposal that I co-authored to illustrate the distinct writing tasks facing the grant writer, and how they enact different ideological commitments. My methodology is based in qualitative discourse analysis and authethnography. While my analysis is not intended to propose generalizable conclusions, it serves to pedagogically illustrate how grant proposals can be approached as rhetorical documents, documents that are the products of different and sometimes competing commitments that create hospitable (and inhospitable) tensions.

Recently, as a consultant, I co-authored a proposal for an organization I will call "Child Care Partners," which trains women to be home child care providers.[2] From a rhetorical standpoint, the *purpose* of the proposal was to win funds from a granting agency (obviously a professional aim), and a sub-purpose was to provide a persuasive critique of the social order that perpetuates the situation for which the funds are needed. The social critique appeared largely in the *need statement,* a component of many grant proposals. We spent several paragraphs of the need statement discussing the situation of poverty in the location in question, and how that poverty affects people's life prospects. For instance, we noted that "[T]he challenges for poor people in [our state] begin at birth," and "about 71,000 children who need caretakers have no access to licensed care, because [our state], like many other states, does not have enough spots available" (Barrett 3).

Through an analysis of our audience (i.e., the intended funder), we honed the kind of social critique that would "sing" to this funder. This honing toward an audience we might think of as a professional act, an act of expediency. In the case of Child Care Partners, we employed a specific version of social change language. We might call it, following Ellen Cushman's work on micro-levels of interaction, social change that engages in challenging one's daily circumstances (12–13), rather than "emancipatory" (14) change that upends an entire social structure. In Cushman's vein, training mothers to operate family daycares is indeed changing the customary, unjust flow of events; the rhetorical act of seeking funds for this project counts as an act of social change too: it is using language to challenge the injustices of daily life. Here, we positioned the organization as way of opening the benefits of the economic order to more people: "Child Care Partners addresses both workforce development and child care in one single swoop" (Barrett 3). In sum, writing the need statement for this proposal was on the one hand an act of professional writing and at the same time a rhetorical attempt to create social change. Bay's premise that service learning can serve as a threshold space is borne out. Moreover, rigid disciplinarity does not apply—whether one is a composition studies student writing a grant or a professional writing student writing the grant, one models the same rhetorical goals.

These rhetorical acts of proposal development, choices designed for expedient and ethical purposes at the same time, offer the service learning student opportunities for social action, reflection, and professional development. Next, in writing the *program statement* or *narrative* of the proposal, the service learning student must describe the cause for which the grant is being sought. Gathering information for the proposal puts students in contact with program leaders and participants. There, students may participate in or observe ideological discourses about the injustices of the current world order that fuse theory and practice in ways that cannot be taught in the classroom alone. Students may come to understand the promises and the shortcomings of real-life social action programs.

As Robert McEachern points out, composition courses and professional writing courses engaged in service learning often emphasize different aspects of these service learning experiences: Composition Studies focuses more on critical reflection, while professional writing emphasizes practical, hands-on experience (213). It should be apparent how proposal-writing provides practical experience, but it also provides ripe opportunity for theoretical discourse: as the service learning student writes, she comes to appreciate the complex relationship between text, author, audience, and reality, concepts from the composition course. You have the social program as it unfolds in the world, the program as it is communicated in operating manuals, memos, and spoken discourse, and the program as written in a grant proposal. Proposal writers will sometimes find that the program they construct through their descriptive choices and rhetorical devices bears only passing similarity to the "actual" program on the ground. Proposal writing can therefore be a helpful way of actualizing academic approaches to framing rhetorical production and ontology, such as James Kinneavy's four kinds of discourse emphasizing different pieces of the communication triangle.[3] For instance, while I drafted the Child Care Partners proposal, I kept in mind the funder (decoder) I intended to persuade, but well before drafting the proposal I discussed the project at length with the Executive Director, thus constituting reference discourse with its focus on realism. Students can also be encouraged to identify stages of the proposal development process where as writers they invoke literary discourse and where they invoke expressive writing.

The construction of the remaining sections of the grant proposal, which can include *organizational information, outcomes,* and *evaluation* sections, involves similar modeling of the rhetorical goals, the evolving text, the social context, and the program in question. Here is where the relationship between text and reality can become one of co-construction: outcomes sections often do configure programs not simply vice versa, because once the outcomes are in place, and funding awarded, staff must strive to meet them. Often in these situations, writing a proposal writes certain aspects of the project along with it. One outcome in the Child Care Partners proposal was a "[research report] discussing the prospects of expanding our model" (Barrett 1) beyond the state in which we operated; lo and behold, a research report became part of the project. The seemingly obtuse theoretical idea that texts can construct reality becomes concretely exemplified through the process of proposal writing.

Finally, the very nature of the rhetorical analysis and enactment involved in authoring a successful grant proposal will steep the service-learning student in the discourses of professional work and the use of specific business skills such as marketing. The student learns the simple skill of reviewing a funder's website—and any memos regarding conversations with program officers—and decides what buzzwords might be inserted into a proposal, for instance. Because the funder I was working with had a "Community" grant program that cited an interest in "children and family services" we ensured that the proposal stressed Child Care Partners' value for both providers and children enrolled. These rhetorical choices are expedient in that we were not thinking about writing the "best" proposal in terms of fidelity to some writerly ideal, but writing the one that would get us the funding.

Grantwriting: Logic of Persuasion and Style

As seen with Child Care Partners, the proposal's rhetorical purpose could be said to be winning a grant, which involved persuading a private foundation to decide in its favor. Proposal writing may therefore best be thought of as deliberative rhetoric, deciding on future action. Our proposal was written in multiple modes of discourse, including narrative, descriptive, and argumentative forms. As James Kinneavy notes, the narrative mode of discourse may serve to introduce a topic and initiate ethical and pathetic appeals in the context of persuasive discourse (268). Our proposal's narrative, abridged here, establishes the organization's ethos:

> Child Care Partners began by helping parents in [city], especially single mothers of young children, meet the [Welfare Reform Act's] welfare-to-work requirements by training them to open family childcares. In time, Child Care Partners established both a licensing component, helping unlicensed caregivers meet health and safety standards necessary for state licensing, and a childcare network, offering an array of support to licensed providers. In ten short years, it has become a leading voice in state policy circles. (Barrett 3)

The argumentative discourse in our proposal drew upon enthymemes and examples that involved the logic of the dual appeals of ethics and expediency. The enthymeme that formed the entire arc of our proposal went roughly like this (excerpts are followed by parenthetical paraphrases):

1. About 71,000 children who need caretakers have no access to licensed care . . . the burden of poverty does not end there . . . wages for [state's] lowest paid workers have fallen over the past 20 years. **(Poor children lack childcare and poor adults suffer from low wages)**
2. Child Care Partners addresses both workforce development and child care in one single swoop. **(Our organization helps poor children get care and poor adults earn wages)**
3. The help of several national funders will be critical not only to provide needed funds but to lend legitimacy to our expansion project. **(We need your money to do our work)**
4. (Therefore, you ought to give us the grant we requested)

The enthymeme, then, involved both appeals to ethics (premises 1 and 2) and expediency in the sense of obtaining material rewards (premise 3 and implied conclusion 4).

Stylistically, proposals conform to the vocabulary, grammar, and mechanics of mainstream English. There is perhaps nothing more important to a grant proposal than impeccable grammar and spelling, for as cultural studies has taught us, the ability to expertly handle dominant discourse is viewed as a window into the capability of an individual or an organization to implement its program and, ultimately, to acquit itself admirably of the funds provided.

Service Learning: Complicating Hospitality

Thus far, we have spoken about the ways in which grant proposal-writing hosts both critique and professional discourses, in a hybridized platform that fuses and confuses disciplinary boundaries. Why, then have I spoken about the *inhospitality* of the service learning space?

Quite often, writers struggle considerably when the demands of the goal of obtaining funds and the goal of changing the world compete with, rather than complement, one another. *Overpromising*—described as one of the most common mistakes of new investigators by the National Institute of Child Health and Human Development—results when one affirms in a written proposal more ambitious goals than are practicable, usually in order to impress a potential funder (Cologna and Cluzeau, par. 12). Many funding institutions refuse to support general operations, perhaps harkening back to their capitalist origins and belief that enterprises should become "self-sustaining"—despite the unwieldy constraints on sustainability imposed by charitable missions and non-private inurement clauses. This tenuous situation causes organizations to have to build "incremental" activities into grant proposals, stretching staffing and budgets to the point where some grants barely confer any benefit at all, and also heralding expedient and highly unethical choices. Confronting a deficit, one organization I served previously used gifts from a prominent donor to pay down debt without acknowledging this use to the donor. (I discovered the questionable practice while reviewing donor correspondences.)

The aforementioned research report for Child Care Partners may have been a mild example of overpromising, in that I suggested advancing the idea in order to appeal to the funder rather than because the project actually called for it. I felt as if the funder needed some piece of the larger project that they alone would fund. The empirical study of fundraising is a new field, and while there is a growing body of research on the effects of, for instance, thank-you gifts on giving decisions (e.g., see Newman and Shen) there is less to be said about the drivers behind foundation decisionmaking. So I worked instinctively, with little empirically predictive basis to justify whether that research report would have increased the likelihood of a grant. The best outcome for Child Care Partners would have been, of course, winning the grant without promising extra work. In situations where that outcome is not certain, writers make choices reflecting their valuation of different potential outcomes. For instance, if I felt there were a greater probability of winning an award with the research report included, I might be less concerned about the extra, seemingly mission-diverting work. However, diverting effort away from mission-related activities might be more of a concern to a program director than a grant writer, meaning that the program director may prefer to risk a declination from a funder rather than propose a grant that would create a burden. A scenario such as this illustrates ethics and expedience working orthogonally to one another, because expedience (taken as a means to an end) should suggest always (or usually) pursuing a given grant, whereas ethics should imply possibly turning one away if it represents a dilution of mission.

Another common problem according to many observers of the nonprofit world (Jonker and Meehan 60) is *mission creep:* expanding the organization's mission in order to obtain funding. Again, lured by the promise of funding, grant writers may expand the organization's programming in order to reach different funding pockets. Child Care Partners was excellent at staying on message. However, government cutbacks caused one potential funder to propose that our organization focus on forging entrepreneurial partnerships with nearby stakeholders. While seemingly plausible, the suggestion represented a different philosophy of child care (market-financed instead of public-financed) and might have been time-intensive and detracting from Child Care Partners' public policy orientation. The leaders opted against that funder's suggestion, preserving their focus on a more progressive and less commercial conception of social change. A more expedient option focused more on maximizing income would have involved exploring the market model, and I was more inclined to pursue the funder's suggestion, being the persuasive writer with the rhetorical uber-goal of winning grants. Now, one could argue that a social venture like this would be not only pragmatic and expedient but ethically valid, which serves to illustrate the richness of service learning as a site for practicing and theorizing hospitality.

While I am aware of no extensive studies on the problems of overpromising and mission creep, informal conversations during my career as well as my own experience tell me that most grant writers have encountered these tensions in their work and have had to make rhetorical choices that positioned the proposal in a particular space of the (in)hospitality zone that Bay speaks of. Professional writers, in my experience, tend to want to err on the side of sacrificing output and mission for more awards, whereas program staff will tend to err on the side of conserving mission and output and "leaving money on the table." These office conversations are often contentious and heated and unfortunately, the typical grant writing environment does not afford the full opportunity for writers and managers to reflectively weigh each (in)hospitable demand and consider its long-term costs and benefits. While the large university I once served has actually *returned* gifts that compromised its academic mission, smaller and fledgling organizations have no such luxury.

One final point of (in)hospitality between professional writing demands and the ideals of Composition Studies are the stylistic sacrifices entailed by grant writing. Often times, grant writers feel compelled to parrot funder language, sacrificing their Pulitzer ambitions for prose such as "asset-based," "capacity-building," and "means-tested." The proposal I have been describing featured wonderful nominalizations and jargon describing "our secondary target population," (Barrett 4) "low quality learning environment," (1) and "innovative training programs" (1).

Although I am sympathetic to Kathryn Rentz and Ashley Mattingly's position that service learning students, at least those earning professional writing degrees, serve as consulting professionals first and change agents second (115), I think that having service learning students reflect critically upon decisions made in cases where competing ends seemed at work, explain why they represented compromises, and perhaps even suggest alternatives builds not only fluency in various discourses, but the ability to critique the discourses from within, rather than simply from without. After all, as Bay recognizes, professors do not sit outside of the discourses of capitalism, and we must train our students to level their own critiques while fully conscious of the implications of their own choices. Furthermore, and as a more pragmatic point, service learning students' reflection will help organizations that do not have the resources to deeply analyze the implications of their choices. What seems like professionally helping an organization by supporting an expanded mission or overstretched scope of work may hurt in the long run.

Conclusion

The crucible of the nonprofit worksite forces connection, consensus, dissensus, and dialogue. The idea that hospitality involves imposition and negotiation is a metaphor that, I have proposed, best captures the way that rhetoric enters into and makes meaning in this crucible.

Furthermore, the disciplines that comprise writing are not and should not be taken to be governed by rigid, essentialist boundaries. As I have tried to show, the writing practices that make up the nonprofit sector expose such boundaries as impracticable and unsustainable. As we prepare college students to enter the real world, service learning opportunities can help students build metacognitive awareness of their own rhetorical choices as agents and as future professionals. And in order to reap the most from our service learning programs, we must understand that these programs do not unfold in uncomplicatedly neutral sites of hospitality but in fractured and decentered locales, fractured partly because of their hosts' dual identities as businesses on the one hand and agents of social change on the other.

While nonprofit workspaces, because of their own hybridity, are a special case for rapprochement, other spaces invite exploration as well as Bay has noted. Social Enterprise Europe, for instance, seeks to expand capitalist practices beyond the sole aim of profitability to embrace social causes, and related endeavors such as microenterprise provide promising avenues for rhetoricians to explore values of ethics and expediency ("What is"). The move away from dichotomous thinking about dubious binaries such as capitalism and academia, professional writing and Composition Studies, and business and nonprofits is surely best accomplished by practicing hospitality through engaged learning and scholarship.

Notes

1. Marc Bousquet, Stanley Aronowitz, Michael Bérubé and others have examined the implications of treating the university as a material enterprise (Grabill et al. 219). Of course, if knowledge is the commodity of the university, then knowledge products such as academic papers and ideas exist in that

2. material framework, and Composition Studies simply *is* professional writing. The boundary collapses altogether.
3. The discussion that follows was conducted with the permission of my client organization, who wishes to remain anonymous. The organization's Executive Director reviewed a draft of this essay prior to publication. My experience with this organization enriched me personally and professionally, and I am grateful to be able to include my observations of our work in this article.
4. Discourse focusing on either the encoder (expressive), the decoder (persuasive), reality (reference), or the signal (literary) (Kinneavy 38–39).

Works Cited

Appiah, Kwame Anthony, and Amy Gutmann. *Color Conscious: the Political Morality of Race*. Princeton: Princeton UP, 1996. Print.

Balzhiser, Deborah, and Susan McLeod. "The Undergraduate Writing Major: What is it? What Should It Be?" *CCC* 61.3 (2010): 415–433. Print.

Barrett, Kenna. "Grant Proposal." Unpublished manuscript, 2010. Print.

Bay, Jennifer. "Writing beyond Borders: Rethinking the Relationship between Composition Studies and Professional Writing." *Composition Studies* 38.2 (2010): 29–46. Print.

Berlin, James. "Rhetoric and Ideology in the Writing Class." *The Norton Book of Composition Studies*. Ed. Susan Miller. New York, NY: W. W. Norton & Company, Inc., 2009. 667–684. Print.

Cologna, Stephanie, and Celine Cluzeau. "'Write Winning NIH Proposals' led by Dr. David C. Morrison." *The NICHD Connection*. National Institute of Child Health and Human Development, 6 Jul. 2012. Web. 15 Sept. 2012.

Cushman, Ellen. "The Rhetorician as Agent of Social Change." *CCC* 47.1 (1996): 7–28. Web. 20 Sept. 2012.

Derrida, Jacques. *Acts of Religion*. London: Routledge, 2002. Print.

Faigley, Lester. *Fragments of Rationality: Postmodernity and the Subject of Composition*. Pittsburgh: U of Pittsburgh P, 1992. Print.

Flower, Linda, and John R. Hayes. "A Cognitive Process Theory of Writing." *CCC* 32 (1981): 365–87. Print.

Grabill, Jeffrey T., James E. Porter, Stuart Blythe, and Libby Miles. "Institutional Critique Revisited." *Works and Days* 41/42 (2003): 219–237. Print.

Haynes, Cynthia. "Writing Offshore: The Disappearing Coastline of Composition Theory." *JAC* 23.4 (2003): 667–724. Print.

Jonker, Kim, and William F. Meehan III. "Curbing Mission Creep." *Stanford Social Innovation Review* Winter (2008): 60–65. Web. 15 Sept. 2012.

Katz, Steven B. "The Ethic of Expediency: Classical Rhetoric, Technology, and the Holocaust." *College English* 54.3 (1992): 255–275. Print.

Kinneavy, James L. *A Theory of Discourse: The Aims of Discourse*. New York: Norton, 1980. Print.

Lanham, Richard A. *Revising Business Prose*. New York: Macmillan Publishers, 1987. Print.

McEachern, Robert. "Problems in Service Learning and Professional/Technical Writing: Incorporating the Perspective of Nonprofit Management." *Technical Communication Quarterly* 10.2 (2001): 211–223. Web. 15 Sept. 2012.

Newman, George, and Y. Jeremy Shen. "The Counterintuitive Effects of Thank-you Gifts on Charitable Giving." *Journal of Economic Psychology* 33.5 (2012): 973–983. Web. 15 March 2013.

Ortoleva, Matthew. "Narragansett Bay and Biospheric Literacies of the Body." *Community Literacy Journal* 4.1 (2009): 59–72. Print.

Parascondola, Leo. "Cheap Labor in a World of Precious Words: What Do Writing Classes Produce?" *Workplace: A Journal for Academic Labor* 7 (2004): n. pag. Web. 15 Sept. 2012.

Rentz, Kathryn, and Ashley Mattingly. "Selling Peace in a Time of War: The Rhetorical and Ethical Challenges of a Graduate-Level Service-Learning Course." *Reflections* 4.2 (2005): 103–122. Web. 15 March 2013.

Rhode Island, University of. "B.A. WRT Proposal November 2010 with appendices.doc." Unpublished manuscript provided by Libby Miles, 2011. Print.

"*What Is Social Enterprise?* An International Definition." Social Enterprise Europe. Web. 15 Sept. 2012.

The Historical Problem of Vertical Coherence: Writing, Research, and Legitimacy in Early 20th Century Rhetoric and Composition

Annie Mendenhall

This article explores historical debates over the relationship of composition to rhetoric, arguing that these debates resonate with contemporary arguments about first year writing and undergraduate and graduate programs in writing and rhetoric. Analyzing early scholars' articulations of the differing aims of undergraduate and graduate studies, this history outlines the challenges rhetoric and composition has faced in establishing a vertical curriculum (from first year writing to a major to a graduate degree). The conclusion provides a heuristic for program development that accounts for the ways institutional structures and cultural contexts shape curricula.

The fabric of institutions intervenes between the material exigencies of life and the speculative scheme of things.

—Thorstein Veblen, "The Evolution of the Scientific Point of View" (44)

A vertical curriculum is the hallmark of a discipline. It establishes curricular coherence by positioning a first-year course as an introduction to the discipline's content, and culminates in a major. That major then serves as preparation for entry into graduate study, and graduate study produces new members of the discipline prepared to teach undergraduate courses, lead advanced graduate seminars, and conduct specialized research. This model of disciplinarity has persisted since the turn of the twentieth century—if not always in practice, then at least in the academic imaginary as the ideal for liberal arts subjects. Historically, rhetoric and composition has not fit this mold; however, recent arguments to reframe the field as 'Writing Studies' imply that the discipline might improve its status by positioning first-year writing (FYW) as an introduction to the discipline. For example, Ellen Cushman suggests that a vertical curriculum would mitigate unfair labor practices and improve the discipline's status by "tap[ping] into the cachet that writing has in many university administrations" (123). More recently, Douglas Downs and Elizabeth Wardle argue that teaching FYW as a "discipline with content knowledge" like any other introductory course might correct misconceptions about writing among the public and administrators, and allow the field to articulate "more realistic understandings of writing" congruous with current research ("Teaching" 553).

But disciplinarity is a tricky subject in rhetoric and composition,[1] and the questions raised by these curricular proposals reveal just how much the location of FYW obscures a clear aim for the course. Is the course an introduction to a major, or does it still serve a purpose in general education? Does it teach disciplinary content or inculcate students into a way of knowing, such as critical thinking? Does it still "teach" writing, and, if so, is what it teaches transferable? The difficulty of these questions reveals how much our hopes hinge on FYW. In this essay, I show how our contemporary attempt to reconfigure FYW (and Writing Studies in general) according to a vertical model raises the ghost of a longstanding debate over the relationship between undergraduate and graduate education. Arguing that material spaces shape our intellectual work, I describe how the structural division of American higher education into undergraduate colleges with attached graduate schools fundamentally impacted the trajectory of rhetoric and composition.

As most historians have framed it, the emergence of graduate schools in American higher education signaled the decline of rhetoric because it failed to establish itself as a discipline (see Connors, Goggin, Kitzhaber). This narrative of decline assumes that had rhetoric been established in graduate schools, the status of FYW would have improved—a claim mirroring contemporary assertions. In fact, as I will show, some early scholars did attempt to define rhetoric as a subject suitable for graduate school by drawing on the discourse of science. However, this position, rather than consolidating the curriculum of rhetoric and composition, brought to the fore tensions over the nature and role of undergraduate education, inciting debate and revealing the tenets of cultural, civic, and practical training at work in undergraduate education. The ideological disjunction between undergraduate studies as preparation for life and graduate education as a research endeavor complicated attempts to define vertical coherence in the curriculum. Indeed, it challenged the notion that vertical coherence was a possible or desirable goal because many individuals resisted the imposition of the research model in undergraduate education. Furthermore, defining rhetoric as a science actually expanded the work of rhetoric across disciplines. This expansion occurred because scholars attempting to situate rhetoric scientifically adopted and mixed the discourse of the natural sciences, social sciences, and humanities (the three major structural divisions of liberal arts disciplines). This dispersal of rhetoric limited its ability to serve as the end point of a vertical curriculum from first-year to graduate school.

This history provides a framework for understanding contemporary challenges with definition. How do we connect the curriculum when undergraduate study serves a vastly different purpose than graduate study? How do we establish a distinct space for the discipline when it claims to encompass and draw from a variety of knowledges? One problem is that we tend not to discuss graduate and undergraduate education in rhetoric and composition together. Even discussions of a vertical curriculum often end with a major. I argue that we need to consider the relationship undergraduate education has to graduate study, and how that historical development has constrained and enabled particular curricular and disciplinary visions.

Curricular Coherence: The Relationship of Graduate and Undergraduate Education, 1870–1930

From 1870 to 1915 universities experienced what Louis Menand calls "the big bang of American higher education" (97). During this time, American institutions adopted graduate schools modeled after the German model of higher education implemented at The Johns Hopkins University in 1876 (followed closely by Clark University, Stanford University, and University of Chicago). This transformation profoundly impacted the structure and credentialing process of American universities by expanding and popularizing graduate education focused on specialized research. Although many composition histories point to the impact of the German model, most reduce it to a philosophical bend toward positivistic research in the natural sciences. However, German higher education approached scholarship with an ideal of continual investigation, without restrictions or market-concerns, for the sake of expanding human knowledge (see Veysey, Rudolph). Because it valued scholarship, the German model institutionalized continual research through publication and the credentialing of the PhD.

American higher education quickly revolutionized in the two decades after Hopkins founding. The impact of this revolution has been well documented: the PhD became a requirement for faculty at major universities; publication became a part of faculty responsibilities; graduate schools were added to undergraduate colleges; and the university underwent massive reorganization as existing departments split or new departments came into existence and formed an increasingly segmented body in need of a new class of administrators. Intense competition for resources encouraged standardization across universities, and as departments standardized, they pushed forward the formation of larger professional organizations that we now associate with disciplines (the Modern Language Association, MLA, being one example).

The primary influence of the German model was structural. As Frederick Rudolph explains, the German model brought to American higher education "a fundamental attachment to the graduate faculty of arts and sciences, to the idea of a body of scholars and students pushing forward the frontiers of pure knowledge" (334). What is particularly significant in this history is that graduate schools were often built on already existing undergraduate colleges with particular missions, constituencies, and trustees. In effect, this arrangement created the conditions of possibility for a vertical curriculum as departments organized around content areas, undergraduate majors developed, and those majors and departments were connected structurally to graduate studies. Before Hopkins initiated this change, undergraduate colleges constituted a collection of decentralized and largely sectarian institutions in the United States organized around a required curriculum in classical languages and moral philosophy (the latter course often taught by the college president). After Hopkins, those institutions remained varied, but the dynamic growth of graduate schools catalyzed the introduction of the modern languages and sciences.

Expanding the range of academic subjects prompted the need for an increasingly segmented university structure. As Patricia J. Gumport argues, the emergence of graduate education correlated with the departmental expansion in the final decades of the nineteenth century. This model created a central dilemma: "If Ph.D. programs were integrated organizationally as a separate level from the liberal education of undergraduate colleges, they also were made parts of departments responsible for undergraduate instruction in a discipline" (229). That is, graduate education served entirely different purposes from, but was organizationally linked to, undergraduate education. Undergraduate departments provided a base for research faculty, supporting their work financially through tuition, but universities desiring increased status lured research faculty with the opportunity to research and work with graduate students. Furthermore, the reproduction of disciplinary specialists in graduate education became a prerequisite for teaching undergraduates, and the undergraduate degree became the prerequisite for entering graduate or professional school.

The impact of this system was profound. The pull of the undergraduate system compelled Hopkins and Clark to add undergraduate programs to their institutions *after* their founding (Gumport 229). But the system was also complicated. Unlike the German system, American universities received little (if any) state or federal funding, so financial problems impeded institutions' ability to value research and graduate education. Indeed, by 1910 Edwin Slosson, editor of *The Independent,* only identified fourteen "great American universities," excelling at the university mission (see Slosson). Because many undergraduate colleges preexisted graduate schools, they already had funding sources, institutional aims, and constituencies whose expectations they needed to balance with university expansion to attract students and philanthropists.

With the expansion of graduate education, increased stress on faculty credentials (the PhD) and productivity (publication) became normal operating procedure in universities. These notions extended into English, and were the subject of debate and controversy. Harry T. Baker, in 1928, wrote, "At one great university in the cow pastures of the Middle West, the attitude to young professors has been informally but accurately phrased as 'Get a Ph.D. or get out!'" (824). The next year, Edwin Berry Bergum remarked, "The contemporary scholar in English studies is a business man. In proportion he is successful, at the top of his profession, he becomes a director of research among subordinates, a bureaucrat on the business model, always tempted to measure success in terms of output" (468). Indeed, Baker and Bergum's comments indicate both the encroachment of specialized research on faculty demands, and the simultaneous resistance to this encroachment, as if it violated certain ideals about intellectual life by measuring it in terms of credentials and publications.

Although it manifested differently across institutions, resistance to the research model revolved around the undergraduate curriculum. For example, Baker argued that graduate study in English led to questionable composition instruction, in which first-year students "adorn their pages with innumerous footnotes, as preparation for writing a future Ph.D. thesis or a learned article for one of the scholarly periodicals which never pay for contributions! It is difficult to see what relation such training has to the writing of plain English for sensible purposes" (822). That graduate education actually transformed the undergraduate curriculum into a kind of disciplinary training seemed problematic to Baker because undergraduates wanted the *practical* education:

> In only one college for men, Harvard, does [English] stand at the head of the list [of most popular majors]. It is generally eclipsed by economics and by social science. The great manly course in most men's colleges is money and banking. And I shall merely say that this is true to note of our American life. The university is 100 per cent accurate in registering American interests. (824)

Although the comment applies to a gendered context, it expresses fear that the research model would remove what the public valued from English: writing instruction. Its role in the undergraduate curriculum seemed to demand something more than an introduction to advanced research methods.

Baker's comment also points to the key role undergraduate education played in building and popularizing the university. As John R. Thelin argues, "Although the university-builders' public pronouncements tended to disparage the historic college as obsolete, in private conversations they acknowledged that their universities were dependent on the colleges' resurgence" (156). Graduate schools needed undergraduates for courses, tuition, and future enrollment in graduate programs. Undergraduates became alumni and incentivized charitable donations to the university (156). Furthermore, between 1880 and 1930, the demographic of boards of trustees changed radically, becoming dominated by individuals with corporate, not academic, backgrounds (238). All of these material constraints impacted (and still do) the range of intellectual possibilities for undergraduate courses. Simply put, the value placed on the undergraduate curriculum necessarily affected the curricular goals of rhetoric and composition.

Science, Rhetoric, and Writing in the Scheme of Modern Subjects

The disconnect between undergraduate and graduate curricula became particularly apparent in universities' championing of 'scientific' discourse, defined vaguely. With the impact of natural scientists like Charles Darwin, inventors and entrepreneurs in various applied sciences, and the advocacy of research as 'pure science' by those returning from Germany, the meaning of the term became increasingly varied. Danette Paul and Ann M. Blakeslee argue that science relied on its connotations of "utility, progress, and individuality" to enter the university (248; see also Wolfe, Gumport). Indeed, an 1890 article in the *Philadelphia Inquirer* indicates the connection of science at the undergraduate level to practical and civic training. Commenting on Columbia President Seth Low's inaugural address, the article asserted, "This is not an age of monasticism, but of hard, earnest work, of material development and of a liberal scholarship that pervades every stratum of society" (122). The article remarked that college provides "a necessary foundation for [students'] duties as a citizen in the ordinary callings" and preparation "to launch upon a successful career": "the young man of to-day wants to fit himself for an active business life. He wants the latest scientific knowledge" (122). Training in the sciences prepared students for citizenship and business insofar as it abandoned the "monastic" education of the past.

The ideal of scientific research was in a period of transition around the turn of the twentieth century. Associated somewhat with the older terminology of natural laws and empiricism, scientific methodology also became linked with the work of natural scientists. To add to the confusion, scientific study was not limited to the outside natural world, but increasingly included the human mind and society (Veysey 134). With new aims for science and the addition of modern subjects to the curriculum, universities underwent structural changes that impacted the curriculum. John Guillory notes that the eighteenth and early nineteenth century educational system based on the division between moral and natural philosophy shifted to a three-part system in the late nineteenth century, dividing modern disciplines into the natural sciences, social sciences, and humanities (26). Thus, science was more than an intellectual issue; it was a structural problem. Where would disciplines be located as they transitioned to this schema or entered the university for the first time?

The confusion over science was exacerbated by administrators' inconsistent attention to research. Roger L. Geiger notes that, even by 1920, research represented an important ideal, but "the manner in which [American universities] sustained their commitment to research was inchoate at best. The major universities thus had a philosophical commitment to the advancement of knowledge but lacked a secure institutional means for meeting that commitment" (2). The impact of this gap between philosophy and institutional resources meant that the undergraduate program, as the financial base of the university, constrained research. In 1908, Gustaf E. Karsten made a similar observation, comparing German and American universities. He argued that the vast American administrative system had not "sufficiently safeguarded and encouraged" scholarship because it was too concerned with the its financial well-being (29). As he explained,

> And when some multi-millionaire gives millions to or for some institution, we see, with rarest exceptions, the old story repeating itself: a big undergraduate teaching establishment is founded . . . and by the time that is done the money is gone and practically nothing is left to build up the greatest work. (29)

Implicit in this account, is that undergraduate education served as the focal point for pressure to meet particular public demands. What emerged in American higher education was a system that forced correlation between two units with different aims.

This structural arrangement of universities prompted changes in rhetoric and composition as it attempted to weather the transition from the collegiate to the university model. Before the introduction of modern disciplines in the university, the collegiate structure revolved around subjects like rhetoric, logic, and moral philosophy, which served to discipline students' mental faculties. Toward the latter half of the nineteenth century, academic reformers increasingly criticized the idea that college taught students mental discipline, arguing instead that college should provide professional training and instruction in the modern languages, arts, and sciences. As the mental discipline model faded slowly from higher education, modern subjects were increasingly added based on content knowledge. Vocational and professional studies were added as well, particularly at land-grant institutions, but were usually structurally separate from colleges of arts and sciences (colleges of education, engineering, etc.). University of California president Daniel Coit Gilman (later the first president of Hopkins) defined the university in 1872 as "the most comprehensive term that can be employed to indicate a foundation for the promotion and diffusion of knowledge—a group of agencies organized to advance the arts and sciences of every sort, and train young men as scholars for the intellectual callings of life" (qtd. in Rudolph 333). With the emphasis on content knowledge and the imposition of new areas of study to replace the classical college curriculum, departments underwent a period of rapid development, emerging or splitting to create a much more compartmentalized system of units (Veysey 23–24). Departments provided a convenient location for linking undergraduate to graduate education, so that the same faculty controlled both areas. But this arrangement also forced a correlation between undergraduate and graduate education that was not immediately obvious. Undergraduate education served to inculcate cultural and civic values and to prepare students for professions, while the new graduate studies in the arts and sciences connoted specialized research. Thus, a fundamental question was how to construct continuity in the curriculum when the educational motivations of undergraduates often vastly differed from the aims of graduate students.

The transition from mental discipline to knowledge discipline precipitated a move from rhetoric as a methodology to rhetoric as an object of study. After 1880, Albert Kitzhaber argues, American rhetoricians abandoned attempts to "indicate the place of rhetoric in relation to other disciplines" in training students' mental faculties (81). Elaborating on this claim, he writes,

> when rhetoric was usually thought to be a separate 'mental science,' a distinctive field had to be marked out for it and bulwarked against the encroachments of such other disciplines as logic, grammar, psychology, and ethics. The most plausible way to do this was simply to show in what ways rhetoric is indebted to these other subjects, yet manages to preserve its own identity and function. (81)

Kitzhaber demonstrates little concern for what happened after 1880 because he, like most historians, views it as a period of reducing rhetoric to composition. However, because the early focus on demarcating rhetoric from other mental disciplines correlated with the tendency to view rhetoric as constitutive of a variety of knowledges, rhetoric was not in a position to transition easily from informing knowledge to establishing a disciplinary territory. This expansiveness was complicated in the late nineteenth and early twentieth century by difficulty correlating undergraduate and graduate studies in composition and rhetoric.

The problem of rhetoric's past as a mental discipline is exemplified in David J. Hill's 1877 *The Science of Rhetoric*. Hill rejected the Aristotelian notion of rhetoric as the study of the five canons. For him, rhetorical science consisted of both a set of laws and a method for effecting mental change. He described rhetoric as comprising "laws of the *mind,* the *idea,* and the *form*" and seeking to act on the mind through language (39). He carefully articulated the differences between rhetoric and other "mental disciplines" such as aesthetics, ethics, and logic—components of the collegiate curriculum in moral philosophy, but saw rhetoric as informing "the methods of investigation . . . in the various departments of thought" such as law, theology, and criticism (3–4). As such, Hill delineated an expansive role for rhetoric. Defining rhetoric methodologically thus positioned it as informing the emerging disciplines and professional vocations, not as its own area of study.

Although Hill's theory did not become as popular as other, more reductive rhetorics, a prominent current of thought arguing for rhetoric as a science persisted into the late nineteenth and twentieth centuries. These voices struggled to adapt a methodological rhetoric to the changing understanding of discipline. Take, for example John F. Genung's[2] argument in 1887 that educators should see in "the art" of rhetoric "a practical value, immediate and universal" as well as a study "large enough for any elaborateness of discipline" (3). Genung attempted to reconcile the practicality and artistry of rhetoric and composition with the concept of 'discipline,' a term connoting, for him, abstract "facts, principles" (4). He did not deny the role of principles in rhetoric, but he favored artistic "construction, creation," as its principle object (4). In fact, Genung wanted discipline to include the production of creative texts as a stated objective. He thus argued that the study of rhetoric might be taught scientifically by having students observe what works well in literature to foster writing ability: "This is not speculation out of some one's head; it is scientific method. Rhetoric is the constructive study of literature, as distinguished from the philological and the historical study" (10). For him, rhetoric represented a particular methodology for studying literature in order to produce it, but also a knowledge base. The resulting vision situated rhetoric as overlapping with literature in content, but providing different methods for its study—methods geared more toward training professional writers. This approach saw investigation as a means not an end, a view that would increasingly seem incongruous with the goals of graduate education in the arts and sciences as primarily the reproduction of an intellectual class (university faculty) not the production of a professional class. Was rhetoric a vocational study or a research subject? If a vocational study, the location of rhetoric within the liberal arts would need to be rethought, especially at the graduate level. If a research subject, then the relationship between rhetoric and composition would need to be more clearly articulated, as would the distinction between rhetoric and literature.

A 1901 survey by the MLA Pedagogical Section on graduate education in rhetoric highlighted rhetoric's territory problem. William Edward Mead, the survey editor, emphasized that the responses at the time were largely in favor of graduate study in rhetoric (xxi). As outlined by respondents to the survey, such a graduate program would involve "historical, psychological, or philosophical, and pedagogical" investigations (xxv). Individual responses elaborated on the variety of content rhetoric comprised. One respondent, for example, defined rhetoric as "a composite of parts of grammar, psychology, logic, literary criticism, and perhaps other studies" (xxv). Another responded indicated that rhetoric encompassed both multiple subject matters ("literature and linguistics") and research methods ("psychology, aesthetics, and sociology") (xxvii). One respondent concluded:

> The relation of Rhetoric to Psychology deserves exhaustive investigation; is full of problems of interest and practical significance. The relation of Rhetoric to Logic, the history of Logic and Rhetoric, the philosophical implications of Rhetoric, are all crying for treatment and discussion . . . A study of Rhetoric on liberal lines I believe may have the highest disciplinary value for graduate learning and does offer problems of profound interest for research. (xxx)

The responses indicate that rhetoric overlapped with a range of departments and disciplines—literature, history, psychology, sociology, linguistics, pedagogy, *in addition to* encompassing mental disciplines, including logic, grammar, and aesthetics. These articulations reflect rhetoric's transition from a discipline associated with mental training and textual production to a liberal art suitable for graduate study—that is, from mental training to research subject. In order for rhetoric to fit within the structure of graduate training in the liberal arts, it had to be reframed as a research subject with legitimate content—an assumption that continues to inform our conception of the field.

The expansion of rhetoric's content raised questions about its position in the scheme of English and other emerging disciplines. As Mead explains, some respondents felt that giving rhetoric "'the false dignity of isolation' would be to diminish rather than to increase its importance" (xxv). The importance of isolation and independence was stressed in other comments. One respondent defined rhetoric as a science, worthy of graduate work, but added the caveat that it is not "equal in importance to those subjects that have an *independent existence,* and if it is to be pursued as a graduate study its relation to other branches of knowledge must be fully realized" (Mead xxvi, italics mine). Another suggested, "There should be no separate curriculum of graduate study in rhetoric," because it already existed as part of literary study (xxx). These respondents perceived rhetoric as a field lacking a natural or obvious object of study or reason for existence, and composed of other more clearly defined disciplines.

Thus, what Guillory has claimed for philology's history also proved true for rhetoric: rhetoric and composition was disadvantaged because it "straddled the new spectrum of the disciplines" (36), always subject to critique for not quite fitting any single "norm of scientificity" (24). Rhetoric retained and repressed prior views of its role as a methodological mental discipline (as Crowley has extensively argued), and that role never integrated well into the content-model of modern disciplines. Thus, the division between rhetoric and composition was forced primarily by *structural* shifts rather than *epistemological* shifts. However, scholars who focused on defining rhetoric as a science tended to push organizational challenges into the background, an historical tendency that has complicated our ability to articulate the relationships among rhetoric, composition, and literature.

"Culture and Efficiency" in Undergraduate Composition

Even as scholars of rhetoric struggled to articulate its content and suitability for graduate study, the pressure placed on the undergraduate curriculum to resist scientism impacted the relationship between rhetoric and composition. In fact, the scientificity of the humanities—which legitimized graduate study—became the object of criticism in undergraduate education. Speaking of both philology and rhetoric, Morton W. Easton cautioned in 1889 that the "science of language . . . is not an exact science" (21). He noted that comparing 'linguistic sciences' with the hard sciences "is but little to the advantage of the former" (21). Rather than diminish its significance, he argued that the lack of correlation actually provided language studies with a unique role:

> What should we say of the teacher of psychology who should confine his work to the anatomical tissues of the brain and nerves? No! *to stop here is to relinquish our distinctive claims to respectful attention.* Language is an art; it is not merely the product of certain historical factors, it is an art, and the study of its application as an art is worthy of our best energies *as educators of undergraduates.* (21, italics mine)

Easton connected the artistic study of language with the undergraduate mission specifically. In fact, Easton suggested that an analogy with the hard sciences would diminish the legitimacy of those studies, perhaps because it dismissed the practical application central to the undergraduate mission. Indeed, the undergraduate study of rhetoric and English provided "the only source of culture in the academical course," mitigating the "tendency of the scientific departments . . . to convert men into mere wheels in the social machine" (22). Undergraduate instructors should be "of a different, and in some respects, of a higher order. To use the terminology of college faculties, he should be, preeminently, a teacher in the 'Department of Arts'" (20). Only in the arts, could the study of language create a "well-rounded man" capable of dealing with "literary wholes" (22) rather than specialized periods or other divisions. Easton's remark reveals a crucial tendency—for the undergraduate course to push back against the specialization the graduate schools encouraged. This tendency would return in twentieth century general education movements, in which reformers proposed courses in common knowledge and American values requisite for properly cultured undergraduates (see Menand). Yet paradoxically, the structure of graduate education made specialized research the credential for teaching undergraduates.

Some individuals strove to connect undergraduate and graduate programs in rhetoric through a vertical research track. For example, Frank W. Scott began his discussion on "The Relation of Composition to the Rest of the Curriculum" by noting that composition did *not* fit the curriculum, nor represent the wider study of rhetoric. Scott argued that this lack of correspondence resulted from the competing aims of the course to improve students' literacy on one hand and to inculcate literary and cultural sensibilities on the other hand (512). The practical orientation of composition positioned it as a "'handmaiden' to the rest of the curriculum" through "a sincere but mistaken attempt to make Freshman rhetoric meet immediate social and industrial needs" (513). Scott argues that the proliferation of specialized writing courses suggests a curricular confusion:

> we have courses in ideas, in the evolution of the Darwinian theory since the death of Darwin, in current events, in advertising, in journalism, in engineering English, in agricultural English, in technique of the short story and of the play, and many other fads and specialties that promise to make competent writers out of students who know no rhetoric. (513)

Scott's understanding of these courses was shaped by his assumption that language is merely a container for thought, and "good English . . . is English for engineers as well as for all the rest of us" (516). Despite this limited perspective on writing, Scott made an important observation: composition was dispersed because it "leads nowhere, in the matter of [instructor] promotion, and, so far as our curricula show, has no scholarly relationships" (518). Scott wanted to return rhetoric to the content of the composition course, and to establish a scholarly agenda. Rhetoric provided "opportunity for graduate investigation and scholarly research" in history, theory, aesthetics, and criticism, which would lead to an advanced degree (519). His observation assumed that verticality would give value to faculty teaching introductory courses, while a myriad of horizontal writing courses would not. Thus, the purpose for the course that imbued rhetoric and composition with disciplinary content indicated underlying concern over the labor pool and status of the course

In contrast, Fred Newton Scott articulated diverging purposes for undergraduate and graduate courses in rhetoric. As he explains in "Rhetoric Redeviva," rhetoric was a science worthy of "advanced study" (413). Concerned with justifying this scientific definition, Scott argued that rhetoric had too long been dominated by Aristotle's "closed science" approach, which conceived of rhetoric as predefined rules with no possibility for original investigation (413). Scott thus viewed the older taxonomic perspective as limited, and attempted to outline possibilities for original investigation in rhetoric for graduate students. However, for Scott, undergraduate students still needed rhetoric to be a "cultural discipline"; only graduate students could "grapple with weighty and complex problems and . . . make independent investigation" (413). Outlining the elements of the rhetorical science, Scott argued that rhetoric required a "unified subject-matter" and a research methodology based upon empirical observation (414). Despite calling for unity, he emphasized the range of fields that rhetoric encompasses—notably aesthetics, sociology, and psychology. Although historians have lionized Scott for validating rhetoric, his own justification for rhetorical study—like that of Hill—defined rhetoric as a compilation of various subjects, while simultaneously relying on a tenuous analogy between the natural sciences and rhetoric. Scott grappled with the issue of relating undergraduate and graduate studies. As he explained,

> In this subject [composition], as in most others, the general educational principle holds good that elementary practice and advanced research are mutually dependent . . . Illustrations of this truth in mathematics, biology, medicine, and other sciences, will occur to everyone. (413)

Scott tries to correlate rhetoric with the vertical curricula of the hard sciences, even though he already distinguished introductory rhetoric courses as serving a cultural purpose. Thus, Scott reproduces the very tension over verticality that still troubles our discussions of it today.

Respondents to the MLA Pedagogical Section's 1901 survey also debated whether composition, as distinct from rhetoric, had any place in a graduate program. A few deemed composition appropriate graduate study if defined as a pedagogical science. One respondent remarked that rhetoric could provide "a scientific base for teaching an efficient use of the mother tongue," specifying that the ultimate aim of graduate study in rhetoric should be "pedagogical," and suggesting like others, numerous areas of study for this pursuit: "the aesthetics of prose, the history of language, and the history of Rhetoric" as well as "the psychology of childhood and youth as related to the problems of language-teaching" (xxviii). Yet because newly founded colleges of education focused on the latter, while the arts and sciences tended to the former, this approach to composition and rhetoric also spanned educational divisions.

Other respondents to the survey thought that including rhetoric in graduate study meant teaching writing at the graduate level; they emphatically discouraged such a trend: "Mere theme-writing, however sublimated or raised even to the *n*th power, ought never to be a part of the credits for a higher degree" (xxx). The problem, as one respondent mentioned, was that Rhetoric might "simply continue the mixed lessons given under that name in elementary text-books" (xxvi)—a comment that implies both that rhetoric lacked coherence and that rhetoric differed in purpose at the graduate level. Composition might merit place in graduate education if focused on training teachers, but not if focused on writing itself. Thus, composition's relationship to rhetoric posed a fundamental problem. If pedagogically focused, it seemed more appropriate for colleges of education, but that would split it from the work of the liberal arts and sciences where it was currently located. If practically focused, it seemed more appropriate for professional training or undergraduate courses than graduate school. In short, the location of rhetoric and composition within the liberal arts fundamentally shaped its credentialing process and curricular content. Instruction in rhetorical practice—that is, composition—was pushed from graduate curricula to undergraduate courses, where it could more easily incorporate vocational and cultural values, and the distinction between the study of rhetoric and literature thus became increasingly unclear.

However, some respondents challenged the definition of graduate education as disinterested investigation without practical application. According to Mead, many indicated that "a graduate school might be made to serve as a school for critical or creative genius; but their plans for the conduct of such a school were not very definite" (xxiv-xxv). One comment in particular elaborates on this point:

> If regarded as an art there would need to be a change in the interpretation of the advanced degrees. For the Oxford doctorate in music the candidate must present a musical composition as part of evidence of proficiency. I do not see why a rhetorical composition, an essay, a novel, a poem, or other literary kind, should not count toward a degree in literature. (xxix)

As this remark indicates, the system of graduate school adapted by American universities discouraged connections between rhetoric and composition, a fact that also lead rhetoric, literature, and creative writing to become increasingly delineated in subsequent decades.

Glenn E. Palmer summarized the conflict between undergraduate and graduate rhetoric in his 1912 essay, "Culture and Efficiency through Composition." Palmer concurred that a scientific investigation of rhetoric, including historical philology, literature, psychology, philosophy, could inform composition. However, this knowledge should never be the sum of composition at the undergraduate level (490). Palmer's motivation for this assertion emerged from his particular perspective that undergraduate education should unify culture and efficiency. As he explained, "After all, is not the purpose of education to enable us to live, and are we not safe in concluding that in the last analysis the most efficient life is that which is cultured, and the most cultured life that which is at the same time efficient?" (488). What is particularly interesting about Palmer's desire to unite culture and efficiency is the implication that undergraduate instruction should mitigate problematic tendencies in American culture. A focus on liberal culture in education could become "dilettantism" while efficiency could be "carried to the extreme of impersonal system and administrative machinery that is rife in many of our state institutions today" (488). Composition thus served as the locus for a number of competing social desires—both public and academic. The fact that an argument for something as simple as changing the content of the FYW course could be perceived as altering perceptions of the discipline among the public and administrators reveal how persistent these desires are still. The potential for a vertical curriculum to improve the labor and status of a course has historically been complicated because FYW exists at the intersection of differing cultural and academic purposes. How we negotiate its location is a question that we still struggle with both because American higher education maintains the structure of undergraduate and graduate education that emerged more than a century ago, and because rhetoric and composition has always had difficulty fitting that structure. These historical debates reveal contemporary challenges we must negotiate—challenges not just of content, but of structure, location, and labor.

Implications for the Present

Ongoing challenges with definition and verticality persist because disciplinarity has *always* been a messy construct in practice. This is particularly true in the humanities, where many subjects retain traces of the early collegiate curriculum and seem to resist the specialization we associate with majors and graduate programs. This messiness has resurfaced recently in the slippage between defining our work as a discipline or an interdisciplinary field,[3] a trend that recalls the history of debate over whether rhetoric and composition is an independent or composite research subject. We might confront the tension surrounding our knowledge base—and its impact on FYW, minors, majors, departments, and various other writing programs—by considering how articulations of disciplinarity shape the location and content of writing and research at all levels.

To that end, institutional histories can provide a heuristic for considering curricular issues. In curricular development, we might think beyond the vertical alignment of courses—following a track from FYW to a writing and rhetoric degree. Instead, we need to think vertically, horizontally, and institutionally about how to create courses and curricula. In other words, minors, majors, and graduate programs increase the field's legitimacy by shaping it into a model discipline, but our work might also operate outside the vertical model to engage other disciplines and communities in writing instruction or interdisciplinary programs of study. As we engage in building programs and courses, we might consider the following issues:

- *Vertical legitimacy:* Does the structure of a course or program reinforce our claim that writing and rhetoric are legitimate areas of research and knowledge at *all* levels—from the first year to advanced undergraduate level courses and graduate studies? Do advanced undergraduate courses provide opportunities for undergraduate research and theoretical engagement in addition to courses oriented toward training students for relevant professional work? How can our understanding of the purpose of undergraduate majors in writing and rhetoric reshape our graduate programs?
- *Horizontal outreach and engagement:* Does the structure of a course or program support our contention that writing is the province of all disciplines and professions? Do our FYW programs and undergraduate writing majors have substantial and sustainable connections to the writing that happens in other disciplines, even if those courses do not feed back into a minor or major? Can minors, majors, and graduate programs accommodate writing and rhetoric-focused coursework from other disciplines and departments? Do programs, courses, and community outreach opportunities actively work to engage public values and knowledge? Do graduate programs account for the range of professional as well as academic careers students might pursue?
- *Institutional values and contexts:* Does the structure of a course or program operate persuasively within a particular institution's culture and history? Do outcomes and assessment practices employ research in rhetoric and composition while engaging local audiences and attending institutional values? How can we adapt program and professional development (FYW, graduate training, etc.) to improve the labor structures unique to our institutions?

The questions I raise here acknowledge that verticality is an important but limited argument for resources. For example, we might consider how the structure of the PhD shapes research and curricula, not just in introductory composition courses, but also in subfields such as technical and professional writing. If that structure prioritizes research, we may need to be more explicit about including and valuing opportunities for community engagement and professional experience as part of graduate training. And how do we balance disciplinary and institutional values? Teaching introductory writing courses as an introduction to writing research—an approach that has influenced my own teaching—provides a sense of vertical coherence by modeling the approach of other disciplines. However, my course still operates within—and must support the assessment of—general education goals outlined by my university. Those goals range from discussing diversity in American culture to teaching "expository" writing and critical thinking. Furthermore, writing instruction in general education is complicated as we involve faculty across disciplines—particularly when a writing program or department has no central administrative control over Writing Across the Curriculum or Writing in the Disciplines (WAC/WID) courses, or when WAC/WID programs replace FYW entirely. We all must draw from values embedded in our local contexts in ways that strengthen writing in its institutional environments. Only by attending to the ways institutional structures shape intellectual work—at both local and global levels—can we articulate how both to work within and expand beyond vertical disciplinary structures.

Notes

1. I use rhetoric and composition throughout this essay because the terminology is more historically appropriate for the texts I discuss than Writing Studies. The moniker *writing studies* intentionally attempts to distance the field from composition as a delegitimized subject (see Cushman). The debate over terminology is outside the scope of this essay, but it is worth considering whether the change in name removes the historical pressures I describe from undergraduate courses, or, for that matter, graduate programs.
2. John C. Brereton describes Genung as "the perfect transitional figure" given his doctoral training in the German educational system and his background as a minister (133).
3. See, for example, the interchangeable use of interdisciplinary and disciplinary in Downs and Wardle, "Reflecting." For another example of the slippage between discipline and interdiscipline, see Robert R. Johnson's "Craft Knowledge: Of Disciplinarity in Writing Studies," which argues that to be interdisciplinary rhetoric and composition needs first to establish a disciplinary knowledge base.

Works Cited

Baker, Harry T. "English and the Ph.D." *The English Journal* 17.10 (1928): 820–824. Print.

Bergum, Edwin Berry. "Modern Dry as Dust." *The English Journal* 18.6 (1929): 465–475. Print.

Brereton, John C., ed. *The Origins of Composition Studies in the American College, 1875–1925: A Documentary History*. U of Pittsburgh P, 1995. Print.

Connors, Robert J. *Composition-Rhetoric: Backgrounds, Theory, and Pedagogy*. Pittsburgh: U of Pittsburgh P, 1997. Print.

Crowley, Sharon. *The Methodical Memory: Invention in Current Traditional Rhetoric*. Carbondale: Southern Illinois UP, 1990. Print.

Cushman, Ellen. "Vertical Writing Programs in Departments of Rhetoric and Writing." *Composition Studies in the New Millennium: Rereading the Past, Rewriting the Future*. Ed. Lynn Z. Bloom, Donald A. Daiker, and Edward M. White. Carbondale: Southern Illinois UP, 2003. 121–125. Print.

Downs, Douglas, and Elizabeth Wardle. "Teaching About Writing, Righting Misconceptions: (Re)Envisioning 'First-Year Composition' as 'Introduction to Writing Studies.'" *CCC* 58.4 (June 2007): 552–585. Print.

—. "Reflecting Back and Looking Forward: Revisiting 'Teaching About Writing, Righting Misconceptions' Five Years Later." *Composition Forum* 27 (Spring 2013). Web. 1 March 2013.

Easton, Morton W. "The Rhetorical Tendency in Undergraduate Courses." *PMLA* 4.1 (1889): 19–23. Print.

Geiger, Roger L. *To Advance Knowledge: The Growth of American Research Universities, 1900–1940*. New York: Oxford UP, 1986. Print.

Genung, John Franklin. *The Study of Rhetoric in the College Course*. Boston: D. C. Heath & Co. Publishers, 1887. Print.

Goggin, Maureen Daly. *Authoring a Discipline. Scholarly Journals and the Post-World War II Emergence of Rhetoric and Composition*. Mahwah, NJ: Lawrence Erlbaum Associates, 2000. Print.

Guillory, John. "Literary Study and the Modern System of Disciplines." *Disciplinarity at the Fin-de-Siècle*. Ed. Amanda Anderson and Joseph Valente. Princeton, NJ: Princeton UP, 2002. 19–43. Print.

Gumport, Patricia J. "Graduate Education and Organized Research in the United States." *The Research Foundations of Graduate Education: Germany, Britain, France, United States, Japan*. Ed. Burton R. Clark. Berkeley: U of California P, 1993. 225–260. Print.

Hill, David J. *The Science of Rhetoric: An Introduction to the Laws of Effective Discourse*. New York: Butler, Sheldon and Company, 1877. Print.

Johnson, Robert R. "Craft Knowledge: Of Disciplinarity in Writing Studies." *CCC* 61.4 (June 2010): 673–690. Print.

Karsten, Gustaf E. "The German Universities." *The Journal of English and Germanic Philology* 7.2 (Apr 1908): 26–39. Print.

Kitzhaber, Albert R. *Rhetoric in American Colleges: 1850–1900*. Dallas: Southern Methodist UP, 1990. Print.

Mead, William Edward. "Report of the Pedagogical Section: The Graduate Study of Rhetoric" *PMLA* 15 (1900): xix-xxxii. Print.

Menand, Louis. *The Marketplace of Ideas: Reform and Resistance in the American University*. New York: W. W. Norton & Company, 2010. Print.

Palmer, Glenn E. "Culture and Efficiency Through Composition." *The English Journal* 1.8 (1912): 488–492. Print.

Paul, Danette, and Ann M. Blakeslee. "Inventing the American Research University: Nineteenth-Century American Science and the New Middle Class." *Inventing a Discipline: Rhetoric Scholarship in Honor of Richard E. Young*. Ed. Maureen Daly Goggin. Urbana, IL: NCTE, 1999. 237–269. Print.

"President Low on College Work." *Philadelphia Inquirer* 5 Feb 1890. 122. Print.

Rudolph, Frederick. *The American College & University: A History*. Athens, GA: U of Georgia P, 1990. Print.

Scott, Frank W. "The Relation of Composition to the Rest of the Curriculum." *The English Journal* 7.8 (1918): 512–520. Print.

Scott, Fred Newton. "Rhetoric Rediviva." *CCC* 31.4 (1980): 413–419. Print.

Slosson, Edwin Emery. *Great American Universities*. New York: The MacMillan Company, 1910.

Thelin, John R. *A History of American Higher Education*. Baltimore: The Johns Hopkins University Press, 2004. Print.

Veblen, Thorstein. "The Evolution of the Scientific Point of View." *The Place of Science in Modern Civilisation and Other Essays*. New York: B.W. Huebsch, 1919. 32–55. Print.

Veysey, Laurence R. *The Emergence of the American University*. Chicago: U of Chicago P, 1965. Print.

Wolfe, Daehl. *The Home of Science: The Role of the University*. New York: McGraw-Hill Book Company, 1972. Print.

Course Design
ETC 408/508: Technical Editing

Michael Charlton

ETC 408/508: Technical Editing is a cross-listed undergraduate and graduate course at Missouri Western State University, an open admissions public university with approximately 6,000 students. 508 is an elective course for students in the Master of Applied Arts in Written Communication degree and highly recommended for those in the Technical Communication and Writing Studies options. 408 is a required course for students pursuing the Bachelor of Arts in English with a Technical Communication emphasis. Prior to Fall 2011 the course's content had been combined with an existing undergraduate course in technical documentation (ETC 420). This was also the first semester it was taught for graduate credit. The program's website describes the course as emphasizing "the role of the editor in organizational settings, including creating successful writer/editor collaboration" ("Course Descriptions"). Stated course objectives include "practice in editing documents for grammar, syntax, organization, style, emphasis, document design, graphics, and user-centered design" ("Course Descriptions"). An unstated course objective for this semester was teaching future composition instructors strategies for responding to student writing and dealing with "correctness" issues.

Institutional Context

The creation of ETC 408/508 was a product of multiple needs within the department. Faculty in composition, rhetoric, and professional writing decided to split the pre-existing course in technical documentation and editing for two reasons. First, the material covered in the course had grown too large for a single semester and the dual objectives of the course inevitably meant that one subject area was slighted in the scheduling and assignments. Second, students in the professional writing program began to receive lower scores from the outside evaluators brought in to critique their graduation portfolios. Comments on student writing indicated a decreased attention to multiple levels of editing from the grammatical and mechanical to rhetorical and argumentative problems. An internal assessment of these comments and the portfolios themselves suggested that our students in professional writing would benefit from increased exposure to editing practices.

As an open admissions institution where a high percentage of entering students are placed into developmental writing programs, we try to place a special emphasis on developing students to be more effective communicators. This may be especially true in the professional writing section, which includes emphases in areas such as technical communication, public relations, journalism, and convergent media. Many of our students are first-generation college students from families without professional backgrounds in similar fields. Students need to be familiarized with occupational expectations for writers, including the role of the editor.

The Master of Applied Arts (MAA) program is less than five years old and currently includes approximately a dozen students, most of whom are either working professional writers looking for an advanced degree as a gateway to promotion, or students interested in teaching composition at the community college level. While numbers have increased, administrative and budget pressures to maximize faculty teaching loads have resulted in courses being cross-listed at the undergraduate and graduate level so that the courses would not be cancelled due to low enrolment. Graduate faculty have discussed this as a challenge to maintaining an appropriately rigorous graduate curriculum, as well as a negative factor under accreditation and program review rubrics. However, programmatic and fiscal realities have entwined these two sections into one.

Experiences with the first three graduate theses in the MAA program led to concerns not dissimilar to those raised by the undergraduate writing portfolios. Namely, students seemed to have difficulty editing their own writing in academically and professionally appropriate ways. Though they conducted interesting studies into topics such as the integration of e-book readers into local libraries, the use of blogging in the composition classroom, and teaching rhetorical concepts to first-year composition students through graphic novels, these theses had not been rigorously edited. Students had difficulties with editing errors from the mechanical to document design to audience and tone. Many students were encouraged to enrol in ETC 508 as preparation not only for their future professional roles as technical editors and composition instructors, but as apprentices in academic research writing.

This last issue, the need for apprenticeship in academic research writing, could be seen as a fundamental separation between the undergraduate and graduate populations for the course. While undergraduate students took the course largely as preparation for the senior portfolio and for workplace editing roles, graduate students were also being prepared to edit their own theses and seminar papers. Though not unrelated fields, professional writing and academic writing have different genres, readers, and expectations. Balancing these two broad categories of writing and editing would be difficult.

Theoretical Rationale

One of my major concerns in designing ETC 408/508 was to balance what I saw as the two major programmatic needs for this course. First, we had a stated curricular need. Students planning to enter professional writing needed to be introduced to the role of editing within that occupational environment. Students planning to teach at the community college level needed to be introduced to editing as it applied to their own career goals and responding to student writing. Second, we had the needs of our particular student population. Negative editing feedback on both the senior writing portfolios and the MAA theses indicated that students needed editing practice not only for professionalization but also in order to become more polished and self-reflective writers themselves. Yet even here I sensed a problem. If merging the undergraduate and graduate courses was already a complicating factor, these two objectives only added to the problem. Students were to be treated as apprentices, professional writers, and teachers all at once.

As a teacher in both composition and technical communication, I was also concerned that the course follow disciplinary standards for editing, reflecting both professional and educational conventions and academic research on the topic. I found through talking to several students prior to the semester that many students came to the course with preconceived notions of what editing is. Some of these were principles with which many writing instructors would agree; i.e., editing is collaborative and/or might involve some version of peer review, editing is a slow and careful process. Other student preconceptions were more problematic; i.e., editing is equivalent to proofreading or is only about grammar, editing is about "correctness" or "placing blame for mistakes" on authors. I knew that one aspect of the course would have to be self-definition. As we worked through the semester, we would work on expanding our definition of what editing is and what editors do.

Of course editing has been central to Composition Studies for decades as process theory stressed the key role such revision-oriented tasks were to play in a reconsidered pedagogy for freshman English. Richard Gebhardt's 1984 essay in *Rhetoric Review* was already able to frame the terms of the debate, as well as many of the names that would become central to later research, such as Sommers, Perl, Flower and Hayes, and Faigley and Witte. True, what has tended to be called "editing" in technical communication is more often termed "responding" or "reviewing" or "commenting" in Composition Studies. Yet these are closely related bodies of theory and practice. For example, consider this passage from Sommers' classic essay "Responding to Student Writing":

> Theoretically, at least, we know that we comment on our students' writing for the same reasons professional editors comment on the work of professional writers or for the same reasons we ask our colleagues to read and respond to our own writing. As writers we need and want thoughtful commentary to show us when we have communicated our ideas and when not, raising questions from a reader's point of view that may not have occurred to us as writers. We want to know if our writing has communicated our intended meaning and, if not, what questions or discrepancies our reader sees that we, as writers, are blind to. (148)

There is a basic similarity between the roles of professional editor, composition teacher, and even peer or student reviewer. All of these commentators are concerned primarily with how the meaning of a text is communicated to its intended reader and in what ways revision might make this communication even more effective or audience-focused. As Sommers points out, the key difference between the professional editor and the teacher is the pedagogical role played by the latter (148). While editors are most concerned with the professionalism of the final product, teachers are invested in seeing students internalize these processes and apply them in different educational and "real world" contexts. This course, with its dual audience, would have to bridge that gap of motivation and purpose.

After looking through both classic and more contemporary research, textbooks, and handbooks on editing, I began the process of writing the syllabus by writing down what seemed to be commonly accepted principles of approaching editing within composition and technical communication:

- Editing is a skill which develops with practice; editing can help writers to recognize their own errors and weaknesses (Pianko and Radzik 220).
- Editing should be approached as a complex and multi-levelled process (Rude xxiv-xxv).
- Editing is a key part of the writing process, not simply an end-of-line or product-oriented skill (Podis and Podis 91).
- Editors should be self-reflective about their practices and should encourage writers to be self-reflective in their own practices (White 122–126).
- Editing should not be approached as simply error correction, especially since that "correctness" can vary given the situation and the reader (Shafer 66–67).
- Editors should move towards a more complex relationship with grammar than simply the "rules" and standards of formal grammar instruction (Hartwell 107–108).
- Editing is about audience; good editors critically reflect on both the writer and the text's intended audience and students need practice thinking of themselves as potential editors and reviewers (Wyngaard and Gehrke 67–70).
- Editors need to identify the goals and objectives of the text in order to comment on it with effective rhetorical strategies and the complexities of the writer/reader relationship are key to negotiating and communicating the meaning of a text (Ede and Lunsford 167–170).
- Editing and writing are field-specific; writers and readers need to understand the role of disciplinary and professional conventions and how different disciplines conceive of writing and the writing process (Carter 385–387).

These would serve as my own stated principles for editing on the syllabus and in course lectures. In-class and portfolio assignments would be structured to reflect these principles, as would the grading rubrics given to students with the assignment sheets.

Even here the issues of cross-listing and of disciplinary differences (technical communication vs. composition, workplace writing vs. academic writing) were present. The principles listed here and on the syllabus were discussed in class mostly because they represented broad overlaps between the disciplines involved. Yet, as students noted themselves, these principles are not as complementary as they may seem. For example, while Pianko and Radzik approach editing as a learned and developed skill, Podis and Podis define it primarily as a process (223; 91). While some writers stress a more personal or rhetorical examination of the individual reader (e.g., Wyngaard and Gehrke), others stress how fields and disciplines dominate discussions of documents (e.g., Carter). Simply put, while process theory and constructivism have clearly come to dominate discussions of editing in both composition and technical communication, there are still tensions both within and between these fields. Given the course description and the focus on "levels of edit" (see below), there was an implied preference for certain of these principles. A course explicitly focused on editing for the workplace is more likely to be invested in Carter's idea of disciplinary and profession-specific standards of editing than a typical advanced composition course might be. Discussions in the course did attempt to problematize some of these assumptions and to point out how some of the internal contradictions here (for example, the skill/process split) could be troubling.

Scholarship in technical communication has tended to stress the "levels of edit" approach to editing far more than the process-oriented model in composition with its brainstorming, multiple drafts, and peer review. This approach was popularized by Robert Van Buren and Mary Fran Buehler's 1980 Society for Technical Communication publication *The Levels of Edit* but radically adapted by later writers. In general terms, texts are reviewed over several passes instead of in a single pass meant to cover every potential concern. Each pass is dedicated to a specific aspect of the text, though textbooks and handbooks have developed their own systems. For example, one textbook might have three passes: the first focused on mechanics, the second focused on content, and the third focused on document design. The textbook for the course was chosen because of its dedication to this approach and because it presented a simple but effective three-pronged approach (essentially passes dedicated to mechanics, then document design and visual readability, and then overall content and organization).

The three major editing assignments were structured around this approach. For each assignment the students were given an example document to be edited and a "level of edit" upon which to focus. In order to stress editing's connection to the "real world," all of the example documents were actual documents used with the authors' permission in need of editing for correctness, visual readability, or effectiveness. I began looking for these documents by examining existing workbooks and textbooks on editing and by asking colleagues for examples. When those documents did not meet my requirements, I broadened by using a search engine and using the desired genre (for example, example proposals, example recommendation reports) as my search term. After combing through several pages of documents in the genre, I located documents which I felt to be structurally sound (that is, they fit the basic expectations for what a proposal or a recommendation report would look like) but which had major editing problems in one of the three levels (for example, grammatical or mechanical issues). I made certain that none of these documents were marked as proprietary or confidential and that they contained contact information for the authors. I then e-mailed the authors with a request to use the document, explaining the purpose of the assignment and attaching a copy of the syllabus. Though I expected some resistance–I was, after all, using these as documents to be revised, not as positive models–I found that these writers were uniformly receptive as long as they could be guaranteed anonymity for both themselves and their employers. I removed personally identifiable information from each and sent them back to the writers for final permission. Once that was granted, they were posted as assignments.

Selecting the documents proved to be difficult, given the broadness of course goals and the multiple audiences within it. I decided that the presence of students focused on composition teaching precluded any highly technical or documentation-based genres, which would stray too far from the types of writing assigned in composition. For example, I considered that genres such as equipment evaluations or lab reports were too far removed from typical persuasive writing since they were designed to be expository and objective in tone. However, the genres selected also had to be within established technical writing patterns in order to prepare majors for this type of workplace editing. The grant proposal seemed a natural fit, as it is both a staple of technical writing programs (in fact, our technical communication MAA requires a graduate course in grant and proposal writing) and stresses typical composition features such as audience, persuasion, and tone. The technical definition also bridged between technical communication and composition, where the similar genre of the "extended definition" is still a common assignment in freshmen textbooks. Finally, the recommendation report, while it did not have an easy analogue in composition assignments, seemed to have strong enough rhetorical aspects (that is, the explanation and justification of a course of action) that it would connect to both disciplines.

Students were shown how to use commenting features such as the Comment and Track Changes functions in Microsoft Word, and even Dropbox in order to introduce them to common technological tools for collaborative writing and editing, as well as introduced to theories on marginal commenting and end-note commenting. These were first modelled in class, both in class lectures with practice documents and during in-class group work with short texts in need of editing. The nature of the class demanded that the example documents for the major assignments fit into recognized technical communication genres (namely, a recommendation report, a progress report, and a proposal) but I also included more common student writing genres such as the essay exam and research report during in-class exercises to familiarize future teachers with editing and commenting on these types of texts.

Students were encouraged to think of editing as a key part of the writing process and as a rhetorical skill. Class discussions and group exercises stressed that the specific exigencies of the given writing situation were the first questions to be asked. Students were asked to go beyond the text to think about why it was written, who it was written for, and what the intended audience was meant to do with the document. Using "real world" documents was particularly helpful here, as they illustrated actual exigencies. Lectures and in-class practice stressed the positive and negatives of specific writing response strategies, such as paired praise-critique or criticism-suggestion models. Comments left on the major assignment documents were expected to fit one or more of these strategies.

In addition, for the first two major writing assignments students were asked to write an accompanying memo to the text's original writer. This memo was meant to serve multiple purposes. First, it encouraged students to adopt a "patterns of error" or "minimal marking" approach similar to those found in much composition theory (Haswell 600–603). The student writer would highlight key or consistent errors and discuss strategies for dealing with these errors in the future, as well as contemplating why these errors might occur and how intended audiences would perceive them. Students were asked to think rhetorically about these choices and to consider what tone and audience approach might best communicate their concerns to the writer, whether they were a student or a co-worker. At the same time, these memos were meant to sponsor self-reflection. Students were instructed to mull over the challenges of editing and how their approaches to editing were changing with increased practice. Finally, class discussions sought to bring this self-reflection back to writing. While they were gaining experience editing other people's documents, were they also gaining experience with their own documents?

Peer review was meant to serve multiple purposes. Most importantly, it was meant to reinforce the idea of editing and commenting as crucial to the writing process. It also gave students practice interacting with the people whose work they were helping to edit. Since one of the major goals of the course was to encourage active reflection on the rhetorical situation and the relationship between writer and editor, this was crucial. Students were asked to pay careful attention to the memos, as this is where the relationship between the writer and the editor became most crucial.

I realized going into the course that cross-listing might create tensions both with peer review and with the presentations. Students would come to the table with widely varying levels of educational and workplace experience. While many in the graduate technical communication track had years of workplace writing behind them, the undergraduates in particular tended to lack this background. I worried that peer review and the question-and-answer sessions after presentations could easily devolve into inexperienced students being told anecdotes by their more "expert" peers about the "real world" of writing. Even in the best situation, where more experienced students were trying to serve a mentoring function, this would create an unfortunately two-tiered classroom. One way I tried to deal with this in theorizing the course and picking out the editing principles to be highlighted was by laying stress on the individuality of each document and each reader. If editing was to be seen not as a universal skill that was learned once and applied assembly line-style to each and every document but as a process that took different contexts into account, then workplace experience could be both a positive and a negative. Students would be encouraged to talk about their own workplace but also challenged to recognize that each workplace is different and that the writing and editing processes of workplace change from place to place and even across time.

Two assignments at the end of the semester were departures from most of the technical editing courses I had examined at other institutions while preparing my own syllabus. For the third major writing assignment, which focused on overall content and organization, students were asked to make a short oral presentation to the class. In this presentation they would deliver their take on the strengths and weaknesses of the example document while treating their fellow students as the document's writers. These presentations were meant to mirror both the classroom and the workplace environment, where teachers or editors might comment on general writing trends and offer suggestions following office or in-class workshops. Students were trained to anticipate questions about their editing processes and decisions. This assignment was also meant to reinforce the collaborative nature of editing, where both the editor and the writer are involved in negotiations over the final shape of the text.

The final assignment for the course was the style guide. While most technical editing courses covered the idea of corporate and organizational style guides and presented them as valuable reference documents meant to set standards for mechanics, style, and organization within a community of writers, few courses seemed to encourage the actual writing of a style guide. I thought this was a crucial exercise for both the future technical communicators and future teachers in my classroom. Presented with an example organization and a list of style rules to be set down (from comma usage to preferred spellings), technical communicators were meant to reflect on writing standards within the workplace. Confronted with a document which required them to both set certain standards for writing and to explain clearly and concisely the reasons for those standards, teachers were meant to think about how they would approach composing materials such as assignment sheets, peer review guides, and grading rubrics in the future.

Critical Reflection

I used three major tools to assess student outcomes from this course in order to determine whether I had met my original stated objectives. These tools were the students' own writing portfolios, discussions with students immediately following the semester, and the students' instructor evaluations. All three tools seemed to indicate that the course had been at least somewhat successful in meeting my objectives, though there were serious challenges to both my theoretical assumptions and my course design.

Student evaluations and their comments in post-semester discussion were largely positive but did consistently note one major problem at the heart of my assignment structure. While students adopted the principle of levels of edit, they felt that the major assignments actually confused the issue. As I have said, each of the first three writing assignments was dedicated to a different level of editing, such as visual readability. Students found it difficult to keep their comments on the assigned level of edit and were frustrated when comments focused on a different level of edit (for example, comments on mechanical errors during the visual readability assignment) were questioned by the professor. Curiously, this seemed most true of students who had some workplace experience with editing themselves. They felt that this restriction to one level at a time was not reflective of the "real world" and seemed "artificial" in comparison to their own work experience. Ironically, too much attention to "one level at a time" undermined the prevailing idea that the levels of edit were ultimately meant to complement each other and work together. They felt that comments from the professor on their own editing feedback could sometimes be less than helpful in this regard. Rather than focusing on the heuristic process of editing, they became concerned about whether they would be criticized for noting a particular mistake on the "wrong" level. Future composition teachers worried that this "levels of edit" approach might not be directly applicable to their writing classrooms, where factors such as document design tend to be secondary. They were far more interested in and receptive to discussions of response strategies and how to approach student writing to encourage student buy-in.

The course simply served too many constituencies and perceived gaps in the curriculum. While the course editing principles stressed how writing and editing are field-specific and how different types of writers and situations require different feedback strategies, the course itself failed to follow those principles. Students on the Writing Studies side, with their focus on teaching college composition in the future, appreciated in-class exercises with student essays and especially seemed to value peer review. They questioned the style guide's place as the final assignment for the course, since its connection to genres like assignment sheets and grading rubrics seemed more tangential. Upon reflection, I agreed with them on this point and decided that the final assignment would be better split into two options, with students in technical communication completing the style guide while students in composition studies would complete an assignment in writing a detailed grading rubric for an example essay assignment. Students on the technical communication side, with their focus on workplace writing, grew frustrated with non-workplace writing genres. However, they seemed to appreciate the oral presentation far more than their counterparts. Many discussed it as good practice for the sorts of small group critiques or employee workshops they might need to conduct in the future.

The most evident progress was in the goal of building a more collaborative writing environment and in making students more reflective about their own writing. Over the course of the semester peer review sessions grew both more supportive and more analytical. While students had at first struggled with presenting their comments and feedback in constructive ways, later peer reviews were both more honest and better received. Practice approaching writers on paper and in the class presentation seemed to have given them a greater awareness of the rhetorical situations an editor or teacher faces. Students who had at first struggled with the levels of edit (particularly the mechanical aspects) had grown more comfortable with them. By the time we had peer review for the style guides students who had difficulty defining terms at the beginning were throwing out example sentences and suggested corrections during group discussion. The memos were progressively better edited themselves as students paid more attention to how their writing would be received by the class and the professor.

One curious note was the role of undergraduates in the course. Cross-listing had been one of my major concerns at the outset and one of the reasons I severely limited external readings, presenting theories and principles of editing like those listed in the section above in lecture format rather than through discussion of theory-driven articles. At the beginning of the semester I had been careful to divide up the students when they went into in-class group work and made certain that at least one graduate and one undergraduate student were in each group. After the first peer review, however, those distinctions began to vanish. The graduate students were impressed by the undergraduates' work. When I had students submit comments on each of the oral presentations, the overwhelming favorite for the best presentation was an undergraduate. In the end, I believe that the cross-listing played an accidental but positive role in the classroom. The mixes of educational and workplace experience in the room mirrored the differing levels of expertise and comfort with writing present in almost any classroom or workplace. While I had worked hard to introduce different kinds of texts and writers into editing practice, the students themselves modelled my point far better than the texts.

My final impressions of this course are mixed. On the one hand, I believe that students did an incredible job creating a collaborative writing and editing environment in which different levels of expertise and comfort were welcomed. On the other hand, I believe that some of the flaws in the course were driven by the syllabus. In the future I have decided to re-write the major assignments so as not to segregate the levels of edit and confuse students about the complementary nature of this approach. Most importantly, while each document for revision would still focus on a particular level (e.g., editing for visual readability), students would no longer be penalized for making comments about another level (e.g., editing for correctness) while editing. Punishing students for trying to deal with all of the problems they recognized in a document seemed both counter-productive and a violation of some of the editing principles stressed by the syllabus. I will continue to think about the ways in which the two major audiences of this course can both benefit from its principles—by bifurcating the final assignment by discipline as discussed above and perhaps by including an example of student writing in the major assignments. I will also expand the theoretical basis of the course by including more theory-driven readings in the assignment schedule. While aspects of editing such as ethics and cultural awareness were touched on, they deserve far more attention. In an age of mixed media and global audiences, it has become more important than ever for our future professional communicators and teachers to learn how to respond and how to help shape the texts which surround us.

Works Cited

Carter, Michael. "Ways of Knowing, Doing, and Writing in the Disciplines." *College Composition and Communication* 58.3 (2007): 385–418. Print.

"Course Descriptions." *Graduate Studies*. Missouri Western State University, n.d. Web. 19 Jan. 2013. http://www.missouriwestern.edu/Graduate/maawc-coursedesc.asp

Ede, Lisa, and Andrea Lunsford. "Audience Addressed/Audience Invoked: The Role of Audience in Composition Theory and Pedagogy." *CCC* 35.2 (1984): 155–71. Print.

Faigley, Lester, and Stephen Witte. "Analyzing Revision." *CCC* 32.4 (1981): 400–14. Print.

Flower, Linda, and John Hayes. "A Cognitive Process Theory of Writing." *CCC* 32.4 (1981): 365–87. Print.

Gebhardt, Richard. "Changing and Editing: Moving Current Theory on Revision into the Classroom." *Rhetoric Review* 2.2 (1984): 78–88. Print.

Hartwell, Patrick. "Grammar, Grammars, and the Teaching of Grammar." *College English* 47.2 (1985): 105–27. Print.

Haswell, Richard H. "Minimal Marking." *College English* 45.6 (1983): 166–70. Print.

Perl, Sondra. "Understanding Composing." *CCC* 31.4 (1980): 363–69. Print.

Pianko, Sharon, and Abraham Radzik. "The Student Editing Method." *Theory Into Practice* 19.3 (1980): 220–24. Print.

Podis, Leonard A., and Joanne M. Podis. "Improving Our Responses to Student Writing: A Process-Oriented Approach." *Rhetoric Review* 5.1 (1986): 90–98. Print.

Rude, Carolyn D. *Technical Editing*. 2nd ed. Boston, MA: Allyn and Bacon, 1998. Print.

Shafer, Gregory. "Re-Forming Writing and Rethinking Correction." *English Journal* 94.1 (2004): 66–71. Print.

Sommers, Nancy. "Responding to Student Writing." *CCC* 33.2 (1982): 148–56. Print.

Van Buren, Robert, and Mary Fran Buehler. *The Levels of Edit.* 2nd ed. Society for Technical Communication, 1980. Print.

White, Edward M. *Assigning, Responding, Evaluating: A Writing Teacher's Guide.* 3rd ed. New York: St. Martin's Press, 1995. Print.

Wyngaard, Sandra, and Rachel Gehrke. "Responding to Audience: Using Rubrics to Teach and Assess Writing." *English Journal* 85.6 (1996): 67–70. Print.

Syllabus
ETC 408/508: Technical Editing

Course Overview

The course will focus on the role of the editor in organizational settings, including creating successful writer/editor collaboration. Students will gain practice in editing documents for grammar, syntax, organization, style, emphasis, document design, graphics, and user-centered design. The course will provide an introduction to technology for creating, publishing, and distributing technical documents.

Principles of Editing

- Editing is a skill which develops with practice; editing can help writers to recognize their own errors and weaknesses.
- Editing should be approached as a complex and multi-levelled process.
- Editing is a key part of the writing process, not simply an end-of-line or product-oriented skill.
- Editors should be self-reflective about their practices and should encourage writers to be self-reflective in their own practices.
- Editing should not be approached as simply error correction, especially since that "correctness" can vary given the situation and the reader.
- Editors should move towards a more complex relationship with grammar than simply "rules" and standards.
- Editing is about audience; good editors critically reflect on both the writer and the text's intended audience.
- Editors need to identify the goals and objectives of the text in order to comment on it with effective rhetorical strategies and the writer/reader relationship is key to negotiating the meaning of a text.
- Editing and writing are field-specific; writers and readers need to understand the role of disciplinary and professional conventions.

Required Texts

Amare, Nicole, Barry Nowlin, and Jean Hollis Weber. *Technical Editing in the 21st Century.* Upper Saddle River, NJ: Prentice Hall, 2010. Print.

Major Assignments and Grading

There will be four major projects. Each is worth 200 points (20% of the final grade).

The first project will involve mostly sentence-level editing, focusing primarily on grammar, mechanics, and usage (what the book terms "Editing for Correctness"). You will be given an example recommendation report and asked to edit it using Word Comment and Track Changes. You will then write a memo to the original writer indicating his or her key "patterns of error" as discussed in class.

The second project will involve mostly editing related to document design and graphics, focusing on texts as visual artifacts (what the book terms "Editing for Visual Readability"). You will be given an example progress report and asked to edit it using Word Comment and Track Changes, as well as making small corrections to the text itself. You will then write a memo to the original writer discussing his or her key "patterns of error" in terms of visual readability and accessibility.

The third project will involve editing related to whole document issues, such as style, organization, coherence, and usability (what the book terms "Editing for Effectiveness"). You will then create a short oral presentation for the class in which you offer feedback on the strengths and weaknesses of this document, including suggestions for improvement.

The fourth project will involve the creation of a style guide, touching on websites and other forms of electronic publishing as well as technologies used to write and edit these texts collaboratively. It will also include concepts from our three levels of edit.

All four projects will be submitted for peer review by the class. Projects not submitted for peer review will not be graded.

Homework, quizzes, and class participation make up the remaining 200 points (20% of the final grade). Homework generally consists of short reading or writing assignments and completing in-class group and individual exercises.

Class participation does not mean simply attending class on a regular basis. It means coming prepared and taking an active and constructive role in class discussions and group work. People who seldom ask questions or make comments in class rarely receive the best class participation scores. If you attend every single class and come prepared and ready to contribute, your grade will reflect that. If you attend every single class but are unprepared and do nothing during discussions or group work, your grade will reflect that, too. This is meant to be a collaborative learning environment. Your participation is crucial. You have something to offer.

Schedule

Week 1:   Introduction to technical editing, including an overview of the three levels of edit and a discussion of common strategies for responding to writing (praise-critique, etc.). In-class work: commenting on multiple sets of instructions for the same process ("how to tie a tie" directions from the Internet).

Week 2: Introduction to editing for correctness, including a review of key grammatical and mechanical concepts. In-class work: commenting on a student essay exam.

Week 3: Further practice with editing for correctness, including an overview of common technologies for responding to writing (Track Changes, etc.) and a discussion of the writer/editor or writer/teacher relationship. In-class work: commenting on a student research paper.

Week 4: Final practice with editing for correctness, including a discussion of "patterns of error" and other strategies for responding to student writing. In-class work: individual work on Project 1.

Week 5: Brief discussion of the role of peer review and collaboration in the editing process. In-class work: peer review of Project 1.

Week 6: Introduction to editing for visual readability, including a discussion of key document design concepts, as well as ethical and cultural issues in editing. In-class work: editing an example travel brochure.

Week 7: Further discussion of editing for visual readability, including a discussion of key document design concepts, such as accessibility and designing for readers with differing physical abilities. In-class work: editing an example technical description.

Week 8: Final practice with editing for visual readability, including more discussions of workplace and classroom exigencies and dealing with the rhetorical situations of writers. In-class work: individual work on Project 2.

Week 9: In-class work: Peer review of Project 2.

Week 10: Introduction to editing for effectiveness, including key concepts such as style, organization, and overall coherence. In-class work: employment correspondence (application letter, portfolio, self-evaluations, etc.).

Week 11: Further discussion of editing for effectiveness. Discussion of orally presenting feedback on writing. In-class work: critique of short example document, followed by short oral presentations of feedback to example document.

Week 12: Introduction to editing online publications, including websites and web-texts (editing and mark-up languages such as HTML). In-class work: peer review of Project 3 and oral presentations.

Week 13: Project 3 oral presentations, followed by group discussions of the presentations' strengths and weaknesses.

Week 14: Introduction to style guides, including a discussion of how the process might transfer to documents like assignment sheets and grading rubrics. In-class work: critiquing example style guides for effectiveness.

Week 15: Further discussion of style guides. In-class work: individual work on Project 4.

Week 16: In-class work: peer review of Project 4. Project 4 is due finals week.

Agency in the Age of Peer Production, by Quentin D. Vieregge, Kyle D. Stedman, Taylor Joy Mitchell, and Joseph M. Moxley. Urbana: CCCC/NCTE, 2012. 184 pp.

Reviewed by Peter Brooks, University of Wisconsin Milwaukee

Agency in the Age of Peer Production is about writing program administrators who want to better understand how and why their own writing instructors utilize peer-production technology designed for cultivating, exchanging, and evaluating writing program materials. Quentin D. Vieregge, Kyle D. Stedman, Taylor Joy Mitchell, and Joseph M. Moxley are the curious administrators, and authors, of this uniquely written tale of assessment, tech, and agency. The authors explore fellow instructor voices who decry the social networking tools, pedagogical resource wikis, and compositional rubric programs the authors established. In the midst of budget cuts and university credibility, the authors conducted interviews and scanned data hoping to assuage their writing program's atmosphere. Ultimately, their writing program moves from what scholar Gerald Graff calls *courseocentrism* (14)—isolated classroom instruction—to Moxley's own *datagogy* (168)—a decentralized system reflecting the ecology of the network.

Like any ethnographic study, *Agency* follows a traditional path of problems, questions, hypotheses, methods, data analyses, and conclusions. The authors' core hypothesis: "If peer production is to assume its own 'age,' then it must be more about values than about tools, which are replaceable and easily outdated" (2). The peer-production tools are smaller programs accessed through Microsoft SharePoint, a writing portal application. These programs include Facebook-like social networking tools, various Wikis used to (re)define programmatic objectives, and an online rubric application which provides student feedback and tracks data. The values the authors discuss were found in the individual interviews and ongoing assessment of their study. For them, formal and informal face-to-face interactions complement peer-production technology, and foster communal and individual agency.

Comparatively, *Agency*'s information and style is unlike the more theoretical techno-utopias such as Henry Jenkins, et al.'s *Confronting the Challenges of Participatory Culture: Media Education for the 21st Century*. While rich in narratives, Jenkins, et al.'s white paper is sometimes overly optimistic on *what can be*, instead of *what is*. *Agency* has its head in the digital cloud of technology's pedagogical potential and its feet grounded by instructors' tales of tripping over and thriving with technology. This is reinforced through the "datalogical narrative" style of *Agency*'s six chapters. The style, rooted in relevant scholarship, builds upon qualitative practices to lift up instructor voices and express a "humanistic and inspirational, not positivistic or statistical" narrative about a writing program in peril and the leadership decisions enacted in order to transcend truncations caused by budget cuts and ubiquitous technology (35).

This unique narrative structure allows *Agency*'s six chapters to be seen as both a professionally designed qualitative research report with step-by-step detail, and a warm, collaboratively written tale imbued with humility, humor, and honesty. As a qualitative report, the authors present components in traditional order. Chapters 1 and 2 frame *Agency's* problem, purpose, methodologies, questions, and hypotheses. Chapters 3, 4, and 5 represent the "personalized interpretation" of the data collected from their own department (35). Chapter 6 wraps up the qualitative study with conclusions and unanswered questions. The authors share their desire to "perhaps provide a [research and programmatic] road map for other university writing programs to follow" (142), yet later acknowledge potential institutional differences (148-155).

Agency's narrative thread illustrates the trials and triumphs of a writing program community. Just as the research structure provides academic credibility, the narrative arc appeals emotionally to writing program stakeholders—lead administrators, programmatic mentors, and instructors of all experience levels—who wish to use peer-production technology. Vieregge, Stedman, Mitchell, and Moxley could have waltzed into any institution, but chose their own—anonymously naming it Research University (RU)—where they held four influential administrative positions. As the authors contend, "we engage[d] with our research participants by unashamedly interacting with them to better our program and investigate the various interactions between individual and collective power" (34-35). Each chapter is filled with this emotional energy and sincerity to learn.

Chapter 1, "Peer Production and Tectonic Shifts in Agency" establishes scholarly perspectives on peer-production technology in FYC programs. The authors draw on Jenkins, Benkler, Nissenbaum, Boyd, Ellison, Brown, and others to establish how peer-production "communities have reshuffled power relations, enabling individuals to influence the shape and direction of modern life, world markets, elections, and public opinion" by allowing "users to add content, which affects the way knowledge is constructed" (9). The authors recognize that this empowerment is not always felt by FYC instructors. From their own instructors, they were anecdotally aware of three empowerment obstacles: courseocentrism, insufficient training, and the "80-20 rule" (15)—20% of users actively engage in peer-production technology while 80% engage occasionally and casually.

These obstacles, coupled with RU's FYC identity, provide the catalyst described by the authors in chapter 2, "Contexts and Research Questions." The authors make clear RU's context: "The majority of our 500+ sections of first-year composition courses are . . . classrooms that have a networked computer, a computer projection system, a document camera, and a DVD player" (23). In order to connect overburdened instructors with techno-rich classrooms, the writing program administrators created a face-to-face mentorship program. One of the main goals was to familiarize instructors on SharePoint and its related peer-production tools. However, instructors saw the face-to-face and the digital as two separate spaces thereby causing *Agency*'s authors to revisit five years of archival data and conduct two years of interviews. Their overarching research question: from an instructor standpoint, what kinds of relationships exist between peer-production technology, face-to-face mentoring, agency, and assessment data?

These individual instructors' experiences are conveyed prominently in chapters 3, 4, and 5, demonstrating a reality familiar to English Departments. Chapter 3, "Creating a Culture of Assessment" shares reactions from the mandatory implementation of the online writing rubric, My Reviewer. The inclusion of an instructor-created newsletter which recasts RU's writing program administrators as "Big Brother" shows how the authors are open to all types of feedback in order to engage the anxiety felt toward assessment (46-49). This thick skin granted them insight into 26 diverse instructor perspectives. The honest responses frame common problems instructors face using online rubrics: the panoptic feel of data tracking, a frustration with inscribing grades then entering data, and the lack of intuitiveness from the software.

The voices in chapter 4: "Managing a Self-Sustaining Network" represent the more optimistic views of assessment and peer-production technology. Refreshingly unexpected, however, is the authors' choice to follow those voices with dissenting ones in chapter 5, "Agency in the Mentoring Program." Structurally, these chapters are similar. Both dedicate whole sections to select instructors who self-identify as "innovators" or "laggards" from Everett M. Rogers model of technological adaptation (86). As the chapter titles indicate, the authors showcase their specific peer-production technology practices and face-to-face mentorship program interactions, respectively.

Chapter 4 focuses on three sub-groups the authors discovered when analyzing interviews. Playfully named after Soap Opera titles, each sub-group characterizes different instructor approaches and attitudes toward the peer-production technology. Individuals like Claudette, from *The Young and Restless*, searches and reads other peers' projects to help construct her own (93-94). Shirley, from the *Guiding Light*, expresses feeling initially overwhelmed then suggests to the writing program administrators changes in personal training to complement technological intuitiveness (105-109). The narratives in each sub-group alter how we see the digital divide, and create a continuum of technological engagement instead of a polarization.

Reemphasizing the authors' commitment toward all kinds of feedback, chapter 5 opens with an instructor stating that "you can't give someone agency" (116). This chapter specifies how the face-to-face mentorship program attempts to address concerns similar to Shirley's. Here, the values seen by the authors start to gravitate together: provide open feedback space, continuously share ideas, promote social interaction, and practice humble leadership. This is where both research and narrative threads converge as if happening in real-time: the authors acknowledge dissenting voices, learn from them, and adapt their writing program accordingly, without reinventing the wheel.

In chapter 6, "Agency, Peer Production, and University Composition Programs," these values are further discussed in the research's results, questions to consider, and implications for programs wishing to use peer-production technology. The authors here earn our applause for overcoming budgetary concerns because they've remained transparent and grounded throughout the whole book, not because they seek it. Their research clarifies how and why instructors maintain a sense of individual agency with communal agency, and the authors' more global implications reflect a humble and active view of writing program leadership.

Vieregge, Stedman, Mitchell, and Moxley are a team of individuals unafraid to use research to show how human agency thrives in a technological world. They are unafraid to place professional writing alongside playful language. They are unafraid to assess their own decisions as administrators. From my perspective, which has seen the inner-workings of Student Affairs and Academic departments alike, this fearlessness represents true educational leadership in an actual learning organization. I look forward to, and hope for, their potential follow up which further discusses the student data they were collecting at the time of writing. *Agency* is a self-reflective collection of researched stories from teachers about a community who changed their writing program through collaborative online/offline spaces/practices thereby resolving budgetary and political concerns while maintaining a focus on what matters: our students.

Milwaukee, WI

Works Cited

Jenkins, Henry, Katie Clinton, Ravi Purushotma, Alice J. Robison, and Margaret Weigel. *Confronting the Challenges of Participatory Culture: Media Education for the 21st Century,* Chicago: The MacArthur Foundation, 2006. Print.

Redesigning Composition for Multilingual Realities, by Jay Jordan. Urbana, Illinois: CCC and NCTE, 2012. 165 pp.

Reviewed by Pisarn Bee Chamcharatsri, University of New Mexico

When I started my graduate studies in Composition and TESOL at Indiana University of Pennsylvania (IUP) in 2006, I had no idea what I was getting myself into. I immersed myself into the interdisciplinary field of Composition Studies and teaching English as a second/foreign language (TESL/TEFL). With my teaching experiences from Thailand, my focal interests resided around second language (L2) writing. It was my first time hearing such terms as *L2 writing, world Englishes, composition,* and *applied linguistics*. As I navigated national and international conferences, I often attended L2 writing-related sessions, as they were a part of my academic scholarship. I often left those conferences thinking of ways to address issues of teaching L2 writers from both theoretical and pedagogical perspectives. I was delighted to see and have an opportunity to review *Redesigning Composition for Multilingual Realities* as I believe this is a long overdue book for the field of rhetoric and composition.

Working from different fields such as rhetoric and composition, applied linguistics, Teaching English as a Second/Foreign Language (TESL/TEFL), and World Englishes, Jordan complicates the term "composition" or "comp" (20). In the introduction, the author suggests the this book is an attempt to continue conversations in teaching, researching, and working with multilingual writers through "advance[d] cross-disciplinary understandings of multilingualism" (4) to better inform pedagogy. The introduction chapter orients readers by defining relevant terms, such as "English" (7), "users" (12), and "composition" (15) that the author will refer to in the following chapters.

Chapter 1 discusses the concept of "compensation" (25) from writing center scholarship. The writing center is a site where multilingual writers seek advice from tutors on their drafts; it is also where multilingual writers negotiate their agencies with tutors. Writing centers are often perceived as fix-it shops for instructors in different disciplines. Through the lenses of "communities of practice" (see Wenger) and *Students' Right to Their Own Language* (SRTOL), multilingual writers are often seen to be novices in composing their written assignments with dialects which are viewed as illegitimate discourses from their instructors. Instead of tutors looking at these dialects as illegitimate, the author proposes that writing center pedagogies and tutoring practices should be spaces where multilingual writers learn to socialize, negotiate, and accommodate their language uses in academic genres.

In chapter 2, the term "competence" (50) is discussed from TESL/TEFL and applied linguistics perspectives. The author synthesizes research from various disciplines and analyzes field notes he has collected from his own studies. Jordan emphasizes that by privileging one variety of English over another, we run the risk of thinking English is a static entity that cannot be changed, which will only be detrimental to multilingual writers. Composition Studies cannot ignore the fact that multilingual writers bring with them multiple competences or literacies to our classrooms. Different communicative competencies—grammatical knowledge, language creativity, cross-cultural background, and negotiating strategies—that these writers bring should be explored through observation during classroom interactions that they have with other students. The author encourages other compositionists to observe these competencies in their classrooms as the discovery of these aspects is rewarding to both students and teachers. Such pedagogical practices are discussed in the following chapters.

"Composition" (85) is the focal discussion in chapter 3. This short chapter describes a cross-cultural composition course that Jordan and his colleague piloted in 2004. The author describes the process of linking two composition classes—one section of mainstream and one section of multilingual writers. Jordan lays out the whole process of the course with some critical reflective remarks. For example, he points out challenges in creating this particular course such as technical difficulties in linking two courses together, as well as time constraints because the two classes were taught by different faculty members. The awareness of students from both classes is positive in that students learn about multicultural issues and challenges. Jordan proposes that composition courses should move towards the framework of intercultural practices by either connecting, mixing, or allowing mainstream students and multilingual students to comment, interact, and discuss their writing assignments together to maximize multilingual students' competencies that they bring into our classrooms.

The last chapter focuses on the concept of "intercultural composition" (119). While the author promises that he will not provide any cookie cutter pedagogies at the beginning of the book, he does suggest some key changes in Composition Studies at the curricular level. Conducting needs analysis and surveying students are suggested as places to start the revision of curricula. Jordan suggests assigning culture-related writing projects and scaffolding peer feedback, as both help multilingual writers gain agency and negotiate their sense of selves in their written works. Based on activities like asking students to write about meta-discourse awareness, producing narratives based on their experiences of language, and the using of "realia" (133) or real life tools and materials, as well as portfolios (136), the author emphasizes that curricula and teachers should ask multilingual students to share their lives, experiences, and competencies.

Redesigning Composition for Multilingual Realities is an attempt to challenge the idealized Standard Written English and promote interdisciplinary research and scholarship from L2 writing, applied linguistics, World Englishes, rhetoric and composition, and literary studies. The book refers to useful and seminal works of each field. New graduate students and compositionists may find this book to be dense and jargonized. However, the book is accessible for those who are interested in intercultural communication. I would like to praise the author in his attempt not to provide any pedagogical implications to readers because we all know that the context of each classroom plays an important factor in (re)designing any composition course to focus on (critical) reflections of language learning experiences. That being said, some pedagogical practices and strategies can be found throughout the book. More importantly, the author attempts to promote the neglected and undervalued personal experiences that multilingual writers bring into our classrooms. As a composition instructor and an L2 writer who values students' personal histories and backgrounds, this book provides a refreshing voice to hear. The insightfulness of this book will become a valuable resource for WPA, composition scholars, L2 writing scholars, TESOL educators, and graduate students.

Albuquerque, NM

Works Cited

Conference on College Composition and Communication. "Students' Right to Their Own Language." *CCC* XXV (1974): 1-32. Print.

Wenger, E. *Communities of Practice: Learning, Meaning, and Identity*. NY: Cambridge University Press, 1998. Print.

Agents of Integration: Understanding Transfer as a Rhetorical Act, by Rebecca S. Nowacek. Carbondale: Southern Illinois UP, 2011. 167 pp.

Reviewed by José M. Cortez, University of Arizona

While the transfer of knowledge across contexts and disciplines is a perennial concern in composition studies—sometimes due to its widespread service discipline frame—and compositionists have been using methodologies like longitudinal studies to understand how transfer operates, Rebecca S. Nowacek aims to introduce a closer examination to supplement existing disciplinary analyses. Her synchronous approach, a close reading of data gathered from an interdisciplinary humanities sequence, provides a stimulating inquiry into the ways that genre plays a role in the transfer of knowledge for both teachers and students. Nowacek argues that "transfer is best understood as an act of recontextualization," a premise from which she builds her framework to develop the "concept of *agents of integration*—a concept that foregrounds the rhetorical dimensions of transfer" (8, emphasis in the original). Writing program administrators, interdisciplinary practitioners, and even experienced first-year writing instructors will find this book stimulating as it explains what she calls an interdisciplinary learning community (LC) model that replaces the traditional first-year writing course in favor of a paradigm where writing instruction resides "within a learning community taught by non-FYC instructors" (129).

The benefit—and challenge—of her study, however, is that it operates outside the first-year writing paradigm, and she admits, "this classroom is not typical of most undergraduate classrooms" (6). Observing a team-taught multidisciplinary arrangement titled *Interdisciplinary Humanities Seminar* offered to first-year honors students, Nowacek collected data from eighteen students enrolled in the second of the three-semester sequence. *Interdisc II*—comprised of literature, history, and religious studies courses—was team taught by professors Olivia, Roger, and Thomas, respectively, who participated in interviews and a focus group and attended each others' classes regularly. In addition, Nowacek attended, audiotaped, and transcribed every class session, used surveys to collect demographic information, collected student papers, and interviewed ten students at the beginning, middle, and end of the semester. In such an intimate research setting with the students and their work, this study is a needed complement to longitudinal studies that sacrifice proximity for longevity, for it allowed Nowacek to provide insight to the ways in which students used transfer of knowledge among courses. The challenge to this methodology, as valuable as it is, is that it will not be easily replicated at other sites because of institutional constraints.

The theoretical framework and its implications are developed in the first three chapters of the book, in which she unpacks the notion of *agents of integration* and extensively reviews her findings. Nowacek grounds her work in the discipline by arguing that composition is void of transfer theory that describes how connections are made rhetorically between comparable contexts. More specifically, she argues that metacognitive awareness of writing and rhetorical strategies "may assist in the process of transfer but is not *necessary* for transfer" (17, emphasis in the original). From there she suggests that research on genre can be combined with research on transfer to explain how the identification of similarities and conventions can be used to facilitate the *recontextualization* of knowledge, relying on the warrant that genres frame rhetorical situations and thus sites of overlap among differing discursive spaces. Nowacek gracefully pursues the similarities between theories of transfer and theories of genre to synthesize her notion of recontextualization, though she is careful to articulate a distinction between the two. Consequently, theories of genre, "which assume that individuals find themselves in fundamentally *similar* situations and draw on socially constructed and constitutive genres in order to minimize the sense of difference in these different situations," is a particularly potent mode of understanding transfer, "commonly understood as the negotiation of very different social and intellectual contexts" (20). For Nowacek, genre is a pedagogical foundation from which to build a generative sense of agency (*agents* of integration, not nodes of integration) and not just a simple closed system of rearticulating knowledge through generic conventions. Thus, she is able to argue successfully that transfer framed as recontextualization is a two-pronged concept; is not just an act of mere application but also an act of reconstruction—a highly rhetorical act.

Nowacek is careful not to valorize genre to the extent of dogma to oversimplify her findings. She challenges compositionists, and even instructors in other disciplines, to recognize their role in the process of transfer, as instructors possess the responsibility to decide whether or not to recognize acts of transfer. Instructors must foster a reflexive awareness of genre to reveal to students that they aren't static conventions, lest students experience negative transfer, or, an incorrect application of prior learning. By downshifting the idea of *agents of integration* into a detailed and complicated discussion of genre, she makes an important finding that careful qualitative researchers won't immediately cast off—the need to develop a framework of transfer that will recognize transfer in all students and not simply its representations in the most invested or the most talented students. In the case of Kelly, a student who was admittedly an honors student only at the request of her family and less worried about her academic work than her social interests, her static understanding of genre prevented her from reframing it to fit the objective of the instructor and the assignment. Kelly was prompted to write a medieval diary for a history course, and the assignment asked her to

> "assume a specific medieval identity in terms of gender, age, social position, and occupation and write a diary entry for a single day." The entry

"should focus on material details like what you do and where you do it, including physical surroundings, tools, who else is present, etc." Roger, the history professor, explained that this assignment was meant to focus students' attention on the lived, material reality that undergirded the "big ideas" students were studying in their religious studies classes. (47)

Instead, inspired by a character from *The Canterbury Tales*, Kelly developed a psychological, personal portrait of a nun instead of focusing on describing material details. This one example illustrates Nowacek's caution of limited understandings of genre and the way they may influence students' success in transferring knowledge. Readers will likely find the case studies most useful for developing prompts that challenge students to rethink genre and its rhetorical potential for aiding in the transfer of knowledge. As a doctoral student teaching at a large state university and learning to make my own connections among disparate bodies of knowledge, I appreciated the challenge to think of genre not just as the exigence of transfer, but also as a means of shaking loose assumptions students may possess by stressing the importance of selling transfer as a rhetorical act. In this way I feel I have another weapon in my teaching arsenal for articulating the need for writing instruction to students as well as colleagues in other disciplines.

Building conclusions from student interviews, Nowacek's results sustain her call for "helping students see the rhetorical domain of disciplines" by instructing students to recontextualize genre knowledge and "sell" their writing to new audiences (128). The series of case studies in her project develop the *agents of integration* metaphor and argue against the perception that students are unable to make transfer without a highly structured curriculum, which also serves to demonstrate that institutional setting has major effect on perceptions of transfer in both students and instructors. Regardless of Nowacek's idealist setting, which is likely impossible for the majority of readers to emulate, the fourth and fifth chapters provide ideas for revising FYC courses to reduce the obstacles of integration. I especially appreciate her frame of recognizing the rhetorical domains of disciplines, which she argues pose a roadblock to integration. Also helpful for instructors and writing program administrators, the investigation offers lines of argument and support for the benefits of genre theory both as a tool in first-year writing courses and as a mode of research in assessment. The framework of students as agents appears to be the most directly applicable concept to traditional composition courses.

Tucson, AZ

Beyond the Pulpit: Women's Rhetorical Roles in the Antebellum Religious Press, by Lisa J. Shaver. Pittsburgh: University of Pittsburgh P, 2012. 163 pp.

Reviewed by Paul Dahlgren, Georgia Southwestern State University

The past few years have seen a number of works, from various disciplinary perspectives, which examine the relationship between religion and rhetoric. Of these works, *Beyond the Pulpit: Women's Rhetorical Roles in the Antebellum Religious Press* stands out among this bunch for the exemplary recovery project it undertakes. Whereas works like *Preaching the Inward Light* have often sought to examine neglected traditions in rhetorical theory, *Beyond the Pulpit* instead seeks to recover the rhetorical spaces women occupied within the Methodist Church in Antebellum America. Building off of Roxanne Mountford's *The Gendered Pulpit*, Lisa Shaver tracks the presence of women in the Methodist press and demonstrates the way this religion offered women an opportunity to enter into the public sphere when most other avenues were unavailable to them. Although some may be reluctant to pick up a book with few clear pedagogical implications, we should engage with *Beyond the Pulpit* for its expert navigation of a number of rhetorical issues including the public/private divide as well as its deft use of underexplored archival material. It might also serve as a way of providing some scholar-teachers with a more capacious understanding of the complex role of religion in the lives our students. Shaver emphasizes the liminal spaces created by religious discourse which both "circumscribed and supported women's rhetoric" (133). Composition Studies needs more nuanced arguments about religion like this one.

Shaver's work represents a sustained investigation of the Antebellum religious press, particularly the Methodist arm of that press which would become an influential force in the United States as Methodism spread. Chapters 1 and 2 focus on one of the earliest organs in that press, *Methodist Magazine* (*MM*) and the memoirs of parishioners contained within this journal (1818-1824). Chapter 1 establishes the importance of these works and explores the way they functioned as a genre. According to Shaver, roughly a quarter of the *Methodist Magazine's* pages were devoted to memoirs written about recently deceased Methodists, many of whom were women. These writings served multiple rhetorical purposes for the journals and their readers. Shaver hypothesizes that the publishers often solicited material from their readers and that these memoirs were mostly what they received. They served as a way of sustaining the readership of the magazine and as a way of sustaining the faith of devout Methodists. She notes: "the concept of dying well and the publication of exemplary death for the edification of others is a long-standing religious tradition preceding Methodism" (19). For Methodist readers these memoirs served as a way of "confirming and increasing" the piety of members of what Shaver argues is "an interpretive community" of practicing Christians (23-4). For Methodists, conversion is an on-going process that continues up until one's deathbed. Paradoxically, through these memoirs, an individual might continue to serve the living even through her death. Shaver argues: "death marked a beginning instead of an end. Through the composition, dissemination, and consumption of their memoirs, deceased individuals were resurrected. Depictions of their holy lives and holy deaths, as well as their own voices, were used to instruct and motivate the living to cultivate a textual church community" (35). Without thinking of the importance of the afterlife in Evangelical Protestantism, we reflexively misunderstand the importance of women's deathbed rhetoric as a sign of the deep misogyny and certainly it is on many levels. However, Shaver argues that antebellum Methodist women were able to take such a seemingly undignified position in the early nineteenth century and slowly transform themselves into far more active participants in the religious press.

Chapter 2 looks more carefully at the memoirs about women parishioners and argues that through death, women were granted a certain kind of authority akin to the authority wielded by the male clergy. Readers will likely be most skeptical of Shaver's argument in this chapter and rightly so, but the argument deserves a serious hearing. In part because the subjects of these memoirs were often deceased, the norm was for them to be written either by a close family member, or, more often, a member of the male clergy, usually a minister. Passing over the role of a minister as a filter for the dominant ideology a little too quickly for this reader's taste, Shaver explores the way that clerical authors "elevated [women] to the role of minister, a position they were excluded from during their lives" (36). Perhaps because of the historical trajectory of this book, this reading becomes more convincing after having read some of Shaver's later chapters.

Chapter 3 finds us moving away from *Methodist Magazine* and towards the *Christian Advocate* (*CA*), which became the flagship publication of the church even though it was only intended to supplement *MM*. Running from 1826-1832, the *Christian Advocate* featured a section at the end of the magazine specifically addressed to women called "The Ladies' Department." This chapter is much more satisfying than the previous one. Here, Shaver explains that "By relegating the Ladies' Department to the back page of the *CA*, and by using the column's content to reinforce women's containment in the home and in the roles of wife and mother, the church used space to exert institutional power" (55). Here we learn about the interplay between Methodist practices and the nineteenth century domestic ideology.

Chapter 4, "Stepping Outside the Ladies' Department," tracks the presence of women in *CA* outside of the back pages originally designated for them. Whereas the previous chapter explored the way domesticity limited women within the church, this chapter argues that "religious activities enabled women to emerge from the domestic sphere and engage in social activism that contravened accepted gender norms" (71). Because the church occupies a liminal space between the public and private sphere, women were able to cautiously cross the gendered spaces that confined them in the rest of their lives. The most common means of doing this was through raising money for the church, often in the form of deathbed bequests. The bequests were not only made by well-off women, but also women of severely limited means, whose modest donations often served as stories of exemplary piety. Perhaps more importantly, women were able to take a leading role in benevolent organizations.

The Ladies' Repository and Gathering of the West (*LR*) a magazine specifically addressed to women, although still edited by male clergy, is the subject of Chapter 5. Shaver explains that *LR*, which was published between 1841 and 1876, was the Methodist response to *Godey's Lady's Book*, arguably the most influential journal in antebellum America, and certainly "the most popular women's magazine of the era" (107). Like many other magazines of its era, *LR* contained diverse material including sentimental fiction, writings on etiquette, poetry, and fashion plates. *LR* also became a platform for advocating equal education for women and men, although it often emphasized the need for practical education above all. The journal was particularly interested in female seminaries as female academies were relatively rare in this time period. That said, Shaver rightly notes that the oldest college for women in the world is Wesleyan College in Macon, Georgia and this is likely no coincidence (114). In a variety of ways, *LR* served as both a voice for Methodist Women and a platform that argued for their fuller participation in political life.

Shaver's recovery work is a welcome addition to work to the field of rhetoric and religion. However, it is not without its flaws. Methodism is often described as "a progressive force" but one could just as easily argue that Methodism only contributed minimally to women's emancipation and that the more capacious rhetorical role women took in that institution merely reflected the more capacious role women had in antebellum life (6). Furthermore, the argument could be made that women only gained a more prominent role in the life of the Methodist church when the church became a less central institution in the lives of everyday Americans. Both of these counterarguments suffer from their own problems. The first surely simplifies the complex story about the interrelationship of religion and social power in this time period. The second suffers from what scholars like Charles Taylor call "the secularism thesis" which suggests that secularization is simply a subtraction of excessive religious elements from social life rather than their displacement in other realms (26-29). Shaver might be faulted for not anticipating and addressing these objections, but these issues should not diminish the importance of her work.

Americus, GA

Works Cited

Graves, Michael. *Preaching the Inward Light: Early Quaker Rhetoric.* Waco, TX: Baylor University Press, 2009. Print.

Mountford, Roxanne. *The Gendered Pulpit: Preaching in American Protestant Spaces.* Carbondale: SIUP, 2005. Print.

Taylor, Charles. *A Secular Age.* Cambridge, MA: Harvard University Press, 2007. Print.

Composing (Media) = Composing (Embodiment): Bodies, Technologies, Writing and the Teaching of Writing, edited by Kristin L. Arola and Anne Frances Wysocki. Logan, Utah: Utah State UP, 2012. 289 pp.

Reviewed by Lauri Bohanan Goodling, Georgia Perimeter College

The collection of essays in *Composing (Media) = Composing (Embodiment)* represents a unique equation for understanding multi-layered composition that dominates writing today. Drawing from the growing necessity to recognize materiality and multimodality in the field of Composition Studies, Wysocki and Arola have honed in on an equally-relevant concept of self: embodiment in writing. This notion of embodiment can be rather abstract—calling to mind the psychological and metaphysical influences in writing—and also quite concrete—understanding the physicality of the writing process.

If one were to create a concept map or word cloud from this book, what might surface are terms such as Otherness, connectivity, re-orientation, re-calibration, re-authoring of self, navigation. Underlying each of these words is the question of how intimately tied the body (sometimes as self, other times as physical entity) is to the composing and revising process. The contributors universally challenge us to question traditional assumptions of being, identity, sexuality, functionality, and, in return, offer us a variety of ways we can instruct our students toward this new perspective.

The book is divided into two parts almost as closely linked as the body and mind. Part 1 focuses on the medium through which information is delivered and how that chosen medium impacts the effectiveness of the message. There is particular attention paid to embodiment in the medium and how that influences the development—and reflection—of an individual's identity.

The collection opens with an essay by Anne Wysocki ("Drawn Together: Possibilities for Bodies in Words and Pictures"), which discusses the marriage of opposites in relation to composing a whole entity. She culls together bits of comic book history (as visual rhetoric) and the theory of opposing forces as outlined by Pythagoras and W.J.T. Mitchell to help readers understand the often competing elements of word and image. Wysocki lays the groundwork for a discussion of what constitutes "high" literature and embodiment in the digitally-rich world we write in today.

Paul Walker further develops the idea of embodiment as he discusses reflection in citizen writing, through a discussion of mass observation journals and blogs. These personal narrative structures are embodiments of the daily lives of people who, like our students, are not self-identified or socially-ranked professional writers.

Few who've taught a class of first-year composition would deny that through writing, our students are consistently composing themselves. This is an idea shared by Matthew S.S. Johnson, who draws parallels between the first-year experience and the practice of constructing avatars in the gaming world. Through game-related role-play (embodiment of avatars), students move beyond what is familiar, explore possibilities beyond the surface, and make conscious decisions that will help shape their identity. These are the very same goals we have for students in many of our traditional class assignments.

Ultimately, the questions posed by David Parry ("How Billie Jean King Became the Center of the Universe") and Jason Farman ("Internet Cartography") involve determining how users mediate the Internet, how the Internet embodies the users' roles as information explorers. Both authors see the Internet as a vast space that can be explored purposefully or aimlessly, either for mindless entertainment or Enlightenment-worthy acquisition of knowledge. Just as it's difficult to read a digitally-networked document such as Wikipedia in a linear fashion, it's also difficult to see how Internet maps can benefit users. Both authors discuss the concept of connectivity as a roadmap for maximizing the potential of the Internet.

We can also teach our students to embody writing through recognition of the physicality of the writing process, as Jay Dolmage discusses in "Writing Against Normal." He notes the language of flawed writing as synonymous with the physically-disabled ("awkward," "not fully developed," "dangling" [112]) and shares ways for us to reteach the process of revision as a dominantly physical act (moving, cutting, trimming, looping text). Through the ideas of increased embodiment in the *process* of writing, he encourages students and teachers alike to reconsider our approach to composing altogether.

As a bridge to the discussion of objects, materiality and mediating of self through writing, the first chapter of Part 2 presents the writer in a new role, as craftsman. Kristen Prins explains that the product—that is, the text and ideas—in the world of multimodal composition is crafted using a vast array of tools and technologies (159).

The next several chapters discuss the role the human body, and the resulting sense of individual identity, plays in the composing of self in the textual and digital world. Through a scripted essay ("Bodies of Text"), which is a performance of sorts, Aaron Raz Link demonstrates how we are embodied in what we write, our physical bodies sometimes exposed and sometimes sheltered by our words. Similarly, well-known Queer Theory scholars, Jonathan Alexander and Jacqueline Rhodes, discuss the role of multimodal writing in helping to shape and introduce body, sexuality and gender identity to the world. The authors imply an intersection of sex and text, even highlighting a techno-sensual navigation experience (212).

Co-editor Kristin Arola ("It's My Revolution") uses Native American pow-wow regalia as a metaphor for social networking-related digital identities. She notes that regalia, much more than a costume, is an "embodied, visible act that [...] represents one's history, one's community, and one's self within that particular moment" (218). This is much like MySpace and Facebook profiles, which she examines to better understand how group identity can sometimes be situated within a particular medium.

The work of the feminist group "Guerilla Girls," which Karen Springsteen explores, also challenges assumptions of a group traditionally objectified and tied to their bodies and physical appearance. She sees online composing as a means to "create new embodied identities" (230), and both Arola and Springsteen welcome opportunities for re-identification and re-presentation of self in the digital world. In fact, one grand takeaway from this collection is that we can all benefit from the opportunities to re-mediate ourselves and our ideas through what we compose for new media.

While each essay in this collection addresses the influence these topics have on the way we teach, the collection is not pedagogically dense. To balance theory with practice for the compositionists who teach first-year college writers, the editors have included at the end of each part four or five classroom activities. These suggested activities invite students to reflect on how they are influenced and shaped by media, and to re-examine their perceptions of media, as well as their place in it (indeed, their experience with embodiment).

Wysocki concludes "Draw Together" by asking how we, as leaders in our classrooms, might work discussions of dichotomies into our class activities in order to encourage our students to consider the role of materiality, mediation and embodiment in their own creations. Perhaps another question prompted by the essays in *Composing (Media) = Composing (Embodiment)* as a whole is how we can embrace the power of digital identity and use it to our benefit.

When reflecting on how far we have come in the area of digital composition and how much has changed in our field, we might consider Vannevar Bush's 1945 piece, "As We May Think." In it, the American engineer and innovator, whose ideas greatly influenced Ted Nelson's work on hypertext and hypermedia, wrote in very forward-thinking fashion about many impending technological and scientific changes as he saw them likely to happen. He encouraged his readers to embrace these changes, to be grateful for them, arguing that the "lasting benefit has been man's use of science and of the new instruments [...and has...] increased his control of his material environment" (1). Today, Bush might argue that technology allows the writer to harness the power of materiality in composition, rather than being slave to one-dimensional writing.

On the subject of writing technology, in particular, Bush said that in order for a writer to effectively adapt to the changing composing technology, "All he needs to do is to take advantage of existing mechanisms and to alter his language" (3). As we go forth into a more multimodal world of reading and writing, it is necessary that we work to both understand this new lexicon and add to it. Perhaps even more importantly, in a case effectively made in the Wysocki and Arola text, we must incorporate multimodality into our English composition curriculum.

Atlanta, GA

Works Cited

Bush, Vannevar. "As We May Think." *The Atlantic Monthly*. July 1945. Web. April 1994. 25 September 2012.

Listening to our Elders: Working and Writing for Change, edited by Samantha Blackmon, Cristina Kirklighter and Steve Parks. Philadelphia: New City Community Press and Utah: Utah State UP, 2011. 193pp.

Reviewed by Cantice Greene, Clayton State University

As part of the NCTE centennial celebration, editors conceived of a project that would encapsulate the years of advocacy and agitation that have described the work of SIGs and caucuses within NCTE and CCCC through the last fifty years. *Listening to our Elders* is the product of that conception. The book is organized by caucuses and accompanied by an online companion that houses interviews and archival artifacts recording position and policy statements that have changed the way we view and do composition in the contemporary university.

Opening with a focus on the American Indian Caucus, the first chapter features two interviews, one with Malea Powell titled "We Wanted to Have an Open and Welcoming Space" and the other with Joyce Rain Anderson titled "Work to Be Done." As a pioneer caucus organizer, Powell highlights the accomplishments of her caucus and the uncomfortable moments as well, such as when the caucus was invited to an event where Indian sports logos made the members feel disrespected. In the following section still on the American Indian Caucus, Anderson introduces the metaphor of the gadfly saying, "Caucuses are meant to be the gadfly" "to 'pester and bite' to make change" (24).

The metaphor of the gadfly reappears in the interview with James Hill of the Black Caucus. He recalled that his caucus often supported many other caucuses within NCTE. He also noted that Black Caucus members often ascended to hold leadership positions within NCTE. Dr. Marianna W. Davis, the lead founder of the Black Caucus, was his central mentor. The mission of the Black Caucus, he said, was to "pave a pathway for African-Americans to gain visibility and become productive members and leaders in the organizations" (49). Hill's interview and the account given by Powell and Anderson recount the willingness of some caucuses to work together. This thread reoccurred in many interviews throughout the book.

An interview with Jeffrey Paul Chan highlights his brief work with the NCTE and the Asian/Asian-American Caucus. As a graduate student he was invited to attend a week long workshop of the 1970 Textbook Review Committee to review contemporary anthologies that represented the American literary canon. Chan noted that his job was simple since after a week all he and his colleague Frank Chin could report was that "nothing represents Asian American experience, not even the Asian experience" (39). But their critique didn't stop there; it culminated in a position paper about that lack of representation, an essay titled "Racist Love." After such an experience in the NCTE, Chan did note that many of the suggestions to make culturally sensitive writing curricula have been incorporated in the teaching of English and American Literature.

The chapter capturing the work and mission of the Committee on Disability Issues in College Composition featured an email transcript from a discussion on the DS-RHET Listserv from 2010. In this dialogue the issues of cost and containment surfaced as reasons why the CCCC was slow to incorporate suggested access measures to make their conferences and events more inclusive. The title of this chapter, "I Simply Gave up Trying to Present at CCCC..." is the sentiment of Patricia Dunn who recounted that early on her proposals on learning disabilities were rejected.

The chapter on the Language Policy Committee featuring an interview with Geneva Smitherman is a mix of Black history, Black activism and the Black Movement of the 60's and 70s; it offers an insider view that has all the action and subtlety of a blaxploitation film from the same time. Smitherman's work in NCTE was a natural extension of her work in the Black Movement and it was connected to her experiences growing up black and traversing the university as a linguist and advocate of African-American Vernacular English (AAVE) at a time when AAVE or Black English (BE) was not embraced. Many know that Smitherman's *Talkin' and Testifyin'* was written in AAVE. The feat of that authoring accomplishment should be inspiring to anyone who recognizes how difficult it is to write for an academic audience in vernacular language. One of the many successes of her work highlighted in this lengthy chapter was her leadership in crafting the "Students' Right to Their Own Language" policy statement. In her interview with Austin Jackson and Bonnie Williams she chronicles the steps that led to the interest in and adoption of that statement.

The Latino/a Caucus chapter, "Chicana Trailblazer in NCTE/CCCC," features a conversation with Corlota Cárdenas Dwyer. Dwyer helped form the caucus that was originally titled Chicano Teachers of English or (CTE) in 1968. Dwyer left higher education in 1982 after being denied tenure from the University of Texas at Austin, but she continued to lead presentations on the teaching of Chicano Literature in all-day workshops before NCTE conventions. She went on to organize an anthology of Chicano Literature, *Chicano Voices,* published by Houghton Mifflin. Ironically, the University of Texas at Austin recently welcomed her archival papers, placing them in their Benson Latin American Library. Victor Villanueva was also interviewed as one of the trailblazing members of the Latino/a Caucus. His fondest memory was of the year he was Chair of the CCCCs. He remembered the Spanish theme and Puerto Rican cultural displays of the conference as the highlight of his career because, as he put it, "our ways were up front, on Main Street" (143).

In some of the interviews, the cultural activists revealed their agitation that they hadn't done enough or that the main goals of the group had not yet been realized. The interview with Louise Dunlap, a founder of the Progressive Caucus, was one that exuded this agitation. The title of the chapter "Combating Institutional Neutrality" is a telling foreshadowing of that dissatisfaction. The interview captured her sentiments this way, "I've been centrally concerned with how academic thinking tends to drift toward the neutral. I call this trend 'neutral writing' or 'neutral thinking'—a kind of neutrality that refuses to take a position on things" (149). Despite these neutral tendencies, the interview reveals that one of the caucus's biggest accomplishments was to lend support to striking hotel workers at the Hyatt Hotel in New Orleans. Activism such as this characterized the short history of the Progressive Caucus that lasted from 1982-1992.

The chapter on the Queer Caucus brought some of the most memorable stories about cultural misunderstanding and cultural harmonizing. Louie Crew brought his humor and good memory to the transcript. His founding of the Queer Caucus emerged from his suggestion that NCTE do a special issue on gay and lesbian issues in 1973. Once he was asked to co-edit the project, his call for papers attracted many of the people who would later serve with him in the caucus. The chapter is titled "Renaming Curiosity/Resisting Ignorance" and the power of naming is a theme that reverberates in the many name changes of the caucus. The names include the Committee on Lesbian and Gay Male Concerns in the English Profession, the Lesbian and Gay Male Caucus, the Lesbian and Gay Professional Caucus, and finally the Queer Caucus. Just as others did, Crew noted the impact of the caucus on what was to be published in textbooks and the books that became the theory books behind teaching writing.

The exchange between William Thelin and Pamela Roeper in the chapter on the Working Class Culture and Pedagogy SIG and Bring-A-Book was one of the liveliest because of the adversarial dynamic. The problem of the working conditions of adjunct instructors is still not satisfactorily addressed within the discipline, and the question of how to best empower or approach a class of working class students is still debated. Roeper named "adjuncts who have spouses who earn good livings…" as those who "impede progress in many ways in the fight for adjunct rights" (177). Although she acknowledged the divisiveness of the statement, her comment and others scattered throughout the book seemed to marginalize conservative thought and traditional middle class lifestyles. Later in the chapter, Thelin admitted feeling that the SIG never really met its potential, yet he acknowledged the Bring-A-Book-Project as successful. Over 3650 books were distributed to eight community literacy resources, a follow-up essay by Bill Macauley revealed.

Overall, the collection of interviews is a powerful historical account of activism in composition from the inception of the field until now. The book's neat organization by caucus or SIG makes it easy to sift through if a reader is interested in one particular group's origin. While you won't find pedagogy spelled-out in these pages, you will find examples of teamwork within the field that has led to academic excellence and longevity.

Morrow, GA

Literate Zeal: Gender and the Making of a *New Yorker* **Ethos,** by Janet Carey Eldred. Pittsburgh: U of Pittsburgh P, 2012. 178 pp.

Reviewed by Kerri Hauman, Transylvania University

Janet Carey Eldred's *Literate Zeal: Gender and the Making of a* New Yorker *Ethos* is an archival research project that focuses on women editors of mid-twentieth century large-circulation magazines, in particular Katharine White of the *New Yorker*. Eldred draws on Deborah Brandt's idea of literacy sponsors in her aim to "get behind the scenes of sponsorship" (180, footnote 6) in order to counter a "liberal elitism" (xv) that has created a false divide between women's magazines and literature, including supposedly more highbrow magazines like the *New Yorker*. This false divide, Eldred argues, has led people to devalue decades of rhetorical and literary achievements gained through women's editorial work. In fact, Eldred argues that mid-twentieth century women editors played an important role in establishing magazines—the *New Yorker* and those typically considered women's magazines such as *Mademoiselle*—as a place to find serious literature, which fostered a growing literacy among middle class Americans.

The preface quickly introduces many players and terms alongside Eldred's aims for the book. Expectedly, Eldred acknowledges that the book's contents are a direct result of what she found (and did not find) in the archives. She explains that although the archives do support a full picture of Katharine White, she has opted to present "a heavy, gilded frame" (xi) that draws attention from White and presents glimpses of other women editors' lives and works. This approach challenges an "exceptional woman" approach that is often criticized in feminist rhetorical history for perpetuating a notion that only a few women were accomplished and worthy of study.

The introduction provides many essential backdrops against which the rest of the book unfolds. The first is the conflicting histories of the work that mid-twentieth century women editors did and the critiques Betty Friedan and other feminists of the 1960s and 1970s leveled against women's magazines. Eldred pithily presents key arguments from these dueling histories, into which she weaves feminist media scholarship that asks readers to "rethink the dichotomy between women's magazines as mythmakers and feminists as unveilers" (5). A second backdrop is the changing college curriculum and career expectations for women of the early twentieth century, and a third is the changing conceptions of literacy at this time as it became a "secular faith" (21). Eldred concludes the introduction with excerpts from White's correspondence and admission that although she believes the women editors she writes about would want to be remembered as "zealots for belletrism" who had a "faith in aesthetics that promised to transcend messy social ills and conflicts" (33), she feels she must present a messier, more critical history to demonstrate these women's work as concurrently "pioneering, remarkable, limited [and] flawed" (34).

In chapter 1, Eldred briefly defines her use of "ethos": not the good man speaking well, but instead, drawing on Michael Hyde, "'dwelling places' that 'define the grounds, abodes or habitats, where a person's ethics and moral character take form and develop'" (40). This definition of ethos provides justification for Eldred's use of various primary and secondary sources (i.e., archival documents, trade journals, memoirs, biographies); she must look across the various "dwelling places" that contributed to women's editors' and magazines' ethos. Next, Eldred substantiates her claim that the *New Yorker* is similar to middlebrow publications, particularly women's magazines. By drawing on text from Edward Bok, editor of *Ladies' Home Journal* from 1889-1919, and *Vogue*, Eldred demonstrates that these middlebrow women's magazines share with the *New Yorker* an aim to provide readers with cultural improvement through the simultaneously instructional and leisurely literature the publications printed and promoted. The bulk of chapter 1 then discusses the *New Yorker*'s developing ethos, which Eldred shows has been criticized repeatedly for vacillating between humor and realism, between the purposes of entertainment and education. This criticism, Eldred reveals, is often a concern about genre, an accusation that the *New Yorker* published a "type" of writing with the attendant assumption that for an editor to acknowledge this—or, worse yet, for an author to write with the aim of fitting this type—would diminish a text's literary value. In the archival evidence provided, readers see the long-standing rhetorical battle between episteme and techné play out. Ultimately, Eldred argues the *New Yorker* survived precisely because it "never strayed too far from its middlebrow ethos" (71), because it did adhere to a recognizable type, despite various editors' and readers' claims that this "type" did not exist.

Chapter 2 continues the discussion of characteristic traits and consequent critiques of the *New Yorker,* particularly regarding its editing practices. Eldred recognizes one widespread critique that *New Yorker* editors overedited, privileging grammatical and factual correctness over literary license. To complicate a simplistic understanding that *New Yorker* editing policies could either entirely help or hurt authors, Eldred presents two examples from the archives: 1) correspondence between White and Isabel Bolton, and 2) correspondence between White and Frances Gray Patton. While the first example serves to illustrate a more heated interaction and the second a more collaborative endeavor, both finally support Eldred's claim that many writers "alternately balked at the restraints of the *New Yorker* system and benefited from the structure and comfort it provided its writers" (97). A theme developed through this chapter, then, is the familiar conflict between notions of an author as an individual genius and recognition of the "social politics, market pressures, individual relationships" (109), including gender and collaboration, that affect authors and authorship.

Chapter 3 compares the *New Yorker* to *Mademoiselle* and other women's magazines in order to overturn two claims: 1) "that women's magazines had no significant content," and 2) "that the *New Yorker* is decidedly not a women's magazine" (116). After acknowledging differences in audiences, Eldred outlines the history of *Mademoiselle* to argue that it shared with the *New Yorker* "a similar movement from a light and witty magazine to a publication that sponsored serious high letters" (116). To counter criticisms that the *New Yorker* began catering more to women in 1961 with a change in its editorial staff, Eldred shows that the *New Yorker* had, in fact, always appealed to women's desires, had consistently contained advertisements similar to publications like *Mademoiselle* and *Harper's Bazaar*, and had even established a long-running, popular fashion column only two years after its 1925 debut. In this chapter, Eldred briefly reiterates the caution from the preface to not oversimplify narratives of women's magazines, and more importantly, her careful analysis demonstrates how one can present a fuller, more complex rendering.

In its discussion of women editors' style and the role of "body politics," the conclusion includes the focused gender analysis I had expected more of in the book. Eldred juxtaposes excerpts from *Vogue* editor Edna Woolman Chase's memoir that discuss her personal discovery of a sophisticated, elegant style with representations of White's body – particularly as it aged and in illness – as seen in White's own writing as well as others' writing about her and her husband. A key point here is that women editors were unable to fully control their image, including the inability to place focus solely on their work to the exclusion of their bodies.

The afterword acknowledges White's careful collecting and cataloging of her work in order to donate it to her alma mater, Bryn Mawr College. Eldred also acknowledges that White's reasons for preserving this work were multifaceted: she sought to reduce the amount of material stored in her house, to receive a tax break, to preserve a text-based literacy in "times of encroaching visual media" (162), to emphasize American literature in a time when British literature was privileged, and to discredit a book published in 1975 that marred the ethos she had so carefully worked to create for the *New Yorker*.

Literate Zeal is a book that crosses several disciplines including writing studies, media studies, communication, women's/gender studies, and American literature. Within writing studies, it will especially appeal to scholars of literacy studies, genre, and feminist rhetoric. Although Eldred does include some mention of how the archives she used affected her final product, I found myself wanting more explanation of her methods and of the methodologies guiding her work. Selfishly, as a scholar interested in the politics of gender and technology, I longed for more discussion of the role of technology in these stories. I also longed to read more discussion of the excerpts that Eldred used to demonstrate White's "woman-centered" (146) and collaborative editorial style. Likewise, issues of race receive a few mentions and footnotes but not much focused discussion. Indeed, as Eldred admits early in the book, there is enough material here for several other projects. Ultimately, though, this does not detract from what is overall an excellent book. Eldred's careful and thoughtful work presents a rich portrayal of Katharine White's work and the contributions women's magazines and women editors made to mid-twentieth century United States literacy and literature.

Lexington, KY

Writing Home: A Literacy Autobiography, by Eli Goldblatt. Carbondale: SIUP, 2012. 258 pp.

Reviewed by Ted Kesler, Queens College, City University of New York

Over the years, Eli Goldblatt gave a literacy autobiography assignment to his undergraduate and graduate students "in order to help them see the intimate ways that reading and writing influence their lives" (3). *Writing Home: A Literacy Autobiography* emerged from his desire to fulfill this assignment himself. This is a well-established college assignment in various fields of study. I, for one, began giving this assignment in the fall semester, 2010 to my cohort of pre-service master's degree elementary education students in my two sequential literacy courses after reading an exchange of e-mails on the listserv of the Literacy Research Association (LRA). The 23 participants in this e-mail exchange expressed several significant reasons for giving this assignment, including: recognizing each individual's distinct literacy journey, discerning and valuing multiple literacies, challenging the misconception of one neutral, universal set of literacy skills, and honoring the social, historical, political, and cultural dimensions that shape our literate lives.

Writing Home is organized into ten chapters that recount Goldblatt's literacy experiences in the first 30 years of his life, mostly in chronological order. Chapter 1, "Tour of Duty," recounts Goldblatt's literacy experiences growing up in seven different homes in four US states and Europe, including Landstuhl, Germany, as the son of an officer in the US Army Medical Corps. Chapter 2, "The Right to Mourn," focuses on his middle and high school years in Silver Spring, Maryland, especially contending with his father's death when Goldblatt was 13. In chapter 3, "Into the Daedalean Dreamscape," Goldblatt describes his first year at Beloit College, where he began studying poetry and classics. In chapter 4, "Following Williams," Goldblatt describes his half year working at a printing press in Amherst, Massachusetts, followed by his half year in San Francisco, then his three years at Cornell University, where he continued his study of poetry and classics. "Following Williams" refers to Goldblatt's decision to pursue a medical career as a doctor/ poet, as Williams Carlos Williams did, and thus following in his father's footsteps. In chapter 5, "Dry Creek Road," Goldblatt describes his year transition between Cornell and medical school. Dry Creek Road refers to the road where he lived with a college roommate, working alongside poor migrant workers in the vineyards of northern California that made Goldblatt realize: "For the first time, I wanted to know a language not for poetry or religion but because other people were speaking and I wanted to join the conversation" (108).

Chapter 6, "White Coat," describes Goldblatt's year at Case Western Reserve Medical School, where he strove "to keep making my imagination engage with the real world" (130). In the end, Goldblatt struggled with reconciling the passion for connection that he experienced as a medical student with the isolation of a writer's life. He chose to leave medical school, but wondered: "Would writing cut me off from lives I valued or from those who valued me?" (140). Chapter 7, "Entering Philadelphia," focuses on Goldblatt's first marriage, his first teaching position as a science teacher in an alternative high school for runaway teenagers, and his first forays into constructing his life as a poet. Chapter 8, "Beyond the Fathers," focuses on Goldblatt's high school teaching experience and the breakup of his marriage. In chapter 9, "Viajeros, Extranjeros," Goldblatt focuses on his eight month journey through Mexico and Central America at a time of intense political turmoil and brutal civil wars. Goldblatt was one of many *viajeros*, or international travelers, and in Nicaragua, where the Sandinistas had recently taken control, *extranjeros*, or foreigners hoping to prove that they could contribute to rebuilding the country in the aftermath of revolution. Finally, chapter 10, "High Five at Second Base," recounts Goldblatt's return to Philadelphia, where "teaching would meld with writing to clarify and sharpen the differences and similarities between working with students and addressing readers" (238), and developing a sense of home. The chapter accelerates his literacy autobiography to the present day. Goldblatt has discovered: "I write to belong, and every piece of writing defines the threads by which we connect with others across time and space. One is clearly always alone and never alone within a written text" (239).

Writing Home is unusual as an academic book. By the author's own acknowledgement, explicit theory is deliberately subverted to give way to narrative. Theory is articulated in the introductory chapter, "From Garret to Tree House," and in the final chapter. Theory then serves as bookends to the narrative of Goldblatt's literacy life. Put another way, Goldblatt's literacy life illuminates the theory that frames this book.

In the final chapter, Goldblatt articulates three central themes that pervade his narrative: *the individual and collective nature of text, the materiality of language*, and *the desire for human connection that words embody* (239). He explains that *the individual and collective nature of text* is "the dialectic of individual and group, in writing as in every other human interaction" (243). Indeed, Goldblatt begins his book with a quote from Bakhtin's *The Dialogic Imagination*: "In all areas of life and ideological activity, our speech is filled to overflowing with other people's words." In a process called *appropriation*, Bakhtin (1981) explains the inherent struggle as an individual filters and takes on the cacophony of other voices in society. For example, Bakhtin states:

> Language is not a neutral medium that passes freely and easily into the private property of the speaker's intentions; it is populated—overpopulated—with the intentions of others. Expropriating it, forcing it to submit to one's own intentions and accents, is a difficult and complicated process. (294)

This is the struggle that Goldblatt's literacy autobiography illustrates. His narrative explicates "the bridge between individual and communal senses of self in language" (6).

Goldblatt gives two meanings to the theme *the materiality of language*. First, he means "[f]inding the words to say what I mean—or unearthing what I mean through the words I say" (245). This meaning was particularly apparent in his chapters of his year in medical school (chapter 6, "White Coat"), when he struggled to learn the language of medicine, and of his eight months in Mexico and Central America (chapter 9, "Vianjeros, Extranjeros"), where he had to learn to communicate in Spanish and contended with "the sheer bewilderment of not knowing how to find the public toilet or what friendship could get you killed" (244). Goldblatt applies this struggle for the right word and for using the quotidian in fresh, new ways to writing poetry: "the poet is in the business of discovering what cannot be known or said except by way of the poem" (245). The other meaning of *the materiality of language* is the fact that written words take up space (whether in digital or paper forms). Goldblatt was reminded of this fact when all the books and journals and notepads in his backpack far outweighed his clothes when he returned to Philadelphia at the end of his Central America and Mexico adventures. Goldblatt explains: "the material being of text is itself a metaphor for the promise of relationship that language offers one human with or among others" (247).

Goldblatt's third theme, *the desire for human connection that words embody*, comes from his realization that "most of my understanding about writing came at painful and joyful moments away from classrooms" (247). Goldblatt celebrates literacy that is enacted within the Deweyan concept of joint activity: collaborative community efforts that are "unconnected to school and off the grid of conventional power differences" (252), when "literacy shrugs off correctness or diction as its defining qualities" (252). He values "writing across communities" (5). Conversely, Goldblatt is disparaging of university settings where he himself spends most of his time. He laments students, including his own son, who are "endlessly rehearsing information that makes no sense of the world students face in their personal lives" and that "the very structures in which we teach tend to render our utterances hollow and our assignments the arbitrary tasks for prisoners serving out life sentences" (253). Goldblatt asserts that "literature, rhetoric, and linguistics grow poorer when they remain purely academic studies" (2). A second dimension of human connection is how "[t]he individual striving of a given artist becomes consecrated by the collective effort of artists over time" (253). This dimension harkens to Bakhtin's dialogic, multivoiced construction of literacy: that our intentional uses of language derive from other people's uses, contexts, and intentions with that language.

It's fair to say that *Writing Home: A Literacy Autobiography* expresses many of the values that the contributors to the LRA listserve exchange articulated. This book provides students and professors one person's fully realized exploration of his literacy, which strongly shows the melding of sociocultural dimensions in each of our expressions of a literate life.

Flushing, New York

Works Cited

Bakhtin, M. M. *The Dialogic Imagination: Four Essays* (C. Emerson & M. Holquist, Trans.). Austin: University of Texas Press, 1981. Print.

Collaborative Learning and Writing: Essays on Using Small Groups in Teaching English and Composition, edited by Kathleen M Hunzer. Jefferson: Mcfarland & Company Inc., 2011. 227 pp.

Reviewed by Sean R. Maddox, California Polytechnic State University

I scratched my head in confusion as the last students filed out of my classroom, unable to understand what had just taken place. I thought the collaborative learning unit on Rhetorical appeals I developed was pedagogically sound. I asked students, with my assistance, to break down how political advertisements use different rhetorical appeals, asked them in groups to craft their own political platforms and advertisements then present them to the class. Finally, we held a vote to see which new political advertisement was most successful in persuading their audience by discussing the rhetorical appeals used. But my initial enthusiasm and confidence quickly faded, as each class became disengaged, quickly rushing through the activity and moving on to non-related matters despite my continual questioning and engagement in the group process. The presentations, not showing complexity and integration of class material, reflected this non-critical thought process and lack luster performance. I racked my brain to try to figure out what happened. But, no matter how hard I tried, I couldn't pin point the possible factor that led to the activity's failure, as other group activities had been successful. I, once again, began to question the effectiveness of collaborative learning.

It was a few days later, sitting on my patio drinking a cup of hot coffee and reading Kathleen M. Hunzer's collection, *Collaborative Learning and Writing: Essays on Using Small Groups in Teaching English and Composition*, I found many of the same questions I had about my collaborative learning activities being asked. How do I choose groups? How do I setup assignments specifically for collaborative learning? What pedagogical considerations do I need to make? How do I insure labor is fair and equitable between group members? But, unlike books and essays which only provide a very narrow lens through which to view collaborative learning, Hunzer provides us with "a practical sourcebook that answers these questions" and "provides us helpful advice" through an in depth collection of varied and crucial theory on the use of collaborative learning in classrooms (3-4). To accomplish this task, Hunzer breaks up the collection into five sections, each one based on answering a common question surrounding the use of collaborative learning within classrooms.

The first part, consisting of four essays, tries to answer the question "why [are] collaborative learning and peer review . . . important"? (3). The section begins with Jason Wirtz's article "Writing Courses Live and Die by the Quality of Peer Review," which provides a general overview of why we should peer review in our classrooms by exemplifying the positive benefits associated with successful peer reviewing, from providing students with the support of a writers community to teaching them about audience awareness to showing them there is no "right" answer. To insure successful implementation of peer review, he also addresses the most common reasons peer reviewing "wants to fail" and clearly articulates the instructor's role in the peer reviewing process (9).

What Wirtz's article lacks in peer review classroom implementation, the other three essays of the first section undeniably make up for it, starting with Anthony Edgington's article "Bringing New Perspectives to a Common Practice: A Plan for Peer Review." Edgington provides a thorough outline for implementing a traditional peer review activity from the very first preparation stages to the final instructor responses and includes sample worksheets, activities, and questions for fellow instructors to consider. Catherine Kalish, Heinert, and Pilmaier explain in detail the implementation of the nontraditional peer-tutorial method of peer review in their article, "Reinventing Peer Review Using Writing Center Techniques: Teaching Students to Use Peer-tutorial Methodology." Jacob Stratmen, in "'It's just too nicey-nicey around here': Teaching Dissensus in Research and Collaborative Groups," discusses the use and importance of dissensus within research groups and collaborative learning, an area highly lacking in research since John Trimbur's initial call for dissensus. The four articles, which make up the first section, provide readers with an array of well thought out and critical answers on why and how we should use collaborative learning and peer reviewing within our classrooms.

The second part, composed of three essays, tries to provide an answer to what is probably the most asked question concerning collaborative learning: "How do I best select groups in my classes?" (3). The first essay "Increasing Participation and Accountability in Group Production of Text through Speed Interviews" examines the use of speed interviews, a common business and dating practice, in choosing collaborative learning groups within classrooms. Mialisa Moline provides detailed explanations, theory, diagrams, and examples on the use of speed interviewing for instructors to consider when it comes to group selection. On the other hand, Kathleen Hunzer's article "Connecting Writing Process with Personality: Creating Long-Lasting Trust Circles in Writing Classes" offers a far more personal approach to group formation through the matching of students based on their personalities and provides examples from her own students and classes for instructors to consider. Mialisa Moline, in her essay "Forming Peer Critique Groups Through Personality Preferences," explores the use of personality tests, like the Myer-Briggs Type Indicator, to help select student group members. This includes a breakdown of suggested personality type combinations for different activities and stages of writing. No matter your classroom or student make up, this section provides any concerned instructor a multitude of ways to form groups no matter the demands of their students and classes.

In the third part, Hunzer explores the use of collaborative learning within electronic environments and tries to answer the question of how to successfully implement collaborative learning within these types of new and quickly evolving class room environments. Starting with a general overview of collaborative learning within digital environments, Cindy Tekobbe's, Yazmin Lazcano-Pry's, and Duane Roen's article "Collaborative Learning and Writing in Digital Environments," provides a theoretical basis for the benefits and concerns of using digital environments within collaborative learning activities and explores the different technologies available for setting up a digital collaborative learning environment. Kelly Shea, Donna Evens and Ben S. Bunting, Jr., and Cheryl Melkun, on the other hand, go into detailed explanations, in their respective essays, on the implementation of specific digital technologies within a class, from the use of course management systems for peer response (Shea) to Google Docs for collaborative writing (Evans, Bunting) to the use of web conferencing for online collaboration (Melkun). No matter your technological preference, Hunzer, through the essays she selects, provides an array of in depth and well thought out options when it comes to the use of collaborative learning within digital environments.

In order to provide a "practical source book," Hunzer focuses the fourth section on examining if "collaborative learning and writing work in all writing classrooms" (4). Although this question, in theory, would be impossible to answer considering the ever changing social nature of any classroom, the three essays of this section center on the implementation and use of collaborative learning and writing within different course types. Randi Browning allows us a look into her use of collaborative learning within her business writing classrooms—in order to replicate real-world collaborative experiences—and in the process provides course design material to actual in-class implementation. Through in class examples and assessments, Florence Bacbac dives into her own Business Communication courses to explore and demonstrate the use, advantages, and disadvantages of computer-mediated communication (CMC) for student collaboration during the writing process. And Kara Alexander shows how team projects can be implemented within writing classrooms in ways that mitigate many of the common problems instructors often face. Unlike the other sections, the question Hunzer sets out to answer here isn't clearly answered. Instead, we're provided with practical examples of how different instructors tackled this question themselves, and, in the process, provided ways to find our own answer for our own courses.

To round out her "practical sourcebook" on collaborative learning, Hunzer examines if "special populations benefit from collaborative activities" in her fifth and final part. Because this area of study within collaborative learning theory is still not thoroughly researched, this section consists of only two essays, Robb Mccollum's "Working Together Towards Greatness: The Cumulative Writing Model and English Language Learners" and Kathleen Hunzer's essay "Anxiety Disorders and the Collaborative Classroom." Mccollum examines the use of a cumulative writing model (CWM), in which students continually repeat the research writing process multiple times over a course, to teach students, especially ESL students, the language of academic writing. Mccollum includes a theoretical base for cumulative writing models with examples, activities, and figures. Hunzer deconstructs the conflicting nature between students with anxiety disorders and collaborative learning environments, which tend to exacerbate them. She provides a thoughtful discussion of the differing anxiety disorders our students may have, the problems they can manifest, and possible ways to approach the collaborative learning environment in order to mitigate these problems.

In structuring the collection around some of the most common questions and concerns any instructor familiar with collaborative learning would have, Hunzer successfully provides a practical sourcebook "to make this amazingly productive pedagogy work smoothly and effectively" (4). By the time I finished the book, it became clear the mistakes I made within my own collaborative learning activity. I failed to make collaborative learning the central focus of my course, relied on a random and uncritical group selection process, didn't emphasize the importance of collaboration enough, and, as a result, the majority of my classes didn't always see the importance of working together. Hunzer's collection provided me with a multitude of pragmatic ways to answer my questions and implement collaborative learning in my classrooms, and for any instructor who uses collaborative learning within their course, or is curious in doing so, I strongly recommend *Collaborative Learning and Writing: Essays on Using Small Groups in Teaching English and Composition*.

Grover Beach, CA

Work Cited

Trimbur, John. "Consensus and Differences in Collaborative Learning." *College English*. 51.6 (1989): 602-616. Print.

Autism Spectrum Disorders in the College Composition Classroom: Making Writing Instruction More Accessible for All Students, edited by Val Gerstle and Lynda Walsh. Milwaukee: Marquette University Press, 2011. 150 pp.

Reviewed by Adam M. Pacton, University of Wisconsin-Milwaukee

Gerstle and Walsh's collection of essays opens with a startling statistic, one that is repeated throughout the book: according to the Centers for Disease Control and Prevention (CDC), up to 1 in 110 children may have Autism Spectrum Disorder (ASD). More startling is the fact that current CDC estimates put the prevalence rate at 1 in 88 ("Prevalence"). This upward trajectory raises a host of pressing questions. Is ASD increasing or are diagnostic instruments finally mirroring prevalence? Is increased awareness of ASD leading to more diagnoses? Is the social construction of the disorder going through a radical reformulation? While these questions are undoubtedly important, *Autism Spectrum Disorders in the Composition Classroom* does not focus on them; rather, the collection addresses two pressing, practical consequences of increasing prevalence rates for composition instructors. First, if prevalence is increasing, then composition instructors will be working with more and more ASD students, and these instructors will have to negotiate the sometimes-choppy waters of accommodation in the effort to teach these students how to write in rhetorically nuanced ways. Second, as the subtitle of the collection suggests, the ways in which we adapt our theory and pedagogy to work with these students should ideally not only make writing more accessible for students on the spectrum, but for all writing students. And this is perhaps the most important message of the book: rather than try to "accommodate" or "include" students with ASD—verbs that can imply absorption or homogenization—we should instead look closely at Composition and ask ourselves "how can we make this better for everyone; how can we continue to reshape, grow, and enrich our notions of what it means to be a writer?" Admittedly, these are not easy questions to answer, but the authors in this collection clearly and compassionately ask them.

The collection is divided into two interpenetrating sections which each contain four chapters: "Accommodation" and "Pedagogy." As Lynda Walsh points out in the book's introduction, there is almost no (real) institutional or social accommodation for students with ASD at most colleges, not to mention a dearth of scholarly attention (8); in other words, there is a gaping hole where there should be theory, praxis, and support. However, this vacuum can be an opportunity. Referring to the original *CCCC* panel that led to the book's creation, Walsh says

> The ideal scenario painted by these papers is not one of disciplining ASD students to behave "normally"; rather, it is one in which the unique abilities of ASD students can productively transform the traditional composition classroom by breaking its margins and multiplying its perspectives in order to make writing education more accessible for all. (8-9)

In other words, the exigency created by the coming influx of ASD students can provide an impetus to continue to reconceive Composition, its ends, and its place within the academy in ways that serve all students.

The "Accommodation" section of the book broadly approaches the ways in which Composition must locally (in terms of individual students) and institutionally (in terms of practices and policies) evolve in order to meaningfully accommodate students with ASD. It is appropriate that the first chapter in this section is Marica Ribble's "Basic Writing Students with Autism in the College Classroom," as many ASD students will begin their composition coursework in basic writing courses. In her chapter, Ribble contextualizes many of the challenges students with ASD face in the composition classroom including the required sociability of group work, largely irrelevant institutional "accommodations," and ignorant or undertrained faculty. Katherine V. Wills, in "'I Just Felt Kinda Invisible': Accommodations for Learning Disabled Students in the Composition Classroom," argues that qualitative research (interviews, in particular) can give composition faculty the insight needed to better meet challenges like those that Ribble describes by

> rethink[ing] pedagogy as a commitment to engage disability itself and remake its social construction one student and one class at a time, minimizing the material consequences of the social construction of disability, illuminating expectations, and questioning normative subjectivity towards full educational access. (43)

April Mann foregrounds this social construction of disability in "Structure & Accommodation: Autism & the Writing Center" and clearly shows how thinking about ASD as a disability in relation to Composition can be incredibly problematic. As she points out, students with Asperger's Syndrome (a form of high-functioning autism) can actually be hyperlexic—they can have well-above average reading and writing skills—but can be disadvantaged by disciplinary norms such as inquiry-based writing, composing for imagined audiences, and conceiving of writing as a series of choices (49-53). However, Mann contends, a number of writing center best practices may have the potential to ameliorate the stresses and difficulties that ASD students may experience as a result such classroom norms. In the final chapter of the "Accommodation" section of the book, "Recommended Approaches to the Neuroimaging Literature on Autism Spectrum Disorders (ASD) for Teachers of Writing," Lynda Walsh and Cheryl Olman provide composition instructors with some context on the relationship between neuroimaging studies, autism, and what such studies may or may not say about such things as "mirror neurons," empathy, linguistic interpretation, and cerebral interconnectedness. In addition to uncovering the limitations of such studies, Walsh and Olman argue that what these studies *can* tell us implies pedagogical approaches that may benefit all composition students such as clear directions for assignments or multimodal instruction.

While the second section of the book is titled "Pedagogy," there is still a fair degree of discussion on accommodation just as the "Accommodation" section contains a fair amount of discussion on pedagogy. That said, the chapters in this section stand apart from those in the "Accommodation" section through their grounding in concrete pedagogical practices and postures meant to materially change Composition as a field and as a constellation of practices. Kim Freeman's chapter, "Channeling the Enthusiasm: Two Narratives of Teaching Students with Asperger's Syndrome in Writing & Literature Classes, with Questions & Reflections," describes her failures, successes, and strategies in working with students with Asperger's Syndrome. Like some of the authors in the other section of the book, Freeman holds out hope that education on, and experience with, ASD can result in fundamental theoretical and pedagogical shifts in Composition. Val Gerstle's chapter, "Reaching the College Composition Student with Autism Through the Cartoon-Enhanced Classroom," represents such a shift. Gerstle argues that working with cartoons (particularly humorous ones) in the composition classroom can capitalize on ASD students' (sometimes) visual strengths and help smooth social interactions while decreasing participatory anxieties. Gerstle believes that cartoons may be used not only as objects to be analyzed by the class but texts to be produced *in* the class. Muriel Cunningham also writes on the benefits of using visual instructional modalities when teaching students with ASD in "Helping Autistic Students Improve Written Communication Skills Through Visual Images," arguing that carefully crafted analytic exercises can help autistic and neurotypical students alike learn how to read nuance in texts. In the final chapter of the section and the book, "'Well, Not Exactly': Asperger's and the Integration of Outside Sources," Jennifer McClinton-Temple argues that the contextually-dependent nature of plagiarism makes the incorporation of sources hard to pin down in any sort of algorithmic or procedural sense, and this can be a sometimes-paralyzing situation for students on the spectrum, many of whom may be quite literal or procedural thinkers (137-38). In addition, McClinton-Temple argues, the simple act of paraphrasing may seem like an absurdity to some ASD students—why put something in one's own words if it was well-written to begin with (139)? McClinton-Temple's chapter provides some workarounds for these issues, such as recasting paraphrase as summary, that may help not just ASD students but all composition students address this difficult and ambiguous facet of academic writing.

As a collection, *Autism Spectrum Disorders in the College Composition Classroom*, serves as a good introduction to a number of the challenges that composition instructors will increasingly face as more and more ASD students fill our classrooms. The book does have its blank spots, however. For example, the contributors tend to only address high-functioning ASD students and students with Asperger's Syndrome. There is little mention of students who will need computer-assisted communication devices such as iPads or students who will have sensory integration issues, students who may have to disruptively "stim," or self-stimulate. There is also sparse theoretical or empirical grounding in the book. Much of the collection reads like anecdote or "lore." These criticisms are not, ultimately, criticisms of the book, however—they are criticisms of the field's silences and lack of responsiveness. They are criticisms of those faculty who have received the "needs more time taking tests" notices for accommodation and left it at that, quietly letting the gates of the academy slam shut in their students' faces. These elisions are an indictment, but the voices of this collection are a corrective; they are the first salvos in a discipline-wide discussion that must take place not soon, but now. The authors in this book are doing what the best of us do and what all of us should strive to do: they are looking at their students as individual writers with their own struggles, strengths, and talents, and asking "how can I do better for them and for all of us?"

Milwaukee, WI

Works Cited

"Prevalence of Autism Spectrum Disorders—Autism and Developmental Disabilities Monitoring Network, 14 Sites, United States, 2008." cdc.gov. Centers for Disease Control and Prevention, 2012. Web. 31 Jul. 2012.

Feminist Rhetorical Resilience, edited by Elizabeth A. Flynn, Patricia Sotirin, and Anne Brady. Boulder: Utah State University Press, 2012. 259 pp.

Reviewed by Kristin Ravel, University of Wisconsin-Milwaukee

Like other ambitious collections before it, such as Glen and Ratcliffe's *Silence and Listening as Rhetorical Arts* and Schell and Rawson's *Rhetorica in Motion*, *Feminist Rhetorical Resilience* (*FRR*) expands on current developments in feminist rhetoric while broadening the field to new possibilities of research. Though *FRR* covers a variety of topics—transnational feminism, literacy, university hiring procedures, eugenics history, and queer theory—all essays are deliberately woven around the goal of composing a feminist notion of resilience. In the introduction, the editors share that their interest in the concept of resilience—one that grew out of their experience at the Fifth Biennial International Feminism(s) and Rhetoric(s) Conference—stemmed from the absence of *resilience* as a term discussed in feminist rhetoric despite its prevalence within subjects such as social work, education, and business. The qualities that make up feminist resilience, as defined by the editors, include agency, mêtis, and relationality; this social and transformative view of resilience opposes common perceptions that prioritize an individual's attributes. Through envisioning a feminist resilience, *FFR* becomes a constructive addition to research in feminist rhetoric and also may serve—due to the diversity of the topics covered—as an introduction to contemporary concerns in the field.

In an effort to reinforce their common goal, the editors strategically structure the book to embody the theme of feminist resilience. The collection includes seven essays, each followed up with a "response" from an author (or, in some cases, authors) and a "reflection" from the chapter's author (or authors) to the response. The call and response nature of this type of organization places the essays within a social, always altering, context where a reader can see the living, breathing creature of conversation underlying scholarly work. At times these responses and reflections serve to reinforce issues or themes within the chapter and at other times the responses and reflections lead to a new perspective or point out shortcomings of an issue. A memorable example of this resilience at work, and the reason I am examining the last chapter of the book first, comes from chapter 7, "No One Wants to Go There" by Jennifer DiGrazia and Lauren Rosenberg. In this chapter, the authors propose that queering the classroom—using queer text, recognizing queer moments, and destabilizing normalcy—offers students a deconstructive lens that may enable them to think more critically and resiliently in their own lives. In the response that follows, Jacqueline Rhodes and Jonathan Alexander offer a well-crafted but less optimistic vision of queering the classroom that disrupts DiGrazia and Rosenberg's argument;

Rhodes and Alexander call out the shortcomings of our institutionalized pedagogy to be able to *fully* engage with the queer. The chapter ends with DiGrazia and Rosenburg's reflection of this critique, which reiterates—perhaps more forcefully—the more idealistic key points in their essay while insisting that in our classroom practice we should work to actively seek, identify, and engage with queer moments in the classroom. It is in these moments of textual engagement—ones that place voices in direct tension with another—when a reader can identity the constantly evolving, mêtistic nature of feminist resilience the collection works to define. Through the authors' efforts to remain reflexive, transparent, and always listening, the reflective work done here to enact feminist resilience would also serve as a productive model for future scholarship.

The first three essays in this collection focus on transnational issues, making them of particular interest to scholars interested in the relationship of communication, power, and global borders. Working toward a transnational feminist perspective that recognizes and respects difference across borders is no easy task for our field and is charged with ethical inquiries. "Vandana Shiva and the Rhetorics of Biodiversity" by Eileen Schell studies the advocacy work of Vandana Shiva and begins to map the rhetorical traditions Shiva employs to effect social change. Through detailing Shiva's work to fight biopiracy, Schell identifies collective versus individual action as an important theme throughout Shiva's efforts and defines her rhetorical reliance and agency as located in a web of collectively organized groups. The theme of collective versus individual action continues in the "The Traveling Fado" by Kate Vieira. Like the first essay, "The Traveling Fado" offers a transnational perspective by asking "how rhetorics are passed down across national and linguistic borders" (60). This essay combines creative non-fiction, immigration experience, and rhetorical scholarship to examine the historical and rhetorical significance of the *fado*, a Portuguese folk song characterized by longing and the impossibility of returning home. With these essays, we see that feminist efforts to decenter a hegemonic Western discourse means to struggle with the complexity of how history is made and who is able to share their experiences.

The third chapter, "Virginity and the Hymen Reconstructions" by Iklim Goksel, continues the transnational conversation but focuses on complicating attitudes about how we define literacy. Goksel borrows from other scholars to define literacy as "critical thinking and authorship" and argues that women's engagement in hymen configurations offers a space for them to take charge of their world's conception of traditional gender expectations of virginity (92). This research, rooted in Goksel's fieldwork in the squatter settlements of Turkey, highlights the sophisticated vernacular literacies and resilience of these women as they develop their own sense of agency despite an economically unstable and patriarchal landscape. The narratives documented by Goksel continues the work to re-envision our traditional concepts of literacy while revealing how these studies are significant in order to better understand transnational issues.

Chapter 4 shifts away from a transnational perspective to focus on the relationships and resilience that takes place between the university and dual-career-couples. "Diversity and the Flexible Subject in the Language of Spousal/Partner Hiring Policies" by Amy Koerber uses the rhetorical concepts of flexibility and resilience as a lens to understand the connections that dual-career-couple policies make between spousal/partner hiring issues and faculty diversity. After providing a historical context of the dual-career problem, Koerber looks at the emergence of the idealized *flexible* subject and the problems that arise when an individual rather than an organization is asked to create changes. Scholars, administrations, and of course, dual-career couples will find Koeber's essay informative for both the history of spousal/partner hiring policies it provides and for the weaknesses it reveals concerning contemporary procedures of spousal/partner hiring.

Chapter 5 and 6 both examine Western history in the time of eugenic rhetoric. Though admittedly an uncomfortable history on which to reflect, both "A Case Study in Resilience" by Frances Ranney and "From 'Mothers of the Nation' to 'Mothers of the Race'" by Wendy Hayden look at women's use of eugenic rhetoric as a means to foster agency and resilience. "A Case Study in Resilience" studies the letters and notes of Fontia R.'s fourteen-year dependence on the Luella M. Hannan Foundation—a resource that primarily assisted middle- to upper-class elderly women with food, clothing, and housing needs around the time of the Great Depression. Perhaps using "dependent" to describe Fontia R.'s experience is inaccurate here since the word suggests she is without control. In the essay, Ranney reveals Fontia R.'s clever manipulation that allowed her to—despite being penniless and jobless—maintain her appearance as a respectable, feminine woman of high social standing. Whereas Ranney's research reclaims an individual woman's resilience within the social context of the Great Depression, "From 'Mothers of the Nation' to 'Mothers of the Race'" reflects on the different ways early feminists used eugenic rhetoric to argue for rights to education, rights to protect women from spousal abuse, and even rights to demand sexual pleasure. Although chapter 6's racial implications make it a delicate issue, Hadyen effectively argues that recovering uncomfortable or outdated rhetoric does not mean affirming it. In fact, as Hayden writes,

> By analyzing the specific rhetorical moments and reading them in the context of the larger web of ideological and institutional relations, such as science and medicine, we gain insight into the rhetorical choices that failed feminist rhetors of the past. (202)

Whereas many, including myself, may have resisted or shied away from these topics of controversy, Hadyen demonstrates it is necessary rhetorical work that will allow us to become better prepared to make feminist choices in the future.

Though *FRR* does not specifically discuss feminist methodologies in great detail, the variety of current topics covered in the collection would be valuable reading for a graduate course on feminist rhetorical scholarship; the emphasis on response and reflection could open up further discussions about the ethics underlying feminist research and scholarship, especially concerning history and transnational issues. The first of its kind to focus on resilience as a feminist value, this collection not only addresses some of the more pressing issues facing feminist scholars today, but it also speaks to the breadth and depth of this scholarship within a contemporary landscape. Featuring a variety of perspectives and conclusions, the voices within this conversation provide hope that feminist rhetorical scholarship itself remains always resilient, always thoughtful, and always transformative.

Milwaukee, WI

Works Cited

Glenn, Cheryl and Krista Ratcliffe, eds. *Silence and Listening as Rhetorical Arts*. USA: Southern Illinois University Press, 2011. Print.

Schell, Eileen E. and Kelly Jacob Rawson, eds. *Rhetorica in Motion: Feminist Rhetorical Methods and Methodologies.* Pittsburg: University of Pittsburg Press, 2010. Print.

Exploring Composition Studies: Sites, Issues, and Perspectives, edited by Kelly Ritter and Paul Kei Matsuda. Logan, Utah: Utah State UP, 2012. 281 pp.

Reviewed by Bryna Siegel Finer, Indiana University of Pennsylvania

In the past fifteen years, many excellent edited collections have made the field of Composition Studies easily accessible, compact, and portable. To name a few, *Cross-Talk, The Norton Book of Composition Studies,* and *The Braddock Essays* all collect the field's most important primary works under varying themes and within a variety of contexts. *Exploring Composition Studies: Sites, Issues, and Perspectives* provides new essays that consider important primary texts in the field of composition, helping scholars new to any of Composition Studies' constituent areas to locate the seminal texts in that area and to see how those texts converse with each other. Written by some of the field's most prominent researchers, the chapters in *Exploring Composition Studies* provide what could be considered to be a quintessential portrait of where the field has been, where it is now, and where it could or should be headed. It is, no doubt, a reference book, much in the way that *A Guide to Composition Pedagogies is,* but while *A Guide* is a reference for teaching, this collection is a reference for scholarship. The collection shows us the different scholarly conversations, as well as the methodological approaches to that research, that are used under the diverse and ever-expanding umbrella of Composition Studies.

In the introduction to *Exploring,* Kelly Ritter and Paul Kei Matsuda make a promise to newcomers to "the enterprise of composition studies" (7): this collection of new essays will ease the "struggle" of trying "to understand diverse and growing constituencies and enduring questions in various sub-areas of composition studies" (1). The book delivers on this promise, and in fact it offers much more than that: insightful conversations about the field's subareas that would be useful to any researcher or teacher, not just newcomers. As a whole, the book helps to define Composition Studies as a growing discipline that covers many constituents, from university-wide initiatives such as writing centers and writing across the curriculum, to pedagogical areas like teaching first-year writing or second-language writing, to administrative concerns like the changing roles of WPAs and assessment. In chapters that are more than just literature reviews, the writers in *Exploring* show not just how individual books or articles have been important in our disciplinary history, but how those publications converse with each other to create the meta-narratives of the field. Further, the chapters, often explicitly, ask readers to consider where these meta-narratives might, should, or will take composition research in the future.

Exploring is divided into two sections. The first section, "The State of the Field," covers narratives of "'locations' wherein composition studies happens"

(8): basic writing, second language writing, professional writing, writing across the curriculum, and writing program administration. The collection's second section, "Innovations, Advancements, and Methodologies," covers concepts and methodologies that span across the "locations" described in the first section: writing-about-writing pedagogies, transfer, assessment, digital composing, ethnography, archival research, and instructor education.

While many reviews of collections will offer a summary of each chapter of the book in the order in which they appear, what I noticed while linearly reading *Exploring* were the various methodologies used in presenting the material. Perhaps an unintended consequence of analyzing the various constituencies of the field is the revelation of the diverse methodological approaches we use in Composition Studies to understand the conversations we are having. The book serves as a methodological guide, demonstrating the various frameworks we use and the ways in which we tell the histories and stories of our field. So, rather than discuss the chapters linearly, which is not the way the book is likely intended to be read, I've grouped the chapters methodologically to show only one way of approaching this text.

Chronological Histories

Several chapters are written as thorough chronological histories. Rita Malenczyk's chapter, "WAC's Disappearing Act" asks, "How has WAC gotten to this point and where is it going?" The chapter traces the WAC movement from its beginnings in the 1970s through its fading as many programs adopt writing-intensive courses and the idea of "infusion of writing within a whole curriculum" (96) loses steam; she shows that although it hasn't disappeared, WAC is quite different now than it was when originally conceived. Another chronological history includes Kathleen Blake Yancey's chapter, "Writing Assessment in the Early Twenty-First Century," in which she describes three waves of writing assessment and identifies themes across those waves. She begins with a historical context beginning in the 1970s and traces the role of assessment through to "the current moment" (172). Similarly, Linda Adler-Kassner and Susanmarie Harrington provide a chronological history of basic writing in "Creation Myths and Flashpoints: Understanding Basic Writing Through Conflicted Stories." They use "flash points," or moments of conflict or change, to punctuate the narrative of basic writing. A few of the flash points they discuss include Mina Shaughnessy's work with basic writers at CUNY, Min Zhan Lu and Mary Louise Pratt's respective critiques of the myths of basic writing, and David Bartholomae's interrogation of the term *basic writing*.

Geographies/Mapping

Another methodology some of the writers adopt in *Exploring* is the concept of mapping or geographies of areas of the field. In "Remapping Professional Writing: Articulating the State of the Art and Composition Studies," Tim

Peeples and Bill Hart-Davidson ask "Where does professional writing fit in?" They present the "shifting geographies of professional writing" (56) through various maps showing how professional writing is related to other areas of the field. Although less literally, Heidi Estrem and E. Shelley Reid map locations of writing pedagogy education (WPE) in their chapter, "Writing Pedagogy Education: Instructor Development in Composition Studies." They locate WPE scholarship in several different scholarly and pedagogical places, including English Education, TA training, FYC, and WAC.

Definition Evolutions

The writers in *Exploring Composition Studies* also provide chapters that explore the evolution of terms used in the field. One example is Christiane Donahue's chapter, "Transfer, Portability, Generalization: (How) Does Composition Expertise 'Carry'?," which reviews interdisciplinary scholarship that intersects at *transfer*, showing how the term is used differently in different disciplines. Barbara L'Eplattenier and Lisa S. Mastrangelo's chapter on archival research defines this particular method of research. They argue for more archival research in Composition Studies; thus, the chapter acts as a general how-to for locating archives as well as archival resources. Similarly, Elizabeth Chiseri-Strater's chapter "'What Goes on Here': The Uses of Ethnography in Composition Studies" defines ethnography as pedagogy, curriculum, and research method. In his chapter, "Teaching Composition in the Multilingual World," Paul Kei Matsuda traces the evolution of the terms used to describe students who are writing in non-native languages. And lastly, Doug Downs and Elizabeth Wardle challenge readers to "reimagine" how first year composition is defined in their chapter, "Reimagining the Nature of FYC: Trends in Writing-about-Writing Pedagogies." By showing the evolution of terms in the field, these chapters all ask "What is this?," "How is this done?," "Why is this done this way?," and "How has this changed over time?"—all important questions to consider as participants in the field.

Methodological Examinations

The fourth methodology used in the presentation of this research is metamethodology, of sorts. These chapters describe areas in Composition Studies in terms of how these areas have been researched. Lauren Fitzgerald's chapter on writing center scholarship "examines examples of the three methodological approaches that undergird most writing center scholarship" (75) in order to highlight the different methodologies available to writing center researchers. Similarly, Jeanne Gunner's chapter, "Scholarly Positions in Writing Program Administration" examines the "different orientations of WPA scholarship" (109) and looks at the roles these types of scholarship have played in molding the scholarly area of writing program administration. Gail E. Hawisher and Cynthia L. Selfe examine multimodal digital research as a particular context for scholarship in "Studying Literacy in Digital Contexts: Computers and Composition Studies"; they question how this type of scholarship is valued in the academy by those who evaluate tenure and promotion applications, and they look at how multimodal scholarship works in relation to traditional print research.

Each of the four methodologies described above—chronologies, maps, definitions, and meta-methodologies—asks different types of questions; the combination of these questions throughout *Exploring*—the whos, whys, wheres, whats, and hows—show the variety of methodologies available in conceptualizing and writing up research about composition studies. We can look to *Exploring* not just for the stories it tells but also for models of how to tell our stories.

Of course, when reading any collection, one must ask: What's missing? What is left out? Only a few areas that come to mind include advanced composition, rhetorical genre studies, public writing, eco-composition, the teaching of writing online, and the burgeoning area of postcomposition. Certainly there are others, and I'm not suggesting that Ritter and Matsuda could possibly have covered them all. But, a book like this begs the questions–what is valued and included when we talk about or try to define Composition Studies as a discipline? What areas are directly under the umbrella, and what lie on the margins or are perhaps not included at all? Who gets to decide what we call Composition Studies? In the same vein, perhaps the most important moment in the book is a footnote in Peeples and Hart-Davidson's chapter on professional writing: "'Rhetoric and composition,' 'composition studies,' 'writing studies,' and 'rhetoric and writing studies' are some of the terms used to define a field of related interests. However, these various terms reflect a range of divergent disciplinary geographies and have, in some instances, been vigorously debated and rearticulated" (53). So ultimately, what is Composition Studies? All of these are good questions to ask as participants in the field, and *Exploring Composition Studies* thoughtfully provokes them, both to newcomers and experienced teacher-scholars reading this book.

Because of the diversity of its contents and approaches, I can see this book on the shelves of all of us who do research in Composition Studies, as well as required reading for graduate students new to the field and those who train graduate students. It's useful for readers who want a summary and analysis of important moments in particular areas before they go deeper into those areas for their own research. Although I would not consider myself a newcomer to the field, *Exploring* invigorated my thinking and re-focused my energy toward the field. The chapter on digital literacy has motivated me to consider uses of different "semiotic resources" (191) in the production and presentation of my own research. The WPE chapter has provided me with ways to think about how we will develop our university's training for TAs in composition courses. *Exploring* has reminded me of an old interest I had in archival textbooks that could lead to a new research project, and it's inspired me to try a WAW approach in my FYC class next semester. As

Andrea Lunsford says in the foreword, the book "aims to map a scholarly agenda for writing studies in the coming years" (viii). Exposure to *Exploring Composition Studies*, regardless of one's experience in the field, will certainly help any researcher at any moment in his/her career, to envision the possibilities for participation in projects that lie ahead, continuing the work that these important scholars have positioned us to do.

Indiana, PA

Works Cited

Ede, Lisa, ed. *On Writing Research: The Braddock Essays 1975-1998*. Boston: Bedford St. Martin's, 1999. Print.

Miller, Susan, ed. *The Norton Book of Composition Studies*. New York: WW Norton, 2009. Print.

Tate, Gary, Amy Rupiper, and Kurt Schick, eds. *A Guide to Composition Pedagogies*. New York: Oxford UP, 2001. Print

Villanueva, Victor and Kristin Arola, eds. *Cross-Talk in Comp Theory: A Reader*. Urbana: NCTE, 2011. Print.

Announcement

Call for Papers: Writing Center Theory and Practice

The Winter 2013 (Vol. 17, Iss. 4) Issue of *Academic Exchange Quarterly,* an independent double-blind-peer-reviewed print journal, is now accepting submissions for its special section on Writing Center Theory and Practice. Articles may explore issues of theory, practice, and experience in writing center work, including qualitative and empirical studies and discussions of pedagogy.

Articles may also consider the following: How writing center professionals cope with change and the eventuality of needing to expand their efforts in response to new economic and demographic challenges. Furthermore, as we move towards increasingly virtual and technologically dependent learning communities, how can these efforts help meet the evolving demands of our students?

In addition to Writing Center Directors and other Administrators, submissions are welcome from professional staff, faculty tutors, and graduate students who work in the writing center. Manuscript length should be between 2,000 and 3,000 words. Please identify your submission with the keyword "Center-2."

Submissions will be accepted now until the end of August; however, early submissions are encouraged as they offer the following incentives:

- longer time for revision
- opportunity to be considered for Editor's Choice
- eligibility to have article's abstract and/or full text posted on journal's main webpage
- opportunity to be considered for inclusion in Sound Instruction Series

For more information, please visit http://rapidintellect.com/AEQweb/center2.htm, or email Feature Editor and Sound Instruction Book Editor Kellie Charron at kajr10@comcast.net

Contributors

Ryan Skinnell is an Assistant Professor of English at the University of North Texas. His research focuses on rhetoric and composition histories and has appeared in *JAC*, *Rhetoric Review*, *Enculturation*, and edited collections. He is currently writing a monograph, *Conceding Composition*, considering the role of institutional objectives in first-year composition's history.

Christine Denecker is an Associate Professor of English and the Director of Dual Enrollment Writing Instruction at The University of Findlay where she teaches a variety of composition as well as English education methods courses. She has authored several articles on incorporating multimodal composition pedagogies in secondary and post-secondary classrooms.

Duncan Koerber teaches in the Professional Writing program at York University, Toronto. His scholarly research focuses in pedagogy and media history. He has been published in the *Canadian Journal of Communication*, the *Journal of Canadian Studies, Journalism History, Sport History Review,* and *Media History* (forthcoming).

Kenna Barrett is a PhD Candidate in English with a specialization in Rhetoric and Composition at the University of Rhode Island. Her research interests include assessment theory, professional writing, and organizational rhetorics. She has served as a professional grantwriter for many organizations, including Yale University.

Annie S. Mendenhall is a PhD candidate in the Rhetoric, Composition, and Literacy Studies program at The Ohio State University, where she has taught courses in rhetoric and composition and worked with the First Year Writing and Writing Across the Curriculum programs.

Michael Charlton is an Assistant Professor of professional writing at Missouri Western State University, where he teaches composition, technical communication, and public relations.

Selected as an Outstanding Academic Title by *Choice* and as *Library Journal*'s Best Reference Pick.

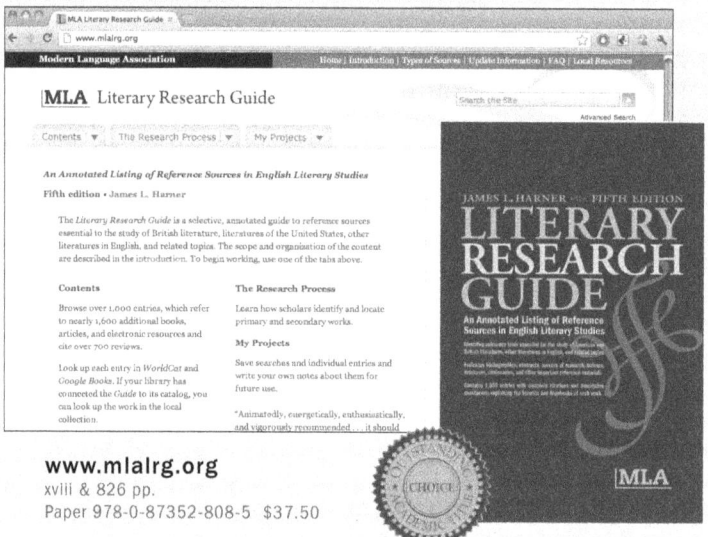

www.mlalrg.org
xviii & 826 pp.
Paper 978-0-87352-808-5 $37.50

The Fifth Edition of the Leading Research Guide in Literary Studies

James L. Harner's *Literary Research Guide*, which Choice calls "the standard guide in the field," evaluates important reference materials in English studies.

In the fifth edition there are substantially more electronic resources, particularly reliable sites sponsored by academic institutions and learned societies, including bibliographic databases, text archives, and other online resources.

This edition also features a new section on cultural studies.

"Essential. All academic collections; upper-level undergraduates through faculty/researchers."
—*Choice*

"Marvellously comprehensive and reliable tool...Every scholar and every library should own this book."
—*Times Literary Supplement Online*

Phone 646 576-5161 ■ Fax 646 576-5160 ■ www.mlalrg.org

Adopt the *MLA Handbook* for Your Spring or Fall Classes.

Check It Out.

MLA members can request a complimentary copy at **www.mla.org**. Each copy includes print and online formats.

Assign It.

Your students can start using the *Handbook* the day you assign it. They can buy access online at **www.mlahandbook.org** (a print copy will be mailed to them) or purchase a print copy online or at their local bookstore (each print copy comes with an online-access code).

Recipient of *Choice* Award for Outstanding Academic Title

The searchable Web site features

- the full text of the *MLA Handbook*
- over two hundred additional examples
- research project narratives, with sample papers

xxii & 292 pp.
Paper 978-1-60329-024-1 $22.00

A large-print edition is also available.

www.mlahandbook.org

Phone orders 646 576-5161 ▪ Fax 646 576-5160 ▪ www.mla.org

Rhetoric & Writing PhD Program

Preparing Rhetoric and Composition Faculty for over 30 Years

Since its founding in 1980, Bowling Green State University's program has prepared more than eighty graduates for faculty careers in rhetoric and composition. Students and faculty in the Rhetoric & Writing PhD Program are committed scholar-teachers who utilize a range of approaches—rhetorical, cultural, empirical, technological—that characterize rhetoric and composition in the twenty-first century.

Some highlights of the Rhetoric & Writing PhD Program:
- Eight core courses in history, theory, computer-mediated writing, research, scholarly publication, and composition studies as a discipline, plus electives in rhetoric and composition and related areas of scholarly interest to students.
- Professional development involving mentoring, collaboration, a monthly colloquium series, and post-prelim groups emphasizing dissertation work and the job search.
- Varied assistantship assignments (FYW, intermediate writing, writing center, faculty research, editorial work, program administration, community outreach, etc.) and competitive non-service fellowships in the fourth year of funding.
- Four-year graduation rate typical for full-time students.
- Placement rate among program graduates approaching 100%.

Rhetoric & Writing PhD Program
http://www.bgsu.edu/departments/english/rcweb/index.html
Facebook Group: BGSU Rhetoric & Writing

Program Director, Sue Carter Wood
carters@bgsu.edu
English Graduate Office: 419-372-6864

Centre for Academic Writing

Academic Writing Theory and Practice: new one-year MA

Taught in England and based on Coventry University's international reputation in the teaching and researching of academic writing, this new Master's programme is designed for graduates and professionals interested in studying, researching, and teaching writing. The focus of the programme is on writing, rhetoric, and literacies research and on how this research informs the teaching of writing. The programme will give students the opportunity to compare academic writing practices across different countries and cultures.

Modules include:

- Supporting Academics, Postgraduates and Professionals in Writing for Publication
- Academic Writing and the Transnationalisation of Knowledge
- Writing Programme Development and Management
- Teaching Academic Writing
- Forms and Practices of Disciplinary Writing
- Researching Academic and Professional Writing: Text Focus
- Researching Academic and Professional Writing: Practices and Processes
- Rhetorical Theory

Apply now to study in 2013

For more information, please visit our website at **www.coventry.ac.uk/CAW** or email us at **writing.caw@coventry.ac.uk**

New Releases . . .

The WPA Outcomes Statement—A Decade Later
Edited by Nicholas N. Behm, Gregory R. Glau, Deborah H. Holdstein, Duane Roen, and Edward M. White. 344 pages. $32 (paperback); $65 (cloth); $20 (digital).

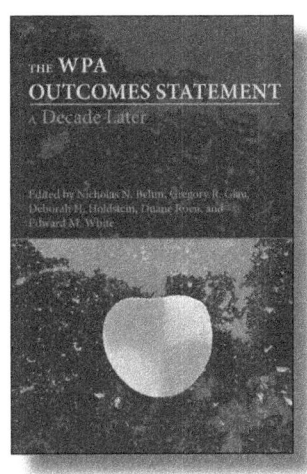

The WPA Outcomes Statement—A Decade Later examines the ways that the Council of Writing Program Administrators' Outcomes Statement for First-Year Composition has informed curricula, generated programmatic, institutional, and disciplinary change, and affected a disciplinary understanding of best practices in first-year composition.

Writing Program Administration at Small Liberal Arts Colleges
Jill M. Gladstein and Dara Rossman Regaignon
290 pages. $32 (paperback); $60 (cloth); $20 (digital)

Writing Program Administration at Small Liberal Arts Colleges presents a research study of the writing programs at one hundred small, private liberal arts institutions. Using grounded theory's mixed methods approach, the book presents a detailed picture of the structures that deliver, support, and lead writing instruction at these institutions.

Also Just Released . . .

Rewriting Success in Rhetoric and Composition Careers
Edited by Amy Goodburn, Donna LeCourt, and Carrie Leverenz.

and with the WAC Clearinghouse . . .

Writing Programs Worldwide: Profiles of Academic Writing in Many Places
Edited by Chris Thaiss, Gerd Bräuer, Paula Carlino, Lisa Ganobcsik-Williams, and Aparna Sinha

International Advances in Writing Research: Cultures, Places, Measures
Edited by Charles Bazerman, Chris Dean, Jessica Early, Karen Lunsford, Suzie Null, Paul Rogers, and Amanda Stansell

www.parlorpress.com

www.ingramcontent.com/pod-product-compliance
Lightning Source LLC
Chambersburg PA
CBHW031321160426
43196CB00007B/609